D1300283

Distraction

Girls, School, and Sexuality

Erin Mikulec and Dawn Beichner (Editors)

ISBN 978-1-64504-044-6 (Hardback)

ISBN 978-1-64504-043-9 (Paperback)

ISBN 978-1-64504-045-3 (E-Book)

Library of Congress Control Number: 2020937662

Printed on acid-free paper

© 2021 DIO Press Inc, New York

https://www.diopress.com

Cover art by Megan Kathol Bersett

Acknowledgments

To my mentors—Janice Joseph, Cassia Spohn, Alida Merlo, Robyn Ogle, and Concetta Culliver—who taught me that women are NOT a distraction.

~ Dawn

This book is dedicated to girls and young women in schools everywhere.

Table of Contents

Introduction

Erin Mikulec and Dawn Beichner

In 2018, an article titled "Is Your Body Appropriate to Wear to School?" appeared in the *New York Times*. The article detailed the experience of 17-year old Lizzy Martinez who, because of a sunburn, chose not to wear a bra to school one day. School officials immediately deemed Lizzy in violation of the school dress code and she was given four Band-Aids with which to cover her nipples in an X pattern. That Lizzy was wearing a heavy long-sleeve t-shirt was irrelevant in this case: her body had become a "distraction," and therefore must be crossed out. Unfortunately, Lizzy's story is one of many when it comes to girls and dress code, and this story is not limited to the United States, as Bates (2015) found in the United Kingdom and Canada and Ongley (2016) found in New Zealand.

Sexist and gendered school dress codes serve as mechanisms of racist and homophobic discrimination. Research has shown that dress code policies directly affect girls of color specifically and at higher rates (Hurley, 2019; Thompson, 2014). The National Women's Law Center (2018) found that schools in the Washington, D.C. area targeted girls through dress code policies that dictate skirt length or even the type of clothing that could or could not be worn (e.g., leggings). The report further found that dress codes also unfairly subject Black girls to policies and possible violations through regulations about hair and hair wraps, which may only be worn for religious reasons. Sadly, this kind of policy is not limited to head coverings but can also apply to braids, extensions (Lattimore, 2017), or hair that is not a "natural color," as in the case of eight-year-old Marian Scott, who was denied having her school picture taken because she was wearing red hair extensions (Schoenberg, 2019).

LGBTQ students also must contend with sexist and gendered dress code policies, as students in Kentucky faced when they were told to change their clothes for wearing t-shirts that said "Lady Lesbian" and "Queer Queen" (Assunção, 2019). When Constance McMillen wanted to take her girlfriend to the prom, the Itawamba School Board simply decided to cancel the event "due to the distractions from the educational process" (Associate Press, 2010). The parents in the school community simply organized a separate private event in lieu of the official school prom, while McMillen, her date, and five other students attended another function, essentially a fake prom, where "all were welcome" (Simpson, 2010).

Regardless of the circumstance, one word is ubiquitous in nearly every new story that features girls and young women in school: distraction. What is a distraction anyway? Distraction is a code word, a cue that means what we're really talking about is girls and young women, their bodies, and their sexuality. This code word carries with it a host of purposes. It is a means of objectifying girls, while simultaneously policing girls' bodies and devaluing their education in schools. When girls and young women are labelled a "distraction" as justification for action taken against them in response to a violation of sexist school policies, it becomes clear that it isn't their education that comes first, but rather their bodies and how their bodies must be held in check, so as not to create disruptions in the educational process of others, primarily boys and young men. Furthermore, it indicates that boys' lack of self-control—their inability to function academically in an environment with "distractions"—is the responsibility of girls and young women. This translates as the need for policies and practices to be put in place within patriarchal school systems that remind girls and young women every day that they must not only focus on their studies but also do their part to maintain a "distraction"-free environment for others, the latter being the more important imperative. School dress codes are filled with gendered language that serves to regulate girls' bodies and reinforce ideas that they must be covered, and be covered according to explicit rules such as the hem of a skirt must reach to the fingertips of an extended arm, known as the "fingertip policy" (Barrett, 2018). A simple search for school dress code policies yields numerous results that explain just what young women may and may not wear. For instance, the 2019–2020 Dress Code policy for Clear Creek Independent School District in Texas outlines the following when it comes to what is appropriate:

Appropriate clothing shall cover midriff, shoulders and upper chest.

Any garment, regardless of what it is called, must be worn no shorter than mid-thigh.

Pants or shorts shall be appropriately sized and worn at the natural waistline and shall not expose skin above mid-thigh.

Shirts may be required to be tucked in unless they are designed to be worn over the waistline and do not exceed four inches below the waistline.

For students in Pre-Kindergarten through 8th grade, tights, form fittingpants, leggings, jeggings, spandex, exercise pants, and yoga pants must be covered by mid length shorts, skirts, or long shirts which cover the bottom.

For high school students, inappropriate tights, form fitting pants, leggings, jeggings, spandex, exercise pants, and yoga pants must be covered by mid length shorts, skirts, or long shirts which cover the bottom. (CCISD, 2019)

Beliefs that girls and young women cannot dress a certain way for fear that they might distract or sexually excite male students or male faculty is a form of victim blaming that perpetuates rape culture. At their core, school dress codes for girls and young women suggest that the female body must be adequately covered or there will be negative consequences—male students who can't focus on their studies, or male students and male staff who become sexually aroused. As young girls become young women, including those on college and university campuses, they continue to be blamed for their clothing and how it may have provoked sexual violence against them. Thus, the belief about their distraction does not end, but instead follows them throughout their lives. (Bates, para. 12, 2015) found that the message of dress codes goes beyond ideas of whose education is more important. She found that not only were girls being told that they were "distracting" to the boys, but also that they made the male teachers "uncomfortable." The author goes on to say that what young women are really being told is that "girls' bodies are dangerous, powerful and sexualised, and that boys are biologically programmed to objectify and harass them." This is perhaps one of the most troubling aspects of examining the larger picture surrounding dress code: that even adult male teachers—who are in school to educate young people—cannot be trusted or rather, expected, not to look at a girl student without harboring inappropriate thoughts or ideas. These patterns of thinking extend to the notion of women and girls who experience sexual assault or harassment as somehow having invited it through their clothing (Barrett, 2018; Bates, 2015; NWLC, 2018; Ongley, 2016).

The idea for this book began with an article about dress code, but soon grew into something much more, exploring the many way in which girls, either through their actions or their bodies, are labeled as a "distraction" throughout their school experiences. The book addresses issues such as adolescent mothers, girls who simply want to learn computer programming, activism of Black girls to address experiences and instances of sexual harassment and violence, the school-to-prison pipeline, international perspectives from Singapore and Turkey, and the problems with how sexual assault is handled on college and university campuses. The book also examines the role of girls and sexuality in private schools, juvenile detention centers, and even young adult literature.

In Chapter 1, Crandall reports that although young adult novels on bullying have become popular instructional aids among teachers in the USA, little is known about their actual usefulness in understanding bullying or helping adolescents who are targets of such behavior. She calls for a rigorous literary analysis of the young adult literature that addresses these topics in which a critical examination can be made of the ideologies of bullying, harassment, female sexuality, and power. Crandall's approach is one that produces a shift in focus from the individual bully and his/her bad behavior to a more nuanced exploration of the complexities of human relationships and the role of power in shaping these differences. In the chapter she examines three contemporary young adult novels that include stories of bullying, coupled with representations of female sexuality that are embedded within the novels. Using a feminist poststructural theoretical framework, she conducts a textual analysis and a feminist critical discourse analysis. Her analysis reveals that sexuality in the novels is heteronormative and that the overwhelming message to female heroines is that sex is more to be feared than celebrated. The analysis also reveals a common theme of predatory sexual behavior. Crandall reflects on how the novels offer limited ideas about female sexuality and power and are more written from the perspective of authors' conceptions of right and wrong.

In Chapter 2, Bailin Wells examines what it is like to be an adolescent woman at an all-girls school in the Upper East Side of Manhattan, New York. Wells critically reviews the literature and condemns past practices of popular and contemporary literature for making broad claims about girls as a monolithic group, lacking intersectional identities. According to Bailin Wells, this approach reinforces White, upper-middle class, heteronormative experiences among girls as being typical and normal. Her research uses a critical-activist inquiry approach to interrogate how ideations of girlhood are constructed and promoted within the school's culture and community. Bailin Wells' case study serves to disrupt the notion that only a single narrative of girlhood exists. Thus, although single-sex schools may share commitments girls' education, assigning them to a singular narrative fails to account for the ways in which individual race, class, and gender identities interact with macro influences of geography, school culture, and school funding. Bailin Wells uses interviews with students and school leaders, as well as participant observation and document analysis, to expand the lens of how girlhood is constructed.

In Chapter 3, Nalls provides a critique of the Singaporean educational curriculum as being heteronormative and marginalizing to the Queer population. She discusses the impact that the curriculum has in silencing the Queer community and denying Queer Singaporeans the birthrights of the national pledge, including the opportunity to vote on decisions that impact their community. Nalls uses critical race theory's counter-storytelling method to investigate the oppressive heteronormative and heterosexist Singaporean curriculum. Her reflective narrative, which discusses what it was like coming out as Queer in a country where being gay is illegal, is a call for repositioning of Queers in Singapore through a universal, inclusive curriculum.

Martin, Boehlke, and Cepec profess in Chapter 4 that when service-learning approaches are paired with feminist pedagogy, the result can be transformational for students. Their chapter focuses on the creation of an afterschool gender studies course, T.R.U.E. Queens, that was created as part of a college course to be implemented in middle school. The resultant "crash course in feminism" was designed with the purpose of combating microaggressions, sexism, and racism within the middle school culture. Not only was the service-learning strategy steeped in feminism and feminist curricula, it targeted historically marginalized students for membership. The resultant case study reveals that the college students who created the course learned many important lessons in leadership, social skills, and the amount of effort required to create lessons on social injustice topics like racism, homophobia, and sexism. Their approach, which provided voice to middle schoolers on the curriculum, provided an alternative to the often hegemonic, predominantly White curriculum.

In Chapter 5 Nuding examines the intersection of middle school girls' desire to learn computer programming while also supporting one another through a "sisterhood." The author, who leads a local chapter of Girls Who Code, a national organization that serves as an afterschool club and program for middle and high school girls, discusses the powerful effect that group has had on her students. The author discusses how media and social norms, which are especially gender-biased in middle school, often reinforce the message that girls are not welcome, or worse, not "suited" to this kind of activity. Nuding describes the afterschool club as a source of positive representation for the girls who attend as well as one of the most popular activities being the "Sisterhood Spotlight," in which the club members learn about women in the STEM field and their accomplishments. Through a focus group with the club members, the author found that these sessions left them feeling inspired to pursue activities and careers in STEM and that the club in general simply normalized coding as something that girls would do. Furthermore, the sisterhood created though the club gave the girls a support network and a place to be heard, unlike other classes "where the teacher never calls on the girls." Nuding's work shows that such clubs and organizations carry far more value than simply providing a place for girls to learn coding, but also a place where girls can become empowered and serve as change agents for themselves and their sisters.

Kaya examines the ways in which girls are sexualized through school practices in Turkey in Chapter 6. As the author points out, although reforms have been implemented to reduce the gendered structure of schools in the country, traditional gender roles are still prominent. Kaya's analysis illustrates how Vocational and Technical Upper Secondary Schools in the country, with their emphasis on traditional gender roles, limit occupational training options for girls and young women to the fields of fashion, design, illustration, and child development, among others. Accordingly, the schools serve as gendered spaces and genderizing spaces that reinforce societal norms and expectations for girls and young women. Moreover, because of the highly centralized nature of the educational system in Turkey, this influence is consistent across the educational field in the country.

In Chapter 7, Farinde-Wu, Graham, and Jones-Fosu invite readers to consider the explicit, implicit, and null policies in schools that uphold institutional racism through higher rates of suspension and other forms of discipline for Black girls. In the case study provided, the authors put theory into practice as they examined an event that took place in a school located in a historically Black neighborhood yet with a predominantly White faculty. The event, a fight that involved thirty girls, made local news with the typical narrative describing the girls involved as "troubled"; however, none of the girls involved were even interviewed, nor did they have the opportunity to share their perspectives with the community. In this way, the girls were further silenced, voiceless, and marginalized. The authors identified a serious disconnect between the White teachers in the school and their Black students, citing the lack of discussion or even recognition of issues related to identity, race, gender, and class on the part of the teachers. The authors assert that educators, especially White educators working in predominantly Black schools, must begin to critically reflect on their own teaching practice and what they bring to the classroom in terms of expectations, beliefs, and ideas, in order to engage in genuine conversation with their students when it comes to Black girls, identity, race, gender, and class.

Kindelsperger and Hallman in Chapter 8 examine the literacy practices of teen mothers and in doing so address the stigma that they face through the intersection of being a parent and being an adolescent. The chapter takes into consideration how this intersection provides a richer source of connection to education, and takes an asset approach, rather than a deficit-based model, to understand education for adolescent mothers. Rather than criticize or punish adolescent girls for becoming mothers, the authors illustrate how this identity serves as a rich fund of knowledge for the mothers as students. The chapter follows two teen mothers and explores their literacy practice and development as it is connected to motherhood. Through their writing, the adolescent mothers expressed their hopes and dreams for their children, and this served as empowerment for the mothers as students. This counterstory to society's ideas and expectations of teen mothers underlies the notion that this population of young women must not be identified as "at-risk" but rather as "at-promise."

In chapter 9 Dunkerly-Bean, Morris, and Bean discuss the adultification of young Black girls, which frames them as being older or more experienced than their White peers. This adultification manifests in the juvenile justice system that convicts and sentences Black girls disproportionately for moral offences rather than criminal ones. The authors introduce Tia, an adolescent girl in the juvenile justice system who engages in alterative literacy practices such as song writing and drawing as both an exploration of her identity and as resistance. Tia's voice is a powerful one, and her work presents the experiences of a young woman caught in a system that both seeks to mediate and punish sexual identity in adolescent girls. Tia's poems and songs as they are presented in this chapter are exemplars of the internal narratives that young women speak as they negotiate their identity, assert their bodies as their own, and recognize the power of those bodies as tools of resistance. This chapter shows Tia first and foremost as a writer and activist and provides an excellent example of the need to support all young women, regardless of circumstance.

In Chapter 10 Wilcox presents a powerful case study that examines Rise Up, a group created by a group of high school girls of color in a social justice course. The group attempts to shed light on and address the alarming rates of sexual violence that girls experience while at school. The group's intent goes beyond simply reporting the sexual violence experiences by girls in their school, and aims also to challenge the narrative that these experiences are normal. The girls of Rise Up asked that education leaders provide classes on consent and develop a way for girls to report incidents of sexual violence. Furthermore, they requested that girls be provided with tools and skills to protect themselves. In addition to policy changes, the girls also demanded that policy language move towards emphasizing the protection of the survivor of sexual violence rather than the perpetrator. The examples provided here in this chapter illustrate the need to address multiple issues surrounding sexual violence and harassment experienced by girls of color in high school. It further emphasizes a needed change in the narrative perpetuated by administrator and district officials, who are often White.

Finally, in Chapter 11 Beichner provides a critical examination of one of the most prevalent forms of gender-based violence in the USA: campus sexual assault. She points out that, despite sweeping rape law reform, many of the problems that plagued sexual assault case processing in the 1970s, remain problematic today—especially on university and college campuses. Among the topics addressed in the chapter, Beichner gives special consideration to the invisibility of sexual assault among LGBTQ students and the ways in which college campuses foster rape culture and victim blaming. She highlights the predominately White male-dominated fraternity subculture and its implicit heterosexism, as well as the power and privilege among college athletes, as key contributors to campus sexual assault. The review also includes an overview of Title IX and how it has changed over time, including the amendments by Department of Education Secretary, Betsy DeVos. Beichner characterizes the Trump administration reform strategy as giving more power to the accused than the accuser. She questions what the long-term impact of such changes will be on the future of campus sexual assault. The chapter concludes with a call for an approach to campus sexual assault that is restorative, centered on the survivor-victims, and intersectional.

Ultimately, the goal of this book is to explore the ways in which girls are sexualized through school practices, beginning early on and continuing throughout their educational experiences as adults. The book examines how schools serve as gendered spaces and genderizing spaces that reinforce societal norms and expectations for girls and young women. The editors and chapter authors shed light on these issues and start a conversation about the challenges that girls and young women—of all ages—face in school every day. The book aims to recognize that girls and young women in school have the right to exist, to take up space, and to be educated free of stigma and punishment for their gender and sexuality. In this way, rather than simply label girls and young women as a "distraction," the editors call on educators and administrators to give voice to girls and young women and empower them.

References

Associated Press. (2010, March). Mississippi: Prom canceled over same-sex date policy. *New York Times*.

Assunção, M. (2019, August). Kentucky students forced to change out of LGBTQ shirts for violating dress code. *New York Daily News*.

Barrett, K. (2018, July). When school dress codes discriminate. NEA Today.

Bates, L. (2015, May). How school dress codes shame girls and perpetuate rape culture. *TIME Magazine*.

Clear Creek Independent Schools. (2019, July). CCISD dress code 2019–2020. Retrieved from: https://ccisd.net/

Hurley, J. (2019, July). My school's dress code unfairly targeted Latina girls, and yours probably does too. National Women's Law Center: Let Her Learn. Retrieved from: https://nwlc.org/blog/my-schools-dress-code-unfairly-targeted-latina-girls-and-yours-probably-does-too/

Krischner, H. (2018, April). Is your body appropriate to wear to school? *New York Times*.

Lattimore, K. (2017, May). When black hair violates the dress code. National Public Radio. Retrieved from: https://www.npr.org/sections/ed/2017/07/17/534448313/when-black-hair-violates-the-dress-code

National Women's Law Center. (2018, April). Dress coded: Black girls, bodies, and bias in D.C. Schools. Retrieved from: https://nwlc.org/press-releases/dress-codes-hurt-learning-for-black-girls-in-d-c-new-nwlc-report-finds/

Ongley, H. (2016, April). School tells girls to lengthen skirts to avoid "distracting" male teachers. VICE. Retrieved from: https://i-d.vice.com/en_us/article/j589xb/school-tells-girls-to-lengthen-skirts-to-avoid-distracting-male-teachers

Schoenberg, N. (2019, November). Naperville photographer comes to the aid of 8-year-old Michigan girl who wasn't allowed to get her school photo taken because of red hair extensions. *Chicago Tribune*.

Simpson, J. (2010, April). Lesbian couple sent to fake prom. *The Atlantic*.

Thompson, N. A. (2014, July). School uniforms and dress code policies most likely to target females, Latinos and Black students. *Latin Post*. Retrieved from:https://www.latinpost.com/articles/16692/20140709/school-uniforms-dress-code-policies-target-females-latinos-black-students.htm

Chapter One

Reading Female Sexuality, Bullying, and Power Relations
in Young Adult Literature

Cara Crandall

When Phoebe Prince, a 15-year old high school freshman in South Hadley, Massachusetts committed suicide in January of 2010, her death was quickly attributed to bullying and harassment she had faced at school. While news reports dug into the social relationships she had maintained since her recent arrival at the town's high school from Ireland, Prince's death led to a vociferous debate about blame and responsibility that continues to this day. Had Phoebe been a naïve newcomer in a town of "mean adolescent women" who targeted her due to her relationships with several boys in town (Cullen, 2010)? Or were reports of Phoebe's own actions as a bully back in Ireland examples of her complicity in the situation in South Hadley (Bazelon, 2010)? This debate crystallized around the decision by local law enforcement officials to charge six of Phoebe's peers with a range of felonies, including harassment, stalking, statutory rape, and civil rights violations. The lives of adolescents can seem unknowable by adults, but when the stakes are so high adults feel compelled to intervene. Did the teens who taunted her deserve criminal punishment? What role and thus responsibility could adults in the school and community play in such a situation? Answering these questions in Phoebe's case reminds one of the most tragic element of her story: Phoebe cannot be saved, no matter how long and loud the debate about her death gets. But what can be learned from the choices Phoebe and the adolescent women she associated with made as they wandered their school's hallways in pursuit of boys and friends?

In the nearly 40 years since academic researchers (Olweus, 1973; Olweus, 1978) first addressed issues of peer relationships and bullying, the topic has become not only a subject worthy of academic study across multiple disciplines but also one that has encouraged a national discourse on bullying in mainstream media with books such as *Odd Girl Out* and *Queen Bees and Wannabees*; in popular films like *Mean Girls*; and at the White House Conference on Bullying in 2011.

E. Mikulec, D. Beichner (eds.), Distraction: Girls, School, and Sexuality, 1-16.

This national conversation has led to an increasing focus on problematic peer relationships, leading legislators in 47 states to pass laws that require school districts to create policies for preventing and responding to bullying. In some states, these laws include consequences for school personnel who fail to report or act on that bullying (Bazelon, 2010). Such legal remedies have arrived at the same time as positive support for bullied children has come about including school-based intervention programs like the Olweus Bullying Prevention Program (Olweus, 2003).

The social import of this phenomenon has not been lost on authors and publishers of young adult (YA) literature, which has experienced a similar growth trajectory in the two decades that saw a rise in bullying. According to Meredith Barnes, a literary agent, "3,000 young adult novels were published in 1997. Twelve years later, that figure hit 30,000 titles" (Grady, 2011). One aspect of the genre's growth and popularity are the multiple sub-genres that have gained prominence, including novels with bullying at the center of the narrative. In fact, "the number of English-language books tagged with the key word 'bullying' in 2012 was 1,891, an increase of 500 in a decade" (Kaufman, 2013). Bullying is, however, hardly new territory in YA books: Robert Cormier's (1974) *The Chocolate War* focused on the tensions between an adolescent boy and his school's power relations and is even predated by books like *The Outsiders* (1967) and *Catcher in the Rye* (1951) that also included episodes of targeting due to difference (Lopez-Robero, 2012). These earlier texts, which solely focused on the lives of young male characters, were part of a movement in the 1960s and 1970s in YA fiction toward what has come to be known as "contemporary realism" (Fitzgerald, 2004) or "YA realism," which includes a set of very specific literary conventions, namely "adolescent protagonists, narration from the adolescent's point of view, realistic contemporary settings, and subject matter formerly considered taboo" (Ross, 1985, p. 175). These books, often referred to as the "problem novel" (Trites, 2000; Fitzgerald, 2004) were written to explore the issues facing contemporary U.S. adolescents in the latter half of the twentieth century and were positioned as responses to the social ills faced by youth but through the lens of literature. Because of their emphasis on male characters, female characters appeared in the narrative only on the sidelines and/or consigned to traditional gender roles. However, these texts were an attempt to answer the call of Michael Cart, when he argued for a

> …young adult fiction…written for and about adolescents and the mind-boggling problems that now plague and perplex them…a new kind of problem novel that is as real as the headlines…enriched by the best means literature can offer…a young adult fiction that takes creative (and marketing) risks to present hard-edged issues so that it may offer readers revelation and, ultimately, that elusive wisdom. (qtd. in Fitzgerald, 2004)

Cart's call indicates a conundrum that YA literature cannot escape, and one that is explored throughout this chapter, when he argues for novels "written for and about adolescents" since these novels will be created by, published by, and marketed by adults. By their very nature, such novels will always foreground adult conceptions of adolescents, their problems, and possible solutions for young people while purporting to represent adolescents' concerns. This conundrum provides one impetus for this chapter's analysis of a select group of YA novels in order to identify and problematize the ideologies of bullying, harassment, female sexuality, and power at work in a medium that purports to explore the lives of young adults, in this case young female adults. This chapter will explore such "wisdom" in order to better understand the work these ideologies do to inculcate adolescents with cultural narratives about sexuality and power.

Additionally, Cart's idea of "revelation" and "wisdom" granted to readers through a literary experience echoes Trites' (2000) description of YA novels as historically derived from the Bildungsroman (coming-of-age novels that end with adulthood), but more clearly understood as Entwicklungsroman (novels of development that end before adulthood) because "the character grows as s/he faces and resolves one specific problem" (p. 14). These novels provide then an "archetypal story" that "is a rite of passage from childhood to maturity" (Ross, 1985, p. 177), providing readers with the experience of growth and change through the eyes and experiences of the protagonist. The conventions of YA problem novels also incorporate "the friend, the first sexual partner, family members, the outcast, and the adult mentor" as part of the narrative while casting "parents …as negative, blocking figures" (Ross, 1985, p. 177). These conventions are coupled with themes that address "identity…the importance of present experience, alienation from the adult world, and isolation" (Ross, 1985, p. 178) all in the service of a novel that picks up any number of contemporary subjects that had been previously been ignored in YA literature: teen sexuality, pregnancy, abortion, and the uses of drugs and alcohol.

Today's titles, though, and the sheer volume published, underscore a preoccupation with peer aggression on the part of American adults, including teachers, librarians, and authors, who are often the source as these books find their way into the classrooms and hands of today's adolescents. Publishers, too, drive this concern with peer aggression and bullying through the creation of their own anti-bullying campaigns at the same time that authors use their websites and Facebook to tap into the "perfect synergy that results: They can promote a cause that most people avidly support while promoting their own products" (Kaufman, 2013). Given this confluence between social issues, literature, and marketing, this preoccupation results as much from exploitation as it does from a compulsion to intervene, understand, and help adolescents.

These "products" are increasingly used in classrooms as teachers and researchers have argued for the inclusion of YA literature alongside canonical literature that has been the staple of American English classrooms for decades (Daniels, 2006; Gibbons, Dail, & Stallworth, 2006; YALSA, 2012). While teachers can incorporate YA novels in their classroom practices for their literary merit or their ability to engage reluctant adolescents in reading, many argue the inclusion of YA literature focused on bullying provides "bibliotherapeutic" (Larson & Hoover, 2012) possibilities in allowing teachers ways to intervene in the "invisible problem of bullying" (Bott, Garden, Jones, & Peters, 2006). Two articles in the Winter 2014 issue of the *ALAN Review* argue for the inclusion of such YA literature, and though each study addressed distinct aspects of the texts through content analysis, both articles positioned YA novels focused on bullying as worthy of classroom study not only as literary texts but also as methods of intervention to prevent or stop bullying within schools. Jones, Dennis, Torres-OvRick, and Walker (2014) looked at 10 novels related to bullying in order to analyze adult interventions in bullying situations. Their content analysis drew on literature that argued for the unique role teachers and other school staff can play in "identifying and decreasing the isolation of students at-risk with bullying," but that also highlighted that "victims of bullying are reluctant to report such incidents to adults" (p. 67). They further urged the use of these novels because they will encourage dialogue between students and adults about the bullying situations within texts, which could then lead "teens [to] learn from adolescent literature how to use adults to intervene to confront the problem of bulling" (p. 67). Similarly, Harmon and Henkin (2014) analyzed 21 YA novels selected because the protagonist had been bullied in order to understand how "such information can serve important instructional purposes" (p. 79). They argue that "teachers should not only capitalize on classroom discussions, but should also use writing opportunities to help students think more deeply about bullying," and they further include discussions and role playing to make text-to-world connections (p. 87). These approaches are offered in the service of "valuable instructional tools for helping teachers address these problems that occur too frequently in the lives of adolescents" because in their analysis the books "provide realistic portrayal of bullying and harassment" (p. 86). YA novels focused on bullying are also seen as offering important lessons for the preparatory work of pre-service teachers (Pytash, 2013) because of their future work with adolescents who might struggle with issues of bullying, harassment, and resulting suicide. Few would quibble with the notion of caring adults stepping in to protect students from or help students deal with experiences of bullying, harassment, or violence. However, our reflex to utilize YA novels focused on bullying as instructional tools for moral behavior; understanding and respecting difference; or understanding complicated issues around power and violence underscores a number of important gaps both in public debates on bullying and the research literature. These gaps, which are addressed in this chapter, include the need to submit YA literature to rigorous literary analysis; to undertake a critical examination of the ideologies of bullying, harassment, female sexuality, and power embedded in the novels as part of the narrative structure; and to problematize the representations of bullying, adolescent behavior, and female characters in particular within these novels.

THEORETICAL FRAMEWORK

This chapter undertakes both a literary and discourse analysis of YA novels in order to critically examine ideologies of bullying, harassment, female sexuality, and power embedded in the novels as part of the narrative structure. However, a narrow emphasis is maintained on novels about adolescent females, bullying and harassment, and female sexuality as examples of "relations of power" because as Foucault (1997) articulated, "in human relationships power is always present" (p. 292). Three contemporary YA novels were selected that present a story of bullying coupled with representations of female sexuality. A feminist poststructural theoretical framework (Weedon,1997) is used in this chapter in order to complete two layers of analysis: a textual analysis of the novels as literary works coupled with a feminist critical discourse analysis in order to understand how these authors and these texts reflect, take up, and possibly resist ideologies of bullying, adolescence, and female sexuality. Poststructural feminist theory is integral to the analysis because this framework will allow a discussion of how "relations of power" are the "contingent, contextual, and the ideological" issues that are at the core of what we have come to identify as bullying (Walton, 2005, p. 61). Further, the analytic tool of "modes of address" is employed to understand how authors hail readers into the subject positions occupied by the female main character and how these modes of address continue, expand, and at times resist contemporary discourses on adolescence, female sexuality, and power (Ellsworth, 1997, p. 22). Modes of address become then almost a welcome to readers, a signal that they will find recognizable characters and situations in the fictional world created by the authors. An example of a mode of address is the setting of the American suburb replete with bored adolescents, distant parents, and peer activities like gossiping, parties, and dating. By situating the reader in such a setting, the author both assumes the reader is familiar with such a place and understands its intricacies. The mode of address then encourages a feeling of intimacy between reader and character as well as reader and text.

Novels in the Study

The novels selected for this study were published between 2008 and 2014, and thus provide insights into the kinds of books adolescent readers will find on bookstore or library shelves. These books constitute a corpus of YA problem novels focused on bullying (Trites, 2000). However, the problem of bullying represented in these novels portray the impetus for this troubling social phenomenon as a problem of adolescence and female sexuality.

The significance of sharing one's version of events provides the narrative structure in the novel *Thirteen Reasons Why* (Asher, 2011), but Hannah, the female protagonist in this novel, has committed suicide before the novel begins. However, she has found a way to tell her story by leaving behind cassette recordings that are strategically created for the people she holds responsible for her decision to end her life. In this novel, Clay, a male friend of the dead girl, listens to the cassettes, each of which is focused on another intended recipient of the recordings and unveils how each person's actions led to her death. Clay's response to the recordings foregrounds the sense of responsibility and shame she hoped her recordings would create. In this novel, technology has made it possible for the dead female protagonist to speak from the grave and by doing so right the wrongs perpetrated against her.

Conflicts between girls who had been friends inform the narrative in the novel *Just Listen* (Dessen, 2008). In this novel, Annabel, the female protagonist, faces sexual violence, but rather than be seen as a victim by her peers, she faces bullying and social ostracism. The sexual violence in this novel positions Annabel not as a victim but as betrayer of her friends' and peers' social codes. Family issues leave her reluctant to tell anyone about her rape. This disinclination paired with her own prior history as a bully prevent her from fighting back when she is humiliated or ostracized by former friends.

In the novel *Tease* (Marciel, 2014), the main character Sara faces legal consequences for the bullying and harassment she and her best friend perpetrate against Emma, the fictional stand-in for Phoebe Prince. While several of the novels in this study address these issues from the perspective of a girl who admits to bullying peers, this novel portrays behavior that results in legal as well as ethical and social consequences. While all of the novels center on the real-world issue of bullying, this novel closely parallels the real-life suicide of Prince and the legal ramifications for those accused of bullying her.

READING SEXUALITY

In addressing the ways power assumes an integral role during adolescence in peer relationships, romantic and sexual relationships must be considered. During adolescence, teens increasingly move into the world of school and the "social worlds" of friends and peers freed from the constrictions of parents and family and begin to explore meaningful relationships with others (Finders, 1997, p. 9). Adolescents find friendships meaningful for many reasons, but as with all relationships power plays a role in how people negotiate the terms of those relationships. This remains true for relationships with others that are focused on romance and sexuality.

Using Ashcraft's (2012) definition for sexuality, which includes the "biological aspects of sex, but also too the emotional, relational dynamics around sexuality," the three novels in this chapter were analyzed for the inclusion of the female main character's sexual choices, attitudes, and experiences as well as the "emotional and relational dynamics" that were set in motion due to sex in the plot (p. 599). Due to the content of these novels, sexuality and romance are uniformly and intrinsically tied to the same-sex friendships and power negotiations.

These novels all utilize heteronormativity (Wagner, 1991) as the backdrop for the plot and as a given for one's sexuality in the fictional world and the real world. Questions about one's gender and/or sexual preferences are never raised, nor is it even acknowledged that such options might exist, so that "compulsory heterosexuality" (Rich, 1980) appears as the "common sense" expectation for gender and sexuality (Gramsci, 1971). No gay characters are included, nor does any character engage in questioning his or her sexual preferences or gender, nor does any character experiment with homosexuality or homosexual sex acts; these exclusions and gaps make heterosexual love, romance, and sexual acts the rule of life and love in these novels. At the same time, the novels explore two aspects of sexuality as defined by Ashcraft but positions them as polar opposites—sexual "biological" acts and "emotional" dynamics of love. In each novel, a clear distinction exists between who the female main character has sex with and who the female main character will find to be their true love, and this distinction is reinforced because this true-love relationship remains chaste or near-chaste. This division is emphasized through the ambivalence and conflict the female main characters experience about sexual choices as well as the ways sex is paired with risky and/or dangerous outcomes, including violence. Concurrently, the possible male partners included in these novels create a similar dyad of dangerous/safe options, so that there are good boys and bad boys, but knowing which is which can be confusing due to the material trappings people normal look to when selecting a partner in contemporary American culture with its emphasis on consumerism. This partner selection has great import in these novels since finding her true love will also allow the female main character to know herself in deeper, more authentic ways made possible through discovering this mate. The implications of such narrative events and discourses will be addressed later in this chapter.

The Boy Next Door: The Predatory Boy/friend

Literature for children and adults abounds with versions of Prince Charming, the attractive, socially accepted, and perhaps even popular young man who offers a female character a story with a happy ending (Botelho & Rudman, 2009). He offers her love, acceptance, and a place in the world he controls, either literally as the prince or as the most popular boy in school. In the novels in this study, all of the stories include a physically attractive male peer that the main character either has feelings for or sees as powerful in the social world of which they are members. This Boy/friend is positioned in these novels as someone who has power in its many forms: social, class, gender, and sexual. In these novels, while this character appears to possess much that would make him attractive as a partner, he is revealed to be a bully or cruel, and in many cases a sexual predator.

This fall from grace occurs for Dylan, Sara's boyfriend, in the novel *Tease*. As she explains, he was a popular senior who was successful at school and played varsity baseball. Her feelings for him are visceral, they will become the impetus for Sara's harassment of Emma because she becomes incensed when Emma and Dylan become friends. Later, it will become apparent to Sara that they are more than friends, and Dylan will admit to his own sense of ambivalence as he ricochets between the two girls. If Dylan's confusion disappoints and hurts Sara, it also leads inadvertently to the continued bullying that Emma faces at their school by many peers, including Sara and Brielle.

Hannah, the protagonist in the novel *Thirteen Reasons Why*, had dreams of romance as well in her relationship with Justin. Instead, Justin betrays her faith by sharing their private moments with other people at school, and by making it seem like they have engaged in more sexual activity than occurred. Justin, like the other male characters in these novels, appears to be a boy Hannah could like: popular, well liked at school, and polite to parents. But Hannah herself will become complicit in Justin's behavior when, at this party, Justin and Hannah do nothing to prevent the rape of Jessica after she has passed out drunk in a bedroom. The sexual harassment and sexual assault become incidents that Hannah, and other female characters, must deal with, but deal with personally, as no justice or redress happens for those who have been targeted. These further incidents, and the power ascribed to these boys in their social world, only push Hannah closer to her final decision to commit suicide.

Rape and its after effects for victims become integral in another of the novels under study, *Just Listen*. The inciting incident in this novel, like the party Hannah attends, is a high school party where teens, drugs, and alcohol mix freely. Will Cash is a serial rapist who attacks the main character Annabel at a party even though she is his girlfriend's best friend. Will holds a power position in their social world, despite or perhaps because of the rumors that he is unfaithful to Sophie with other girls.

In all of these novels, a young male character is presented who seems to embody all of a young woman's desires: good looks, charm, sexual magnetism, and material things like social status, money, and academic standing. But whether the young male characters are involved in a romantic relationship with the main character or merely know her through their social world, they end up betraying these young women and acting in predatory ways. Every Boy/friend in these novels wants to be sexually intimate with the female character, and he will do so with or without her permission. In two of the novels, a sexual assault takes place, and in one of the novels, the backstory of the main character's best friend includes sexually assault. This event provides insights into her behavior, their relationship, and even the main character's choices. Even in the examples of romantic relationships, elements of manipulation and coercion occur, leading the female characters to question the motives of their partners and even their own sexual desires. What becomes apparent in this study is that the Predatory Boy/friends who seem to offer so much in the way of partnership provide negative examples of heterosexual relationships. But in novels that are clearly taking up a heteronormative script, such maneuvers by authors seem puzzling until one recognizes another male character present in all of these novels, the Other Boy.

The Boy on the Margins: The Other Boy

In all of the novels, another male character provides the female character with a different experience of an opposite-sex relationship. However, from the outset of the novels, this young man, whom this study labels the Other Boy, is presented as marginalized and for various reasons an outsider to more popular and powerful peers in the social world. This young male character is marked as Other in the novel by a variety of mechanisms: race/ethnicity, class, social status, or sexual orientation. What sets this boy apart as Other even more is the way he is positioned in the social world of the female main character as someone she has paid little attention to before but comes to see in a new way. The female main character either knows the Other Boy as an opposite-sex friend as in two of the novels or as a school peer who has either been known in passing or has been the target of bullying and/or ostracism by others, including at times the female main character, which occurs in five of the novels. The transformation in the relationship between the Other Boy and the female main character occurs as part of the plot but plays an integral role in the transformation of the female character as well. In fact, the Other Boy, who will become the object of her affections in every one of these novels, provides many of the insights and reflections that propel the character development of the female main character. Without him, such change might not be possible because the Other Boy appears to know the female character so well that he understands her better than she knows and understands herself. His position as Other allows him to see her and their social world from a supposed objective and more distanced perspective in the workings of the novel, so that he becomes an observer/sage about their social world and her. But this character is also part of a dyad with the predatory

Boy/friend in which male characters are either good boys or bad boys, a dichotomy which will be discussed at length later in this chapter.

When Annabel is ostracized by her friends and other schoolmates, this peer isolation brings her into closer proximity to Owen Armstrong, a loner at her school. While Annabel does not know him well at first, she is well aware of what has been said about him. Once she has opened her mind to the possibility of Owen as a friend, their relationship becomes much more the longer she spends time with him. His attitudes on life provide her with new ways to think about her life and how she behaves, and she understands his effect on her is profound. Annabel not only becomes friends with Owen, but she also learns from him about how to deal with her own feelings, including anger, and how to give voice to what she feels.

When Sara attends summer school to make up for the classes she could not finish following Emma's suicide, she ends up as lab partners with Carmichael, a peer who "during the school year, [she] wouldn't have talked to" (Maciel, 2014, p. 43). When the school year resumes, Sara remains ostracized for her role in Emma's suicide. Her only possible friend becomes Carmichael, and as they continue to spend time together, they become friends. Carmichael also begins to take on the role of observer/sage who provides Sara with comfort as well as pushes her to understand the depth of her role in Emma's death, something she resists for most of the novel. But like with all of the Other Boys in these novels, Sara's feelings for him morph from appreciative and friendly to romantic. Carmichael presents a fresh take on how Sara understands a romantic relationship, but also how she sees her situation and herself and because of his perspectives Sara changes her attitudes about how she handles relationships and thus herself.

Romantic feelings draw Hannah and Clay together, though they never become romantic partners and remain only friends. His role in the novel is one of observer of much of the action, an after-the-fact observer, whose understandings of what happened to her allow him to become the observer/sage, but not in a way that will ever benefit Hannah, adding poignancy to her story and setting up the ending for the novel: "I wanted to know her more than I had the chance" (Asher, 2007, p. 10). On her tapes, Hannah's description of Clay reveals how she felt about him as well as make clearer how he is the Other Boy.

One other common feature of the main character's relationship with the Other Boy is the way this relationship remains chaste or near-chaste throughout the novels. Even in the case of novels where the two are physical with each other, these interactions never veer toward intercourse or sexual intimacies. They may and do kiss; they snuggle and feel close to one another; and bodily responses are described. However, the ambivalence and rapacious nature of the main character's relationship with the Predatory Boy/friend is absent, thus setting up a conflict between the male partner who will use a woman for his own sexual needs and the male partner who truly understands and loves a woman. This dyad and its implications will be discussed later in this chapter, but they are parallel with the ways the novels introduce and discuss the sexual choices and sexuality of the female main characters.

DISCUSSION

Mode of Address: Female Sexuality

In her qualitative research project focused on the lives of thirty women in the Northeastern United States, Phillips (2000) explores "hetero-relational subjectivities," which she argues "all women regardless of sexual orientation or sexual identity are engaged in" because all women in a "male dominated society must spend enormous amounts of energy sifting through the complex and pervasive messages about pleasure, danger, and entitlement regarding sexuality and male power" (p. xi). These "pervasive messages" are the very sorts of modes of address that the authors of the novels in this chapter study operationalize in their novels as parts of their fictional worlds, and they do so because such discourses are at work in the cultural and social contexts that readers must live with and negotiate in the real world. One aspect of Phillips' research is particularly resonant for the modes of address employed in the construction of the male characters in these novels. While this chapter study identifies and analyzes these male characters as the Predatory Boy/friend and the Other Boy, Phillips theorizes a similar male dyad found in the research she completed with the women participants in her study. For Phillips, this dyad also echoes the sense that there are "'good guys'" and there are "'bad guys,'" and as such these "...categories do not overlap"; she connects this dyad to what she terms the "normal/danger dichotomy discourse" of sex and violence in Western societies (p. 52). Thus, not only does the heteronormative script play a role in discourses around "hetero-relations," but it also frames a particular take on that script, which then sets up specific discourses around sex and romance omnipresent in many cultural artifacts, including these novels.

Female adolescents, be they in the novels under study or the real world, can find good boys and bad boys, and figuring out what boy belongs to which category becomes vital not only to finding a healthy and happy romantic relationship with the good boy, as Phillips argues and these novels make clear, but also to protecting one's self from the bad boy. This added dimension to discourses around men and sexuality makes clear that woman's safety hinges on her discernment in selecting a romantic or sexual partner. Inherent in these discourses, then, is an element of victim blaming, because if a woman does not carefully choose between these good and bad boys, she will have no one to blame but herself (Phillips, 2000). Such tensions in these novels exists as the female main character must identify the actual failings and rapacious nature of the Predatory Boy/friend and the moral rectitude and wisdom of the Other Boy, an outsider she has already judged and cast aside or regularly ignores. Only once she has seen the error in her ways does the female main character find true happiness and love. But her desire and/or interactions with the Predatory Boyfriend first will lead to serious consequences, which she alone must pay: ostracism, sexual violence, and even death.

In these novels, Prince Charming ends up being a sexual predator, despite his attractiveness, and becomes the bad boy despite what looks good on the surface. But how could the female characters have made better choices? Herein lies the true conflict at work in these novels: They remain at their core morality tales because these novels, like much cultural production and YA literature in particular, serve multiple purposes, the least of which may be to tell a good story. As Trites (2000) argues, the didactic quality of YA literature, especially the sorts of realistic novels used in this study, consists in teaching lessons and helping adolescents assume their role as a healthy, functioning adults. In addition, the use of the Other Boy does not critique or destroy the romance myth of Prince Charming but merely shifts its locus from the attractive, good guy that the female main character (and thus the adolescent reader) has assumed is worthy of her time and attention, to the Other Boy, whose characterization includes aspects that make him appear weird or different, or plagued by social isolation or anger issues. He may be an outsider in many ways and has previously struggled in relationships in the social world of peers, but now he becomes the observer/sage who saves the female main character not only from the Predatory Boy/friend but also from herself and her circumstances. This sense of danger differentiates the male characters in these novels as well as the ways sex and sexuality are constructed.

Trites (2000) argues that YA literature "[shares] the same ideological message that sex is more to be feared than celebrated" (p. 85), and this message is apparent in all of the novels in this study. These novels include rape and predatory sexual behaviors, forms of sexual activity not as celebration but as a response to violence and fear; peer pressure; or a character's knowledge that sexual activity is an expectation for adolescents within her peer group.But nothing connected to sex in these novels celebrates desire, pleasure, or physical intimacy. Quite the opposite: These novels may suggest an open or empowering attitude toward adolescent sexuality because the novels recognize and include the adolescents are engaging in sex, but in fact they represent to their readers and hail them into subject positions that see sex as dangerous, unhealthy, and deadly.

For Foucault (1990) this "deployment of sexuality" (p. 106) as a discursive practice transmutes sex and sexuality from "bodies and pleasure" (p. 157) to a potent method of repression and control. If, as he argues, "sex is placed by power in a binary system" (p. 83), this binary of pleasure and pathology appears in each of these novels as if the authors intended to write a morality tale because the narrative arcs of these novels make clear for adolescent readers that "sex leads to disaster" (Trites, 2000, p. 93), reinforcing social control over bodies through the not-so-subtle reminder that adolescents perhaps should leave sex where Foucault argues society has centered it: within the family as part of the marital contract and reproduction and even then as "an object of great suspicion" (p. 69).

Of the various discourses of social control, perhaps none is as anxiety-provoking as female sexual desire, which is why Foucault (1990) argues the female body was understood to be "saturated with sexuality" and had to be contained and controlled. This understanding framed female sexuality as pathological, the territory of the medical sciences, and needed for reproduction but not a woman's pleasure (p. 104). Constraints on women's sexuality may not be new, but readers might find them surprising in novels published in the span from 2002 to 2014, in a time decades after the feminist movement of the 1970s. For adolescent readers, like many people, choices around sexual activity can be anxiety-provoking and fraught, especially in light of concurrent fears of pregnancy and sexually transmitted diseases, which are both real concerns and parts of the discourses used to control and pathologize sexual activity. Rather than provide readers with ways to celebrate "bodies and pleasure," these novels remain true to the genre of YA literature by asserting that through the experiences of these female main characters, as Kraus wrote in 1975, "'the sexual act itself is never ...joyful, and any show of intimacy carries a warning of future danger'" (qtd. in Trites, 2000, p. 93). The modes of address in these novels around partnership and sexual activity do little to resolve or salve those anxieties.

All the novels in this study include female main characters who do not willingly have sex but are coerced or forced into doing so by a variety of factors, least of which is their own desire. Instead, peer pressure and social expectations; wanting to the please the boy they are interested in; and sexual violence propel these characters toward sex. Every female main character suffers as the result of sex, from the internal conflicts about the decision to have sex to rape. Sex has risks. But in place of such dangers, true love and a more chaste relationship offer the characters not only a second chance at romance but more importantly the opportunity to know herself better, although such self-knowledge is only possible through her relationship with her male romantic partner. If the opposite sex partner she was initially attracted to has betrayed or hurt her, the Other Boy rescues her from such sadness and from her own misunderstandings about herself. These elements of sexuality, romance, and the Predatory Boy/friend/Other Boy dyad become integral pieces to the resolutions of the novels.

While the novels focus on the relationships between female characters, each also portrays sexual or romantic relationships with opposite sex peers. As has been discussed previously, a very clear dichotomy has been constructed in these novels around the suitability of these partners. The female main characters seek emotional intimacy but are stymied when the object of their affection cannot engage in such intimacies. At the same time, the female main characters make choices regarding these relationships and sexuality, and their desire for physical intimacy becomes clear. Yet, such feelings are portrayed in the novels as contradictory in that the female main character appears to want to be sexually active, but she also articulates numerous fears and misgivings about engaging in sex. This generalized ambivalence does not negate their yearning for physical intimacy but raises the issue of how problematic sexuality can be. None of these characters have healthy sexualized lives, nor is there any discussion or exploration of understanding sexual relationships. Moreover, three of them are victims of sexual violence. Sex activity then is paired with danger and many problems occur as a result.

This admission of female sexuality, paired with their involvement in bullying and cruelty to others, confronts readers with characters who are living outside of the boundaries adults have constructed for what is socially acceptable for adolescent behavior, especially female adolescent behavior. It is no surprise then that each of the girls in these novels faces some sort of strife, or punishment, that forces her to reconsider her relationships, her choices, and who she has become. This morality tale aspect of the novels becomes clear as the books conclude because the characters in these books have a happy ending (discussed in more detail below), which gives readers a sense of hope that forgiveness and redemption are possible. But each female main character has done things she must first be sanctioned for.

As the narrative arc bends toward a conclusion, whatever setting the author has used in the fictional world shifts into the now, a narrative time when the main character takes stock of all that has preceded this moment. In this moment, resolutions and insights to both inter- and intra-personal conflicts are possible, and the main character, as well as the reader, is positioned both at the end of a journey and at the start of another. In these novels, the female main character describes a sense of accomplishment as well as new understandings of her situation, how she came to be in that situation, and the truths she now knows about herself. These understandings provide her with a new way to live in this fictional world. But as cultural artifacts, these novels also offer readers insights into the real lives they lead, but these insights are immersed in discourses that take up, refract, and perpetuate ideas about the female subject, power, sexuality, and morality, and as such are not nearly as freeing as the novel's endings might suggest. If the female main characters feel liberated through the work they have undertaken throughout the novel, such freedom to imagine new possibilities are not without reflective and intellectual work on the part of readers, and much of that work remains constrained by the discourses used in these novels because these discourse frame not only the fictional world adolescent females read about, but the worlds they inhabit.

CONCLUSION

No matter the gender of the audience, adolescents read for all sorts of reasons, including entertainment and as part of the required school curriculum, and "literature matters because it teaches how perspective can be brought to bear on experience" (Blackford, 2004, p. 1). These connections between our real lives and the fictional worlds we visit when we read offer worlds "like our own" as well as serving an "ideational function…in the cultural, ideological, philosophical, or ethical issues being addressed by the narrative" (Phelan & Rabinowitz, 2012, p. 7). As readers, we enter settings and meet characters much like us, who engage us through language and confront us with all sorts of meanings, which we can then take up as our own because "rhetorical narrative theory considers the narrative text not just to represent but actually to constitute a transaction between an author and a reader" (Warhol, 2012, p. 10). This transaction can inform our perspectives on myriad issues a text places at the center of its plot. Given the import of the relationship between the reader and a text, adults would be wise to take a more critical approach and provide methods for more critical analysis of such texts that shape young people's understandings of themselves, their relationships, and their lives. Without this critical inquiry into narratives and the ideologies within these narratives, we run the risk, as Walton (2005) argues, of offering students "conceptualizations of bullying" that are merely "definitional" and do little to uncover "the contextual and ideological" issues (p. 10). Instead, these novels create categories of behavior that teach young women a great deal but offer limited ideas about female sexuality and power. The critical stance so important to interrogating these novels would serve young readers to question the possibilities afforded female characters in the fictional worlds they inhabit as well as a perspective from which to critically examine their own lives.

REFERENCES

Ashcraft, C. (2012). But how do we talk about it? Critical literacy practices for addressing sexuality with youth. *Curriculum Inquiry 42*(5), 597–628.

Asher, J. (2011). *Thirteen reasons why*. Razorbill Books (Penguin).

Bazelon, E. (2010, April 30). Bullies beware. *Slate*. Retrieved from http://www.slate.com/articles/life/bulle/2010/04/bullies_beware.html

Bazelon, E. (2010, July 20). What really happened to Phoebe Prince? *Slate*. Retrieved from http://www.slate.com/id/2290797/

Botelho, M., & Rudman, M. (2009). *Critical multicultural analysis of children's literature: Mirrors, windows, and doors*. New York: Routledge.

Bott, C. J., Garden, N., Jones, P., & Peters, J. (2007). Don't look and it will go away: YA books—a key to uncovering the invisible problems of bullying. *The ALAN Review 34*(2), 44–51. Retrieved from http://scholar.lib.vt.edu/ejournals/ALAN/

Blackford, H. (2004). *Out of this world why literature matters to girls*. New York: Teachers College Press.

Cullen, K. (2010, January 24). The untouchable mean girls. *Boston Globe*. Retrieved from http://www.boston.com/news/local/massachusetts/articles/2010/01/24/the_untouchable_mean_girls/?s_campaign=8315

Daniels, C. L. (2006). Literary theory and young adult literature: The open frontier in critical studies. *The ALAN Review 33*(2), 78–82.

Dessen, S. (2006). *Just listen*. Penguin.

Ellsworth, E. (1997). *Teaching positions: Difference, pedagogy, and the power of address*. Teachers College Press.

Finders, M. (1997). *Just girls: Hidden literacies and life in junior high*. Teachers College Press.

FitzGerald, F. (2004, September). The influence of anxiety. *Harper's 309*(1852), 62–70.

Foucault, M. (1990). *The history of sexuality volume 1: An introduction*. Vintage Books.

Foucault, M. (1997). Ethics: Subjectivity and truth. *The Essential Works of Foucault*, 1954–1984 (Vol. 1). Paul Rabinow (Ed.). The New Press.

Gibbons, L., Dail, J., & Stallworth, B. J. (2006). Young adult literature in the English curriculum today. *The ALAN Review*. Retrieved from https://scholar.lib.vt.edu/ejournals/ALAN/v33n3/gibbons.pdf

Grady, D. B. (2011, August). How adult young adult fiction came of age. *The Atlantic*. Retrieved from http://www.theatlantic.entertainment/print/2011/08/how-young-adult-fiction-came-of-age/242671

Gramsci, A. (1971). *Selections from the prison notebooks of Antonio Gramsci*. (Q. Hoare & G. Smith, Trans.). International Publishers.

Harmon, J., & Henkin, R. (2014). The portrayal of bullying in young adult books: Characters, contexts, and complex relationships. *The ALAN Review 41*(2), 79–89.

Herman, D., Phelan, J., Rabinowitz, P., Richardson, B., & Warhol, R. (2012). *Narrative theory: Core concepts and critical debates*. The Ohio State University Press.

Hill, C. (Ed.) (2014). *The critical merits of young adult literature: Coming of age*. Routledge.

Jones, J., Dennis, L., Torres-OvRick, M., & Walker, S. (2014). Content analysis of adolescent literature related to bullying. *The ALAN Review 41*(2), 66–78.

Kaufman, L. (2013, March 27). Publishers revel in youthful cruelty. *New York Times*. Retrieved from www.nytimes.com/2013/3/27/books/bullying-becomes-hot-and-profitable-topic-for-publishers. html

Larson, J., & Hoover, J. (2012). Quality books about bullying in the young adult tradition. *Reclaiming Children and Youth 21*(1), 49–55.

Lazar, M. (2007). Feminist critical discourse analysis articulating a feminist discourse praxis. *Critical Discourse Studies 4*(2), 141–164. doi: 10.1080/17405900701464816

Lopez-Ropero, L. (2012). "You are a flaw in the pattern": Difference, autonomy, and bullying in YA fiction. *Children's Literature in Education 43*(2), 145–157. doi: 10.1007/s10583-0119145-0

Maciel, A. (2014). *Tease*. Balzer + Bray.

National Council of Teachers of English (2011). NCTE Position Statement. Resolution on Confronting Bullying and Harassment [online post]. Retrieved from http://www.ncte.org/positions/statements/confrontingbullying

Olweus, D. (1973). Hackkycklingar och oversitaire. Forskning om skolmobbing. (Victims and bullies: Research on school bullying.) Almqvvist & Wicksell.

Olweus, D. (1978). *Aggression in the schools: Bullies and whipping boys*. Hemisphere Press (Wiley).

Olweus, D. (2003). A profile of bullying at school. *Educational Leadership*, 12–17.

Phillips, L. (2000). *Flirting with danger: Young women's reflections on sexuality and domination*. New York University Press.

Phelan, J., & Rabinowitz, P. Narrative as rhetoric. In Herman, D., Phelan, J., Rabinowitz, P., Richardson, B., & Warhol, R. (Eds.), *Narrative theory: Core concepts and critical debates* (pp. 3–8). Ohio State University Press.

Pytash, K. (2013). Using YA literature to help preservice teachers deal with bullying and suicide. *Journal of Adolescent & Adult Literacy 56*(6), 470–479. doi: 10.1002/JAAL.168

Rich, A. (2003 [1980]). Compulsory heterosexuality and lesbian experience. *Journal of Women's History 15*(3), 11–48.

Ross, C. (1985). Young adult realism: Conventions, narrators, and readers. *Library Quarterly 55*(2), 174–191.

Trites, R. (2000). *Disturbing the universe: Power and repression in adolescent literature*. University of Iowa Press.

Walton, G. (2005). The notion of bullying through the lens of Foucault and critical theory. *Journal of Educational Thought 39*(1), 55–73.

Walton, G. (2011). Spinning our wheels: Reconceptualizing bullying beyond behaviour-focused approaches. *Discourse: Studies in the Cultural Politics of Education 32*(1), 131–144. doi: 10.1080/01596306.2011.537079

Warhol, R. (2012). A feminist approach to narrative. In Herman, D., Phelan, J., Rabinowitz, P., Richardson, B., & Warhol, R. (Eds.), *Narrative theory core concepts and critical debates* (pp. 9–13). Ohio State University Press.

Warner, M. (1991). Introduction: Fear of a queer planet. *Social Text 29*, 3–17.

Weedon, C. (1997). *Feminist practice & poststructuralist theory* (2nd ed.). Blackwell.

Cara Crandall
Glenbrook Middle School

Chapter Two

Counter-Narratives of Girlhood: Interrogating the Ruptures, Complexities, and Challenges of "Being a Girl"

Emily Bailin Wells

All-girls schools are commonly framed as institutions meant to empower girls to be their best selves in environments that foster compassion and excellence. In independent private schools, notions of language, privilege, and place are closely tethered to history and traditions and are woven into the cultural fabric of the institution, creating certain expectations and archetypes of the "ideal girl." Girls' identities and experiences of girlhood are multifaceted, hybridized, and constructed through their ties to various and simultaneous shifting, partial, and social locations (Bettis & Adams, 2009; Zaslow, 2009). Conversely, much of the popular and contemporary literature on girls from the last 30 years not only takes a protectionist stance, focusing on the negative and worrisome aspects of peer culture and adolescence, but also often makes broad claims about "girls" as a monolithic group (e.g., Cohen-Sandler, 2005; Pipher, 1994), failing to account for factors like intersectional identities, and how literacy practices, contexts, and environments inform who girls are and who they want to be. In a similar vein, framing girlhood as a universal phenomenon flattens their experience, which, understood from a critical standpoint, largely reinforces White, upper-middle class, heteronormative experiences of girls and girlhood as "normal" and/or "typical." It is also important to acknowledge the treatment of "girl" and "girlhood" as concepts that are overwhelmingly cisgendered, and often heteronormative, in nature. Therefore, this study employed a working understanding (as opposed to a firm definition) of "girlhood," conceptualized as the various temporal, ecological, cultural, and discursive storylines that intersect to construct and define the experiences of being a girl, and the places and spaces within which these experiences occur.

This chapter draws from a qualitative case study at the Clyde School, an elite, independent private all-girls high school in Manhattan. The study interrogated how ideations of girls and girlhood are constructed and promoted as part of the school's institutional identity and how high school students in turn understand,

E. Mikulec, D. Beichner (eds.), Distraction: Girls, School, and Sexuality, 17-34.

negotiate, subscribe to, and/or resist dominant narratives of what it means to "be a girl" across the contexts of school and life. The study consisted primarily of interviews with 17 students and five school leaders. The language, beliefs, values, and practices that collectively work to construct a school's institutional identity were examined using a critical analysis of discourse; in turn, how students perceive and challenge notions of what it means to be a student at the Clyde School were examined.

In this sense, the study took the form of critical-activist inquiry—research that seeks "not to prove or disprove, but rather to create movement, to displace, to pull apart and allow for resettlement...it seeks [to identify] what is possible and made manifest when our taken-for-taxonomic certainties are intentionally shaken" (Rolling, 2013, p. 99). Brown and Strega (2005, in Rolling, 2013) explain that critical-activist inquiry "produces resistance narratives—counter-stories to authoritative grand narratives that are critical, indigenous or local, and anti-oppressive. To be critical is to activate new discourse overwriting prior theory and practice" (p. 109). The hope is not necessarily to gather narratives that will stand in direct opposition to the "majoritarian story" (Solórzano & Yosso, 2002), but rather will work to disrupt the idea that only a single narrative exists—one that compresses experiences and silences the intersectional relationships between young people, institutions, and society. It is in these moments of disruption that we might begin to untangle and re-examine the cultural, discursive, and systemic practices that work to construct place in an all-girls school like Clyde and then begin to collaboratively engage in reimagining what these spaces could look like when multiple narratives are embraced to create more authentically inclusive places and spaces.

CONCEPTUAL FRAMEWORK

Literacy/ies as Socially Situated Practices

Many scholars (Hull & Nelson, 2005; Jewitt, 2005; Vasudevan, 2009) argue that literacy is multimodal—visual, spoken, written, gestural—and critical skills are needed to analyze and understand a range of media such as newspapers, television, film, Internet, radio, and magazines (Hull & Nelson, 2005; Janks, 2010). As a result, they feel that the practice and process of "reading" is deeply situated in social and cultural contexts and, as critical theorist Paulo Freire (2000) posits, consists of learning how to read both the word and the world critically (in Janks, 2010). There is power in engaging young people in new literacies practices that account for, value, and revolve around their lived experiences and perceptions of the world.

Evolving from the new literacies movement, contemporary scholars of critical literacy continue the push to expand verbo- and logo-centric definitions of literacy to consider the body (Johnson & Vasudevan, 2012) and artifacts (Pahl & Rowsell, 2011) as texts that require critical literate practices to be read, interpreted, judged, analyzed, and negotiated. Embodied literacies practices are personal, political, and rife with assumptions and subjectivities. Kamler (1997, in Johnson & Vasudevan, 2012) understands the body as a text that is "produced by socially circulating norms for gender, race, sexuality, class, age and ability" (p. 35). In this sense, we read bodies by drawing from personal knowledge, lived experiences, discursive practices, media representations, and so on to make sense of who we are; to determine where we fit into micro and macro social orders; and to communicate particular ways of being through speaking, dressing, or gesturing that can reinforce or challenge social norms and power imbalances.

Identity/ies in Practice

From a sociocultural perspective, identities are "mediated, constrained, and juxtaposed" (Johnson, 2012) with intersecting subjectivities (e.g., race, socioeconomic class, gender, sexuality, religion, ethnicity, ability, etc.) that are socially constructed and reinforced through sources such as mass media, popular culture, and school (Collins, 2000; Johnson, 2012). It is during adolescence that young people begin to situate themselves in both local and more global contexts (Noguera, 2012), drawing from the discourses available—behaviors, beliefs, social cues, dress, gestures—to perform and experiment with identity. Identities offer "different ways of participating" in various sorts of social groups, cultures, and institutions (Gee, 2005) such as a being a "good student," a "star athlete," a "people person," or in the case of this study, a "Clyde Girl," an institutional archetype that embodies the ideals of a student—and therefore a girl—at Clyde. How we understand ourselves and others is fundamentally shaped by our daily interactions and lived experiences in the places, contexts, and institutions we occupy (Nukkula, 2012). Within a sociocultural framing, identity is both an internal understanding of self as well as a set of practices outwardly expressed through, among other things, literacies. Literacy/ies practices, therefore, become the tools and modes of communication engaged when writing our own identities into being and reading—constructing and deconstructing—the identities of others.

Place and Institutional Identity

Harvey (1996, in Conley, 2016) aptly notes that place "has to be one of the most multilayered and multi-purpose keywords in our language," functioning as metaphor, material, and territory (p. 50). Mollie Blackburn (2001) understands space as a dialogic between place and people; space refers to "people within a place and the ways in which that place brings people to life" (p. 64). She goes on to say that if a space does not allow for particular articulations or expressions of self, then that space stops being a space for that particular performance of identity. Borrowing from Gruenewald (2003), Tupper, et al. (2008) contend that if researchers understand places are what people construct of them, that people are "place-makers and that places are a primary artifact of human culture, then it seems reasonable that schools might play a more active role in the study, care and creation of spaces" (p. 1066). Given the significant amount of time that young people spend at school, examining the affordances of space(s) and place(s) are crucially important when considering how young people talk about and situate themselves within this setting.

Additionally, Charlotte Linde (2009) is concerned with the social and linguistic mechanisms used by members of an institution to work the past, or construct its collective identity, seeking to tell "an integrated story about stories within institutions: how they are formed, retained, passed on, changed, and used to affect both the narrators and the institution being narrated" (p. 14). One aspect of her study entailed looking at how people tell their own stories within an institution to reveal:

> ...small links and minute traces between individual stories and stories of the institution that indicate how people are inducted into institutional membership and ... learn to shape their stories to harmonize with the events and values of the main institutional narratives. (Linde, 2009, p. 4)

The practice of "working the past" highlights the importance of understanding an institution's identity—the context of a school's history, traditions, and discursive practices, and how they inform a collective of individuals in the present—in order to further explore how ideas of girlhood, and subsequently membership and belonging, are disseminated, reinforced, and perceived at the Clyde School.

The "All-Girls School" as Place

The literature that focuses on the institutional identities of all-girls schools in the United States is complicated. Girls' schools are often celebrated not only for providing equitable access to education but empowering girls physically, emotionally, and intellectually. For instance, in providing a historical context for the Oakland-based all-girls school she co-founded, DeBare (2004) explains that all-girls schools "typically view their mission as extending beyond academics to address the social and emotional challenges facing girls, such as issues of self-esteem, body image, and sexuality" (p. 309). Similarly, McCall (2014) finds that the Parker School, an elite, private school for girls, "represents an ordinary world of learning where girls feel smart, special, cared for, and privileged" (p. 178). Like the Clyde School, the Parker School is committed to reaching and supporting every girl and providing "every opportunity" to their students (McCall, 2014).

All-girls schools, like other social institutions, construct institutional identities over time and in relation to their members (Linde, 2009), producing discourses, or "configuration[s] of knowledge and its habitual forms of expression" (Cazden et al., 1996, p. 75) that reflect particular interests, values, and beliefs. As a result, examining how literacy, identity, and place intersect and operate within a particular context is an important dimension to consider in research about the constructions of girlhood and discourse around expressions of self in single-sex schools.

Framing the "all-girls school" as having a particular institutional identity and history of constructing girls and single-sex education in particular ways requires a closer look at the historical relationship between girls and all-girls schools. Highlighting the dialogic power of belonging that exists between an institution and its members, Gee (2000) writes:

> When an identity is underwritten and sustained by an institution, that institution works, across time and space, to see to it that certain sorts of discourse, dialogue, and interactions happen often enough [and] in similar enough ways to sustain the identities it underwrites. (p. 105)

While single-sex schools may share many commitments and goals to girls' education, they do not necessarily operate in a uniform manner, nor do they exist in dichotomous opposition of one another (DeBare, 2004; McCall, 2014). And while the narratives of encouragement, opportunity, and access in girls' schools may function in supportive and productive ways at times, they also run the risk of conveying essentialized images of institutions and populations in ways that silence inequities and differences, subsequently reinforcing dominant beliefs and hegemonic practices. Citing Deal's (1991) work delineating public schools from private schools, Proweller (1999) explains that, unlike the public school where community is "typically melded through an explicit set of regulatory practices, the private school binds individuals together through a common set of cultural codes that regulate student socialization inside and outside of school" (p. 780). Implying universal experiences across public, private, and parochial "all-girls schools," assigning them to a singular narrative, fails to account for the historical and contextual nuances of the institutions—how factors like race, class, gender, geography, school funding, and so on intersect and impact a school's culture, community, and identity.

The [hidden] ethos of privilege in Manhattan's elite private schools

One of the most significant challenges of conducting research in elite, private, independent schools lies in the ability to "access and then mine surface forms that embody social relations of privilege, inequalities, and hierarchies that are typically invisible because they have been so thoroughly institutionalized" (Proweller, 1998, p. 221). For instance, Amira Proweller (1998) finds that the "fabric of cultural life" at Best Academy is knit together by "social relations of privilege," deeply embedded and embodied in the structures and practices of the institution (p. 221). Her work examines how adolescent girls play active roles in shaping who they are on a daily basis, challenging the traditional view of young people as passive recipients of the institutional structures and discourses available to them when it comes to identity formation. Proweller must, however, work through the tensions of utilizing a poststructural framework within an institution steeped in traditional conceptions of success and belonging:

> Full support for academic excellence creates a climate that fosters confidence, independence, and self-reliance among girls because of and not in spite of the fact that they are female. Through a curriculum that promotes values of individualism, academic excellence, moral behavior, and community service, female students are being prepared for their place in the [upper middle-]class continuum. (p. 202)

Sara Lawrence Lightfoot (1983) describes a similar feeling on the campus of St. Paul's, an elite boarding school in New England. She notes the school's "supreme orchestration" of events and people, arguing that only a school with abundance, privilege, and a sense of institutional security can anticipate and coordinate life in this way. The experiences and memories of the institution are rooted in tradition, which seems to influence the present (Linde, 2009). Traditions, Lightfoot (1983) argues, function as active artifacts that reinforce a discourse of "it has always been that way" (p. 225), making it difficult to question or re-examine the relevance and inclusiveness of a school's customs. This phenomenon is particularly salient when it comes to critically analyzing (and pushing back on) the language, beliefs, customs, and assumptions that have circulated throughout a school community and culture for years.

METHODOLOGY

This critical case study used qualitative research methodology to explore how notions of girls and girlhood are constructed, understood, and promoted at an elite, private all-girls school and to investigate how high school students perceive, navigate, and investigate constructions of girls and girlhood within their school and life worlds. To restate, "girlhood" refers to the various temporal, ecological, cultural, and discursive storylines that intersect to construct and define the experiences of "being a girl," and the places and spaces within which these experiences occur. The study focused on how teenage girls read and write their realities in a particular environment using multimodal literacies practices. Specifically:

RQ1: How are girls and experiences of girlhood institutionally constructed within an elite, private, independent all-girls high school in New York City?

RQ2: How do high school students and school leaders read (interpret, perceive) constructions of girls and girlhood at an elite, private, independent all-girls school in New York City?

Data collection included semi-structured interviews, two multimodal media-making activities with sophomores, participant observations, and document review. In total, 17 students were interviewed (10 seniors, two juniors, and five sophomores), as well as five school leaders. Because this study sought to amplify the diverse voices, positionalities, and identities of the student population, youth participants are further introduced below (Table 1). While not all participants are included in the findings discussed in this chapter, the table below provides a full composite of the dynamic and diverse group of young people involved in this study. A combination of theoretical and quota sampling methods was used to recruit student participants based on a variety of access points and personal relationships that I had to students. Theoretical, or theory-based, sampling entails examining individuals "who can contribute to the evolving theory" of your study (Bloomberg & Volpe, 2012, p. 104). All participants (and the school itself) have been given pseudonyms to protect confidentiality.

Table 1. Student Participants' Identifiers

Student	Grade	Identifiers
Raine	Sophomore	Female; speaks French, English, and Italian
Karl	Sophomore	She/her at Clyde (any pronouns for online persona); Chinese-Canadian; upper-middle class; gay; lives two blocks away from Clyde
Olivia	Sophomore	Straight; she/her; White; female; Jewish; upper-middle class
Lila	Sophomore	Pansexual; part-Asian, quarter Filipino, part White; cis-gendered
Jenny	Sophomore	White; female; straight; privileged; lives on the Upper East Side
Naomi	Junior	Female; she/her; Black; lower-middle class
Maya	Junior	Black; girl; pansexual; lives in Brooklyn
Caroline	Senior	She/her/hers; girl; White; straight; lives on the Upper East Side; Jewish
Annie	Senior	Queer; adopted; female (woman, girl, whatever); Christian; mental health issues; lower-middle class
Maria	Senior	Cis-gendered; female
Kate	Senior	White; female; not straight
Lucy	Senior	White; upper class; female; straight; Catholic and Jewish
Megan	Senior	White; American; Jewish; she/her/hers; straight
Lauren	Senior	She/her; straight; Irani-American; middle-class; White
Lydia	Senior	White; Armenian and Irish; female; she/her; upper-middle class; lives in diverse neighborhood in Brooklyn
Rachel	Senior	White; female
Simone	Senior	Black

The primary method of data analysis for this study was a critical analysis of discourse (McCall, 2014). Engaging in critical analysis of discourse, McCall (2014) emphasizes "the centrality of discursive practices in relation to larger social structures" (p. 118). Discursive practices are the "spoken and unspoken rules and conventions that govern how individuals learn to think, act and speak" in the social positions they occupy in their lives (Alvermann et al., 1997, p. 74), such as student, girl, athlete, New Yorker, etc. For McCall, critical analysis of discourse serves as a productive approach in helping her to identify storylines (Søndergaard, 2002), "a condensed version of a naturalized and conventional cultural narrative, one that is often used as the explanatory framework of one's own and other's practices and sequences of action" (p. 191). Storylines function as lenses through which to consider how an idea is constructed and subsequently how it conveys how to be and what to do in a given setting or circumstance. Storylines helped to trace the ways in which students talk about and make sense of themselves, their experiences as students and girls, and their school surroundings. Using critical analysis of discourse also aided in analyzing the storylines that construct the school's institutional identity and discourses involving belonging and empowerment from the adult perspective.

This case study was designed to provide participants with an opportunity to offer stories and, more importantly, counter-stories of girlhood: the representations, pressures, and idealized expectations about who they are and who they are expected to be in the context of the Clyde School. Solórzano and Yosso (2002) define counter-storytelling as "a method of telling the stories of those people whose experiences are not often told" (p. 26). Counter-stories provide a space for people to engage in creative reflections of self-expression and self-definition.

Many scholars (Hull & Nelson, 2005; Jewitt, 2005; Vasudevan, 2009) argue that literacy is multimodal—visual, spoken, written, gestural—and critical skills are needed to analyze and understand a range of media such as newspapers, television, film, Internet, radio, and magazines (Hull & Nelson, 2005; Janks, 2010). As a result, they feel that the practice and process of "reading" is deeply situated in social and cultural contexts and, as critical theorist Paulo Freire (2000) proposes, consists of learning how to read both the word and the world critically (in Janks, 2010). There is power in engaging young people in new literacies practices that account for, value, and revolve around their lived experiences and perceptions of the world.

Evolving from the new literacies movement, contemporary scholars of critical literacy continue the push to expand verbo- and logo-centric definitions of literacy to consider the body (Johnson & Vasudevan, 2012) and artifacts (Pahl & Rowsell, 2011) as texts that require critical literate practices to be read, interpreted, judged, analyzed, and negotiated. Embodied literacies practices are personal, political, and rife with assumptions and subjectivities. Kamler (1997, in Johnson & Vasudevan, 2012) understands the body as a text that is "produced by socially circulating norms for gender, race, sexuality, class, age and ability" (p. 35). In this sense, we read bodies by drawing from personal knowledge, lived experiences, discursive practices, media representations, and so on to make sense of who we are; to determine where we fit into micro and macro social orders; and to communicate particular ways of being through speaking, dressing, or gesturing that can reinforce or challenge social norms and power imbalances.

FINDINGS AND DISCUSSION

Below is a selection of counter-narratives from the case study that speak directly to the complexity and tangled-ness of girlhood. Counter-narratives provide a space for people—participants and readers alike—to engage in creative reflections of self-expression and self-definition. The first illustrates how students work to reclaim and reimagine the school-sanctioned archetype of the "Ideal Girl"; the second challenges the expectation of wanting or needing to bring one's full self to school; and the third examines the binary that students present between the school culture and the school community at Clyde, and considers the implications of disconnection within the places and spaces that young people occupy. Again, these counter-narratives reveal that the identities and lived experiences of this group of girls are nuanced and complicated, challenging many of the dominant storylines (Søndergaard, 2002) that circulate throughout the school.

Re-imagining Notions of the "Ideal Girl"

As a highly competitive all-girls school in New York City, Clyde's institutional identity is largely defined by its commitment to academics and knowledge; to a certain rigor, intellectuality, and curiosity; and to promises of helping girls "find the best versions" of themselves (as stated in the Clyde viewbook). In some discursive communities, there are constructed archetypes used so often that they begin to function as "revealing windows into a [particular] culture's conventional and dominant conceptions of identity" (Williams, 2011, p. 204). Archetypes can function as conduits for institutionally-sanctioned expectations around behavior, performance, and membership meant to motivate and encourage students to do and be their best.

This research focused on two deeply embedded identities at the Clyde School, the "Clyde Girl" and the "Every Girl," five idealized archetypes that embodied the most desired and valued characteristics, behaviors, and involvements of a quintessential student at the school. For some students, the archetypes were empowering and comforting labels, forces that pushed them toward a higher standard academically, extracurricularly, and socially. For others, the labels held rigid conceptions of what was valued and who belonged at Clyde—subsequently serving as barriers to representation and inclusion. Borrowing from Gee's (1990) notion of membership as it relates to "big-D" Discourse, the Clyde Girl and Every Girl function as symbolic representations of belonging at Clyde—the ways of being that were sanctioned as desirable, respectable, and supported, and in turn granted full access to membership in this discursive community. The idealized archetypes held particular values, perceptions, understandings, appreciations, and actions and served as a gatekeeper of "normalcy," reinforcing hegemonic expectations of excellence, empowerment, and belonging. These expectations denoted the rules of membership— the ways of knowing, acting, believing, speaking, and valuing— required to identify as, and fit the criteria of, the idealized archetypes. Kate, a senior, explains that the quintessential Clyde Girl is a term "that's kind of ... in the zeitgeist of Clyde." She and another senior, Lydia, share:

This girl gets straight As in every class, she does like 10 gagillion extracurriculars, she is really happy and like, very just, outgoing. There's definitely an image of what the Clyde Girl should be and like, frankly, there are just very few of us [who] fit into that mold ... and ... the Clyde Girl is usually White, wealthy, cis-gender, heterosexual, very...it's like a very narrow idea of what the Clyde Girl should be and there are obviously so many deviations from that? ... And, I mean, luckily, I haven't really had to... 'cause I am White and wealthy and like, cis-gender, [but] I don't identify as straight so that has been something that is kind of interesting.... (Interview, 3/15/17)

I've always assumed it's like, a blonde, blue eyed, smart, athletic, but also artsy, funny, quiet, but not too quiet girl. She's ... made up...she's not a real person. I think it's like Blake Lively in Gossip Girl...the ideal version of what that girl is... it's hard to be so inclusive and have everyone be the quintessential Clyde Girl... In middle school and freshman and sophomore years, I was really struggling a lot to be the Clyde Girl and, I just, when I showed up the first day, I wasn't that already and I knew that, so it was like, "I don't know how to mold myself to be this when it's just never gonna fit." ... 'cause the Clyde Girl is born that way. Like, she's a Clyde Girl from day one. She never mushed herself to become it. She is just naturally that. (Lydia, Interview, 3/8/17)

These standards of being reinforce normative beliefs and values about who is appreciated and/or what is expected among students at Clyde. Synthesizing how girls understand the archetypes demonstrates a need to continue critically deconstructing and reflecting on the connections between literacy, identity, and place in relation to empowerment and belonging.

Students further complicated the Clyde Girl archetype by increasingly reclaiming and reimagining it at the time of data collection:

I think we all came to an agreement that it shouldn't be like one type of person ... when you're defining a large group of people, it's really hard to do because it's not going to fit over everyone.... It's more of like an applaud to all students that go here. It's like, well, Clyde students are ones that want to learn, are eager to learn, and to kind of do it their own way, yeah? And they are outspoken compared to other people.... (Lydia, Interview, 3/8/17)

I feel like there's a consensus amongst everyone that like, you are here because you want to make something of your life and you want...I mean, there are some people who may take this education for granted? But I feel like pretty unanimously everyone just like, really wants to...just gain more knowledge and like, ask questions about the world and I think that's kind of what the teachers kind of push us...to keep digging into discussions that like, force us to think outside of maybe our experiences as well? I think that's kind of what it means. If I could put a label on every single person, I feel like that would be what it means. (Kate, Interview, 3/15/17)

Instead of dismissing the Clyde Girl phrase all together, these participants chose to reclaim it, demarcating what an actual or real Clyde Girl looks like today from their perspectives versus the institutionally-sanctioned image. Their conceptions moved away from gender, race, and cultural capital and instead focused on the identity of "student," not "girl." Lydia, Rachel, and Kate, for instance, all centered their re-definitions of the typical and/or ideal student around intellect: the student that embodies everything about Clyde is one who thinks critically, asks questions, and makes their voice heard. This is a testament to how even reclaimed notions of the Clyde Girl remain socially situated within the school context and demonstrate that students indeed share many of the values upheld by the school. The important takeaway here is not that students fully rejected the images and messages at Clyde but rather wanted to share in the ownership of the values, practices, behaviors, and ideals that circulated within and outside of the school building to tell the story/ies of the Clyde School. They wanted to feel heard.

Bringing Your Full Self to School

The second counter-narrative involves "bringing your full self to school," a phrase deeply embedded in the Clyde School lexicon to convey inclusivity and acceptance. It was a well-intentioned mantra frequently used by school leaders and in admissions and development materials, meant to encourage students to feel as though they could express every aspect of themselves freely and openly upon entering the building. As the head of school explained, "I think parents send their daughters to girls' schools so that they don't have to hide any parts of who they are" (Mr. Bennett, Interview, 1/24/17). But, as students evidence below, the notion of bringing one's full self to school every day is not as simple (nor as coveted) as one might think.

"I try to bring my full self to school every day, but there's always some setback, or like, I'm always more scared to do something than I think I am," Maya shared with me during her interview (4/10/17). Maya struggled with being perceived as shy and non-talkative: "I physically can't [speak up] sometimes ... I think it changes with school. Like, I can actually feel my throat close up.... I think it's just, uh, actually, that might have to do with people's perceptions [of me]" (Interview, 4/10/17). At the same time, Maya also credited Clyde for helping her to push herself to try new things and share more of herself. She found that some aspects of her full self were more accepted at home, and others were more accepted by her peers at Clyde.

With the exception of two participants, students reported that they did not feel like they could bring their full selves to school every day, nor did they necessarily want to:

> They say they want us to bring our full selves, but then when we do they're like, 'That's too much of you. That's ... wow, we did not need all of that information.' And like, you hear that all the time. 'You're laughing too loud,' or 'Why are you in this room? What are you doing? Why are you writing stuff on the board? Why are you listening to that music?' ... Don't tell people to bring their full selves to school 'cause they're not doing it anyway and there's a lot of people who don't want to bring their full selves to school ... why would someone bring the rest of them if they [the school] is not supportive of what they did bring?... That's where I think people get confused, and I think that's detrimental for young girls kind of

like, figuring out who they are in general but then also have a school that's like, 'We want to empower you, but you can't do this, or this, or your bra strap is showing, that's bad.'... so that's where it gets conflicting ... just say what you mean. (Lydia, Interview, 3/8/17)

Sharing the sentiment of many, Simone and Rachel spoke to the expectation of asking people to bring their full selves to school when it was a generally unnatural and unfeasible thing to do:

I [don't] think that there was a time when I could bring my whole self to school, but I think that's a universal thing... I don't blame them [the school] for wanting that ... obviously people hide parts of themselves.... I don't think it's a bad thing that people want that to happen in the administration...that Clyde is so warm and it would be so ideal that people could be at a point where they bring their full selves. Like, I don't disagree with it. I [just] think it's unrealistic... (Interview, 4/12/17)

I never really understood what it meant to bring your whole self to school, to be honest.... It's a very scary thought to bring your whole self to school...I don't think I've ever brought my full self to school. I don't think I've been my full self anywhere...Um, but at the same time, being uncomfortable at a place where you're supposed to be challenged is okay, so I don't know ... I think I feel my full self when I'm...able to talk about my opinions and being able to, you know, have my voice heard. (Rachel, Interview, 5/2/17)

Lastly, a few participants talked about how the uniform reinforced certain stereotypes and prohibited people from truly or fully expressing themselves. Dress as a discursive practice conveys ways of knowing and belonging through visual and material modes. A school uniform possesses its own codes of belonging, in the same way that one's own style communicates an understanding of identity and place.[1]

I have this like, more snazzy sense of fashion that can't ... like, be confined to like this and that [referring to her uniform]. I like wearing ... little waistcoats and things like that ... it's not like the uniform really constricts me but like, I still don't feel like I'm ever able to bring my full self to school just because like, there are things that I would like to do with my hair, to do with my clothes [that I can't]. (Karl, Interview, 3/13/17)

... I feel like Clyde can be [a] truly feminist [school] once they like, get rid of the uniform and just start letting us like, bring our full selves to school. Because they always say like, "...you can bring your full self to Clyde," but I don't know how true that is necessarily. (Kate, Interview, 3/15/17)

If the notion of bringing one's full self to school is not a realistic nor coveted option for students, what function does it then play in the school's rhetoric and culture? Participants recognize that the idea of bringing one's full self to school is a positive and respectable goal for the school to have, but it poses the question as to how and in what ways it reinforces the idea that the bodies, selves, and identities of young women are and should be regulated and monitored by an institution.

"Us" and "Them": School Culture versus School Community

The final counter-narrative concerns the demarcations that students see between Clyde's school culture and school community. This finding is significant when thinking about the places and spaces that girls occupy, what institutional supports and barriers they face in the midst of figuring out who they are and who they want to be in their lives. Borrowing from Phillips (1996), school culture refers to the "beliefs, attitudes, and behaviors which characterize a school" (p. 1). A school's culture is abstract, yet also tightly bound to notions of physical space. For instance, Clyde is a "visionary place—a testament to Clyde's promise that every girl will have every chance—at every moment, in every space—to find the best version of herself" (school viewbook, p. 31). As McDowell (1999) argues,

> ...places are made through power relations which construct the rules which define the boundaries. These boundaries are both social and spatial—they define who belongs to a place and who may be excluded, as well as the location or site of the experience. (Quoted in Bettis & Adams, 2005, p. 5)

At Clyde, place not only represents physical spaces, but what students are able to do in them.

Like the school culture, the school community at Clyde had both tangible and intangible aspects to it. The tangible aspects refer to the people within the institution who participate in, engage with, and help create and maintain the culture; the intangible refer to a sense or feeling of being part of a collective within a bounded system—the institution. While there was some relationship between the school culture and school community, many students talked about them as largely unique and separate entities. For students, the "school culture" often seemed less accessible and relevant to them than the "school community," but both clearly played critically central roles in their everyday experiences and perspectives of belonging at Clyde. Students overwhelmingly understood the school community as consisting primarily of their friends and peers as well as their teachers and advisors; the community was a source of support and acceptance. The administration was very rarely, if ever, included in students' explanations of community; yet, when discussing school culture, students often personified the school culture as "they," referring to the administration who, in their eyes, was largely synonymous with the construction and (re)production of the culture.

> Clyde is such an open, like, very inclusive community, but I feel like there's a lot of work to do ... in terms of like, creating the diverse, inclusive community that we talk about a lot.... Like, every girl kind of supports each other, but sometimes we don't acknowledge, like, each other's differences.... I guess from the admissions standpoint, [the Clyde culture is] like, every girl's supported, um, every girl has a voice, and we want to hear it. Um, but then the culture within Clyde is ... very much geared to the experience of ... a girl. And sometimes that can get a little bit weird ... because not every girl chose the same experience. And so, sometimes the culture can be a little bit uniform.... (Rachel, Interview, 5/2/17)

Lila articulately differentiated the dichotomous relationship between culture and community at Clyde: the school culture was rooted in history, traditions, and operated as an intangible aspect of the school's identity and operation; the community was active, current, and personified as a united collective that was evolving in rich and important ways. She said:

> The [school] culture is … [laughs] not as amazing [as the school community]. I guess the culture is more built from an older time rather than the community? It's students who shape the community, which means we keep it modern, we keep it on top of everything. The culture at Clyde, a lot less so. I guess, I've been having a lot of arguments saying how some of the ideals that we have at Clyde just … no longer match who is at Clyde anymore…. (Interview, 3/8/17)

> I think it's a well-knit community and everyone is very supportive, and a lot of people love Clyde … But I think my own experience is kind of different because I don't necessarily fit into the normal like, Clyde Girl, Every Girl-type thing. And so, like, a lot of my friends would agree with me, I think, that Clyde's a very safe and comforting community if you fit this little, like, mold … And it's been challenging kind of to navigate, because no one's gonna be like, "No, you're gonna be … an outcast or whatever." But there's this underlying kind of feeling that's definitely present. (Annie, Interview, 4/18/17)

The comments above illustrate the often contradictory aspects of the school climate that students grapple with every day. While there was an overall feeling of safety reported by students, it was largely attributed to relationships with peers and faculty members—the school community—not as much to the institution—the school culture. The messages surrounding the ideal archetypes, bringing one's full self to school, and the divisions between culture and community, all contribute to how students are made to understand notions of girlhood and their roles at Clyde. The nuanced and seemingly minor instances, interactions, and constructed environments are the aspects of the school climate that require greater attention and further research.

LIMITATIONS

There are always potential limitations in choosing to conduct a study in a school, as it requires flexibility on the part of the researcher and the ensuing research project. A school—as an institution, a culture, a community—is a living organism that is both constantly constructing and adapting to its environment. Schedules can change, new opportunities or access points for data collection can arise, just as tangential class discussions can derail lesson plans but result in important conversations about life. As scholars questioning traditional notions of scholarship (e.g., Dyson & Genishi, 2005; Luttrell, 2000; Vasudevan, 2011) argue, the imperfections and messiness of qualitative research (and the inevitability of limitations) are necessary for a study to evolve and emerge. More than anything, the research must be allowed to breathe. This was a particularly salient point given that a significant focus of this study was on the ecological dynamics of the Clyde School.

Because this project was a single case study and not a comprehensive exploration across multiple sites, the intention was not to represent or make broad claims about the experiences, perspectives, and identities of girls at the six elite private all-girls schools in New York City. The goal of case study research is not generalizability, but rather transferability: "how (if at all) and in what ways understanding and knowledge can be applied in similar contexts and settings" (Bloomberg & Volpe, 2012, p. 31). Conducting a single-site case study afforded more time in a particular culture and community, deeper relationships to develop with members of that community, and ultimately allowed findings and recommendations that were tailored to a specific population and institution.

Furthermore, this study makes the case for further research in elite, independent, private all-girls schools in New York City, a set of institutions which remain largely uninterrogated and absent from the literature on gender and schooling. A multi-site case study involving a selection from the other six elite all-girls schools in Manhattan would be a strategic and important next step for this research. Studying other all-girls schools would help to strengthen the data collection instruments and theories used over time, layering findings from other institutions atop this initial study, and thickening understandings of constructions of girls and girlhood in Manhattan's elite all-girls schools.

CONCLUSION

These findings serve as a testament to the fundamental flaws that can exist in institutional language and practice, no matter how well-intentioned. The takeaway from this set of counter-narratives should not necessarily be that the institution and school leaders are to blame for crafting narratives and expectations meant to motivate, empower, and enliven its students and the larger school community. Clyde, like any other school, is deeply committed to being the best institution it can be, serving its members and fulfilling its promises. Yet, the data presented seek to demonstrate how grand statements and deeply-rooted traditions meant to unify a population can actually overlook and silence the immense diversity and wonderful complicatedness of students' identities and experiences that make young people such dynamic individuals. In this sense, and if nothing else, this study serves as a call to honor the new, complex, and multimodal literacies practices that young people are engaging in every day. These practices provide insights into who they are and what is important to them. As Bettis & Adams (2005) argue,

> Adult feminist scholars must know what the day-to-day habits of life are for adolescent girls. And if these daily habits include talk of who is nice, who is not, and how to change a tampon, then that talk and focus must be taken seriously, explored, played with, explained, and theorized. (p. 3)

Again, the purpose of critical activist inquiry is to disrupt the idea of an institution operating within a single dominant narrative and serve as a reminder that it is in the moments of disruption that we might begin to untangle, examine and re-imagine the practices, language, structures, and systems that work to construct notions of girls and girlhood in particular ways. Participants' responses raise questions of power and language at an institutional level and the impact that discursive practices can have on students' understandings of their roles and expectations through a gendered lens. The evidence presented illustrates the tensions that a school faces between embracing an evolving landscape of identities and literacies while still holding tightly onto history and tradition.

In the fields of gender studies and youth literacies, far less attention has been paid to the internal cultures and discourses of elite private all-girls schools, particularly those located on the Upper East Side of Manhattan. The roles of institutions are often used to frame research studies, but the focus ultimately rests on the students—how they are shaped by the spaces they occupy or how they learn to navigate their ways out. These are important contributions that highlight students' perspectives and help us to re-imagine possibilities for change. At the same time, by only placing young people at the center of the conversation, we shift focus away from the institutions where the negotiations are happening; where language plays a significant role in constructing normative and Other practices and behaviors; and where power structures are in play. Further research that holds focus on institutions themselves—how they construct knowledge, meaning, and membership through discursive practices and sociopolitical structures—primarily from the perspectives of young people, is needed. This would provide fuller, more contextualized narratives and allow us to consider the possibilities and potentials for creating and sustaining more authentically inclusive school spaces. Such spaces are crucial in helping girls continue to redefine and reimagine their roles in society and school, to disrupt the status quo, and to have their voices heard. They have so much to say.

REFERENCES

Alvermann, D. E., Commeyras, M., Young, J. P., Randall, S., & Hinson, D. (1997). Interrupting gendered discursive practices in classroom talk about text: Easy to think about, difficult to do. *Journal of Literacy Research 29*(1), 73–104.

Bettis, P. J., & Adams, N. G. (2009). *Geographies of girlhood: Identities in-between*. Routledge.

Blackburn, M. V. (2001). *Reading and writing for social change: Exploring literacy performances and identity work with queer youth* [Doctoral dissertation]. Retrieved from ProQuest Dissertations & Theses Global. (Order No. 3015297).

Bloomberg, L. D., & Volpe, M. (2012). *Completing your qualitative dissertation: A road map from beginning to end* (2nd ed.). Sage.

Cazden, C., Cope, B., Fairclough, N., Gee, J., Kalantzis, M., Kress, G., ... Nakata, M. (1996). A pedagogy of multiliteracies: Designing social futures. *Harvard Educational Review, 66*, 60–92.

Cohen-Sandler, R. (2005). *Stressed-out girls: Helping them thrive in the age of pressure*. Penguin.

Collins, P. H. (2000). *Black feminist thought: Knowledge, consciousness, and the politics of empowerment* (2nd ed.). Routledge.

Conley, T. L. (2016). *Mapping new(er) connections in a premature place: A case study on youth (dis) connection, mobilities, and the city* (Doctoral dissertation). Retrieved from ProQuest Dissertations & Theses Global. (Order No. 10117106).

DeBare, I. (2004). *Where girls come first: The rise, fall, and surprising revival of girls' schools*. Penguin.

Dyson, A. H., & Genishi, C. (1994). *The need for story: Cultural diversity in classroom and community*. National Council of Teachers of English.

Gee, J. P. (1990). *Social linguistics and literacies: Ideology in discourses* (2nd ed.). Routledge Falmer.

Gee, J. P. (2000). Identity as an analytic lens for research in education. *Review of Research in Education, 25*, 99–125.

Gee, J. P. (2005). *An introduction to discourse analysis: Theory and method* (2nd ed.). Routledge.

Hull, G. A., & Nelson, M. E. (2005). Locating the semiotic power of multimodality. *Written Communication, 22*(2), 1–38.

Janks, H. (2010). *Literacy and power*. Routledge.

Jewitt, C. (2005). Multimodality, "reading," and "writing" for the 21st century. *Discourse: Studies in the Cultural Politics of Education, 26*(3), 315–331.

Johnson, E. (2012). Performative politics and radical possibilities: Re-framing pop culture text work in schools. *Journal of Curriculum Theorizing, 28*(1), 158–174.

Johnson, E., & Vasudevan, L. (2012). Seeing and hearing students' lived and embodied critical literacy practices. *Theory Into Practice, 51*(1), 34–41.

Lightfoot, S. L. (1983). *The good high school: Portraits of character and culture*. Basic Books.

Linde, C. (2009). *Working the past: Narrative and institutional memory*. Oxford University Press.

Luttrell, W. (2000). "Good enough" methods for ethnographic research. *Harvard Educational Review, 70*(4), 499–523.

McCall, S. D. (2014). *What kind of "girl"? Curricular knowledge and the making of girls and young women in two all-girls schools* (Doctoral dissertation). Retrieved from ProQuest Dissertations and Theses Global. (UMI #: 3622268).

Noguera, P. (2012). "Joaquín's dilemma": Understanding the link between racial identity and school-related behaviors. In M. Sadowski (Ed.), *Adolescents at school: Perspectives on youth, identity, and education* (pp. 23–34). Harvard Education Press.

Nukkula, M. (2012). Identity and possibility: Adolescent development and the potential of schools. In M. Sadowski (Ed.), *Adolescents at school: Perspectives on youth, identity, and education* (pp. 11–22). Harvard Education Press.

Pahl, K. H., & Rowsell, J. (2011). Artifactual critical literacy: A new perspective for literacy education. *Berkeley Review of Education, 2*(2), 129–151.

Phillips, G. (1996). *Classroom rituals for at-risk learners*. Educserv, British Columbia School Trustee Publishing.

Pipher, M. (1994). *Reviving Ophelia: Saving the selves of adolescent girls*. Penguin.

Proweller, A. (1998). *Constructing female identities: Meaning making in an upper middle class youth culture*. State University of New York Press.

Proweller, A. (1999). Shifting identities in private education: Reconstructing race at/in the cultural center. *Teachers College Record, 100*(4), 776–808.

Rolling, J. H., Jr. (2013). Arts-based research primer. Peter Lang.

Solórzano, D. G., & Yosso, T. J. (2002). Critical race methodology: Counter-storytelling as an analytical framework for education research. *Qualitative Inquiry, 8*(1), 23–44.

Søndergaard, D. M. (2002). Poststructuralist approaches to empirical analysis. *Qualitative Studies in Education, 15*(2), 187–204.

Tupper, J. A., Carson, T., Johnson, I., & Mangat, J. (2008). Building place: Students' negotiation of spaces and citizenship in schools. *Canadian Journal of Education, 31*(4), 1065–1092.

Vasudevan, L. (2009). Performing new geographies of literacy teaching and learning. *English Education, 41*(4), 356–374.

Vasudevan, L. (2011). Reimagining pedagogies for multimodal selves. *National Society for the Study of Education, 110*(1), 88–108.

Williams, B. T. (2011). Collages of identity: Popular culture, emotion, and online literacies. *National Society for the Study of Education, 110*(1), 200–219.

Zaslow, E. (2009). *Feminism, Inc.: Coming of age in girl power media culture.* Palgrave Macmillan.

Emily Bailin Wells
Teachers College at Columbia University

FOOTNOTE

1. Clyde's uniform consisted of a choice of three pleated skirts (navy, grey, and light blue), a solid-colored collared shirt or school-related top (athletic/sports teams t-shirts and/or sweatshirts), and either sneakers or low-heeled, closed-toed shoes. While it is more flexible than other dress codes—and the uniform is meant to promote equality amongst students—many still felt there were significant restrictions for expression.

Chapter Three

Queer and Normal: A Critical Analysis of the Hidden Curriculum of Heteronormativity

Irdawati Bay Nalls

"Our Pledge"

We, the citizens of Singapore,

Pledge ourselves as one united people.

Regardless of race, language, or religion,

To build a democratic society,

Based on justice and equality.

So as to achieve happiness, prosperity,

and progress for our nation.

"Our Pledge" is a legal document and binding contract between Singapore and her citizens. In this agreement, there is a promise that all Singaporeans will act as one united nation regardless of our differences in race, language, or religion. The goal is to build a society that is democratic, based on a system that is just and subscribes to the concept of equality for all citizens. This ensures Singapore's progress forward as a nation so that her people can live in happiness and prosperity through hard work and play. Despite these democratic ideals, there is a hidden curriculum that defines citizenship. Indeed, racial, linguistic, and religious identities are protected under citizenship; however, what is not promised in the pledge is that of sexual orientation. Does a Queer person not have rights to Singaporean citizenry? This critical reflective narrative applies critical race theory and critical pedagogy to investigate the hidden curriculum of heteronormativity in Singaporean society. Specifically, it unveils how heteronormativity plays out in an education-driven, meritocratic, post-colonial Singaporean society, and how such heteronormative behaviors, laws, and policies masked behind a hidden curriculum impact Queer

E. Mikulec, D. Beichner (eds.), *Distraction: Girls, School, and Sexuality, 35-48.*
© 2021 DIO Press, Inc. All rights reserved.

people. Drawing from critical race theory's (CRT) methodology of counter-story-telling, this chapter illuminates the painful journey that Queer folks must navigate in order to survive in a hetero-normed society.

I begin by offering my identity and positionality as a way to situate the analysis of this chapter. I am a Queer, mixed-heritage Singaporean female in the field of education. Queer Studies is of particular interest, especially in studying the operations of heteronormativity, for three reasons.

First, in acknowledging my marginalized identities and critical dispositions as female in academia (hooks, 1994) and as a woman of color in a post-colonial white supremacist educational system (Lewis & Manno, 2012), my unique racial and gender positioning gives me insight into the mechanisms of race and patriarchy in education. In fact, Black women and women of color in general, as Collins (1989) suggests, have a unique sensitivity to the operations of race and gender, which often go undetected by men and Whites. As such, I embrace my racial and gender identity and acknowledge the application that it provides for my analysis.

Second, given that my research delves into critical theoretical analyses of how hegemonic mechanisms of race and gender impact education, it behooves me to apply such scholarship to the realm of heteronormative curriculum. Essentially, I apply my scholarship to "name the world, to change it" (Freire, 2012, p. 88). That is, if I am to be genuine with my approaches to socially just education and undoing oppressive education, then I must also commit to finding ways to name new social ills beyond race and gender, a process that Freire (2012) argues "is not possible if not infused with love" (p. 89). Therefore, the application of this scholarship to unveil heteronormative curriculum in Singaporean society is how I enact my love for the Queer community that is in itself a "commitment to their cause—the cause of liberation" (p. 89).

Finally, regardless of my sexual orientation which, when exposed, is often used in a way to discredit or project bias onto one's analysis, I operate with the presumption that hegemonic heteronormativity operates. That is, much like how CRT recognizes the endemic nature and permanence of race and White supremacy, the presence of heterosexism, homophobia, and heteronormativity exists as social norms that go unnoticed and uncontested in Singaporean society. Just as scholars of color, and specifically women scholars of color are "presumed incompetent" as taken from the title of a book by Gabriella Gutiérrez y Muhs (2012), due to white supremacy and patriarchy, I am aware that such hegemonic mechanisms can also be applied to work in the Lesbian Gay Transgender Bisexual Queer (LGBTQ) community. As such, I proceed with these subjectivities in mind never forgetting both my positionality and where they are situated in a power structure of race, class, gender, and heteronormativity.

QUEERING THE CURRICULUM

Sumara and Davis (1999) challenge heteronormative pedagogy in their discussion a critical pedagogy that moves towards a Queer curriculum theory. Following Foucault, they believed that "knowledge about sexuality [is] the primary link to all other forms of knowledge" (p. 201). With this understanding, Sumara and Davis (1999) argue for a curriculum that considers four key aspects to help begin the process of developing spaces for exploration of complex relations of sex and epistemologies. These four aspects coincidently match the four keys aspects of sex education in Singapore. The difference is that the curriculum in Singapore fails to critically consider the positionality of the Queer community as it privileges heteronormativity as the standard practice and norm of sex education, discussed subsequently in four aspects, physical, emotional, social, and ethical.

The first key aspect of sex education in Singapore discusses the physical issues of sex. In a Queer curriculum theory, this looks at how "sexuality is understood as a necessary companion to all knowing" (Sumara & Davis, 1999, p. 203). Currently, the curriculum in Singapore explores heteronormative (also known as straight) knowledge and identities. Anything that is considered deviant to heteronormative knowledge and identities, such as Queer identities, are made invisible within the curriculum (Ministry of Education, 2013). This gives rise to the continued stereotypical perceived identities of Queers in Singapore, because of the lack of dialogue on knowledge and identities that are not considered "normative." As reported in the Singapore Survey Report (2012), 60.2% of Queers faced discrimination at school and workplace. Queers are continually misjudged, and their identities stereotyped, as they are not given the space to explore their identities with Others who are different from them. Queers have not been given the opportunity to own their Queerness because they are still perceived as deviant and non-conforming (Singapore Survey Report, 2012).

The second aspect discusses emotional issues of sex in sex education in Singapore. This ties in with two aspects highlighted in the Queer curriculum theory that Sumara and Davis (1999) summarize as sexuality being understood as a companion to all [ways of] knowing.

Human subjects continue to interrupt common beliefs of what constitute the experiences of desire, pleasure, and sexuality to better understand the complex relationships among these experiences.

These aspects highlight the importance of exploring the complexity of human emotions among heterosexuals and homosexuals. The space to explore such emotions provides affirmation that no emotions are deviant. Experiencing desires, pleasures, and sexuality among homosexuals is as common as those experiences that heterosexuals encounter, of which none is more normative, or deviant compared to the other. More than anything, the discussions of such experiences will only affirm Singaporean youths of their sexual emotions, be it towards someone of the opposite gender or of the same gender.

The third aspect of sex education in Singapore discusses the social issues of sex, also described by Sumara and Davis (1999) as:

> Questioning the very existence of heterosexual as a stable category. Taking an interest in understanding and interpreting differences among people rather than noting differences among categories of people.

This aspect of sex education is most crucial to be explored among Singaporean youths, Queers or otherwise. Based on the given curriculum prescribed by the Ministry of Education in Singapore, the social aspect in sex education is defined as sexual norms and behaviors and their legal, cultural, and societal implications. However, this definition only considers heterosexual activities as the norms and normative behaviors. As such, the current curriculum fails to provide a safe space for the discussion of homosexual activities (Ministry of Education, 2013). Rhetoric adopted for the discussion of homosexual behaviors is associated with the legality surrounding the issues. This is refers to Penal Code Section 377A. As a result, Queer youths continue to feel marginalized and alienated for being different. The Queer community continues to remain at the periphery of Singaporeans' social, political, and cultural scenes as they are made aware of their tolerance as long as they conform to what is perceived as normative by society. Queers are not provided the safe space similar to the one discussed in Leonardo and Porter (2010), where one can openly discuss issues of their sexual orientation. They are constantly being taught that the norm is being heterosexual. Straight Singaporeans are also not given the opportunity to explore their own sexual identities or question the perceived stereotypical identities of Queers. Not getting access to such ontologies and epistemologies has led to the current situation where they (straight Singaporeans) continually perceive Queers negatively unless they have had the opportunity to interact with Queers themselves. Their perception of Queers otherwise has been limited to what was taught in schools: being Queer is illegal, deviant, and non-conforming.

From a societal perspective, such teaching and learning practices where Queers remained invisible and the only rhetoric used in school to discuss Queers would be associated to their illegal status will only continue to perpetuate the stereotypical perceived identities of Queers. Both straight Singaporean youths and Queer youths are continually punished and deprived of knowledge as they are not offered a safe space to discuss issues of their identities because being Queer is illegal in the eyes of the Singaporean law (Section 377A). Schools do not and cannot provide a safe space for the engagement of such discussion when topics on Queer identities are made invisible from the curriculum (Ministry of Education, 2013). Hemmings (2004) highlights the importance of identity formation among youth in schools. Her study affirms the important roles that school plays in the shaping of youth identities. The current sex curriculum in Singapore is depriving youths of such experience.

The last and final key aspect of sex education in Singapore discusses the ethical issues of sex. This ties in with the previous discussion that talks about the social and cultural aspects of teaching and learning in the sex curriculum in Singapore. The current curriculum draws a clear black and white line between what is ethical and what is not. Performing heteronormative is ethical and otherwise is not. This is not always the case. However, the lack of discussions and opportunities for debates on such issues are not included in the colonial curriculum where the teacher is the authority figure giving out information to the students, who never question and only absorb this knowledge as the gospel truth. This should no longer be the case with critical pedagogy that allows students in different positionality to challenge the status quo and raise questions through a critical lens (hooks, 1994).

REFLECTIVE NARRATIVE

Societal norms fossilized in educational practices have subjected me, a patriotic Queer Singaporean woman, to a non-conforming experience both as a student and an educator. Coming out of the LGBT closet at the age of 13, while living in a country where being gay was illegal (Lim, 2010), I faced strong rejections from my mother. The cliché often expressed by conservative parents to their Queer children, "I would rather you dead than gay," was uttered out of love to a pre-teenager who thought that God would never love me as His own because my own mother could not accept me as her own. I was rejected since I was a little girl of 13. Three years before that, I was just struggling to fight the Devil within me that made me feel this unnatural magnetic attraction towards girls. I was constantly reminded of how sinful I was as a human being through the microaggressions from my mother who reinforced my guilt for being Queer. Growing up, I believed that I was sinful because neither my mother nor God could accept my being Queer. I felt rejected as I struggled to cope with my identity, a Queer pretending to be straight. I ended up hating who I was.

It was not helpful that I failed to get any support from the convent where I received my formal education. Neither the school counselors nor the teachers were supportive of my Queer identity. In fact, my then teacher, Ms. Goh, and Chemistry teacher, Mrs. Koh, advised me that I would perform better academically if I were "normal" and more feminine as girls should be.

As I grew from a pre-teenager to a young woman, I was hoping that I would mature, and the hatred around and within me would subside. However, I was disappointed when I started teaching. Joining the workforce, I soon realized how sinful and unacceptable I was perceived to be by my fellow colleagues. I was breathing in heteronormativity as I entered the education field. Even though many years had passed since I came out of my closet, the journey towards acceptance, both for myself and those like me, had often been painful and sometimes even humiliating.

A Queer Educator

One of the most humiliating experiences that I had while working was at the convent where I was teaching Math class to secondary school girls aged thirteen through sixteen years old. One afternoon, during my teaching career at the convent, I was told off by two Sisters, because of my identity and not my work ethics. These Sisters were also the school Principal and Vice-Principal at the convent. Sister Josephine, the Vice-Principal then, claimed that I was an amazing Math teacher who not only taught well, but also knew how to inspire the girls. Contrary to the misinformed beliefs in Singapore classrooms that boys are better than girls at Math, results showed that under my tutelage, the girls at the convent not only enjoyed Math class, they were also performing very well on tests.

Despite my professionalism and my strength in teaching, I was still reprimanded at work. I recall being brought into Sister Josephine's room that dreaded afternoon, as if I were one of the convent girls who had misbehaved, and told that even though I was a great teacher, my choices in life were less than desirable to become a more positive role model for the girls at the school. I was advised to transfer myself to another school to teach and was also kindly advised to be discreet about expressing my sexual orientation in my future schools (should I not be able to change my orientation). To begin with, I was not even open about my sexual orientation at the school that I was teaching. I was "caught" because my then-partner was seen driving me to school every morning, and that alone was unacceptable.

Five years had passed since that first humiliating experience where I was asked to leave a school, not because I was a lousy teacher, but because I was perceived as a lousy human being. Just two years before I came to the United States, I was teaching at another mission school, an all-boys school. Again, I found myself sitting in the principal's office another dreaded afternoon because someone had out-ed my sexual orientation to the school administrators. Going through the same internal rejection again, I knew what I needed to do to keep my job, and that was to lie through my teeth to prove that I was "normal." I did, but I was caught in my own lies as the school principal and vice-principal confiscated my phone to read through the personal text messages I had saved on my mobile device. As I sat in the office with my head hanging down, feeling ashamed for being who I was, a Queer educator, I knew what was going to happen to me. I was going to be dismissed again. But the principal was "kind" to me. She expressed this kindness through her desire to want to "treat" me for my Queerness. My treatment was that I was ordered to be counseled by the school pastor for an hour daily so that I could be healed and accepted into God's grace. Once I was considered better by the straight community, I could be accepted into society and the house of God, like the other teachers who were already loved by God because they were unQueer. Heteronormativity was imposed on me by the mainstream straight community, who saw my undesirable sexual orientation as deviant (Warner, 1993). That was the only reason why I needed to be treated of my Queerness, to be normalized.

Back in my beloved country, Singapore, I was asked to hide, or better yet discard completely, a huge part of my identity because acquaintances had informed me that society views my Queerness as being a less than desirable adult role model in the education field. I was told that if I wanted to teach, I must not be me. Being me was wrong, sinful, and un-adult-like. As a young adult then, I felt rejected all over again whenever I had to sit in the principals' office, like I were a 13-year-old pre-teenager whose mother had just told me that I was better off dead. The old wound that I tried so hard to nurse was bleeding, again! And the acceptance I sought was far from my reach.

Living on the Periphery

The journey towards acceptance, both for myself and those around me, has not been easy. I was and still am afraid to tell people who I really am. I wanted to fit in, be the ideal Singaporean, but I also wanted to be me, Queer. The voice of double-consciousness (Du Bois, 2009) is a concept I understand very well. The need to be part of the Singaporean society was so great that I went through a period of time pretending to be a heterosexual woman so that I could be "normal" and accepted by mainstream straights. As I pretended to be who I was not, I saw the acceptance I yearned for when I looked into the eyes of people who claimed to love me, my mother included—like I said, claimed to love me for who I was not. I was not good enough to be me; therefore, I had to become someone whom I was not, just to be loved, and to be accepted.

For years, I struggled with myself, with God, and with society as I battled with my Queer identity and the perceived ideal identity of being a Singaporean. Why couldn't I be a Queer Singaporean? I wanted to change my life and those like me. I wanted to be accepted no matter whom I choose to love. The ongoing battle had been trying for me and people like me in Singapore. Many activists before me have failed, and I know that many more after me might fail. But I do want to believe that none of us will give up the fight to be treated like every other Singaporean, to have the rights that all Singaporeans are entitled to, to claim our birthrights, to be called Singaporeans without a worry in our minds that we could lose our jobs because of who we are. Deep in my heart, I was afraid, hurt, repeatedly disappointed, and very tired, but I held onto the beliefs that I was not a lesser being just because I was different. Some days, I believed myself. Other days, I just felt like throwing in the towel and fit in because I did not want to be reminded of my repeated rejection.

Since I was 13, my mother reminded me that I was an outcast, a rejected minority because of my sexual orientation, which is a huge part of my identity. My teachers were not affirming. Instead of educating me, they reminded me of how my Queer identity and my less feminine personality made me less of the role model convent girl. Joining the education field as a teacher myself with the hope of making a difference, an opportunity I was denied as a student, again… my Queerness was rejected as I was reminded of my worth-"less"-ness. My rejected identity was the main reason why I came to the United States. My rejected identity made me run away from the country I love, my birth country, but not yet my birth right. I just wanted to stop being a minority who was continually marginalized because of who I am, a Queer woman. I had thought that here in the United States, I could finally become a part of the larger society and be who I am without having to hide my identity. I thought that maybe I could stop pretending to be who I am not, a heterosexual woman, just so that I could escape discrimination from the dominant members of society. The United States is supposed to be a land of equal opportunity based on ability. I am educated and capable. I wanted to be just accepted, and not merely tolerated. I didn't want to live on the periphery of societal norms and practices anymore. However, here in Colorado, I soon realized that I am not only Queer, I am also a woman of color and a Multilingual. I am far from the ideal WASP (White, Anglo-Saxon, Protestant) and may I add monolingual English-speaking American majority. Struggling with my new Asian American identity has been difficult enough without having to come out of my LGBT closet. The microaggressions that I have been subjected to in my own country still send shivers down my spine, so that I now lack the courage to come out of my LBGT closet without first being assured that I am in a safe space.

I ran from one country where my identity made me an "illegal citizen" to another country where I may not be an "illegal citizen," but I am more often than not immediately judged based on the way I look and speak. How can I add my sexual orientation to the list of judgments that society already holds against me based on my race and accent? Why did God make me different? I may be queer, but I am normal. Accept me!... so that I can return Home.

CHANGES THROUGH EDUCATION OF THE MASSES

I am a patriotic Queer Singaporean educator who was, is, and will always be passionate about shaping the future of Singapore. I am very invested in shaping the identities and changing the stereotypical perceived identity of Queer Singaporean youths so that they will be offered options that I was denied at 13 when I came out of the LGBT closet. Having obtained my first degree in education from Singapore and taught in mission schools in Singapore, I had experienced microaggressions both as a Queer student and educator. Because of my experiences, some of which I have shared through my narratives in this chapter, I am passionate about being the change that challenges the status quo in regard to the treatment of Queers in my beloved country, Singapore.

For a long time, I too had adopted the colonized mentality (Memmi, 1992) of my fellow Singaporeans, living on the periphery of Singaporean society as I struggled with my Queer Singaporean identity. Having shown a critical perspective through my tertiary education in Colorado, I am able to re-situate my positionality as I negotiate my identities as a Queer Singaporean educator re-claiming my birthrights and the birthrights of those like me. This can be accomplished by re-framing the current pedagogy in Singapore schools to create a more critical pedagogy (Freire, 2012) that considers the positionality of the mainstream as well as the marginalized community in Singapore.

Critical Pedagogy

Freire (2012) offered an enlightening framework to define what he calls the pedagogy of the oppressed. He clearly outlined the scope to describe pedagogy of people engaged in a fight for their own liberation. It is a critical pedagogy similar to the one Memmi (1992) suggests where the oppressed are in a position that gives them the power to free the oppressors by first freeing themselves. Freire referred to this process as a revolutionary action, where the oppressed and the oppressors are in communication to negotiate the healing process. Allen (2004) used Freire's book to discuss the curriculum of critical pedagogy.

Allen (2004) helped me reposition my role as an educator as I reflect on the current curriculum in Singapore in respect to heteronormativity (Sumara & Davis, 1999). Using critical Whiteness theory, Allen suggested that the way to cure Whites of their exercise of white supremacy is to stop the spreading of White ontologies and epistemologies as the privileged knowledge. This form of pedagogy, where White ontologies and epistemologies are privileged, has resulted in internalized racism because even people of color continue to perpetuate such forms of teaching and learning. A situation where hegemony of teaching and learning practices arise when the described practices of spreading White knowledge are made standard (Gramsci, 2010) among Whites and people of color.

In Singapore, such a curriculum where a hegemony of certain teaching and learning practices are made standard exists with respect to heteronormativity. Singaporean educators are not encouraged to discuss issues pertaining to homosexuality in the classrooms due to the law 377A in Singapore, and this is worsening because of the strict control on free expression in Singapore (Human Rights Watch, 2013). In addition, gay men are criminalized for performing sodomy, while heterosexual couples are spared from such criminalization even when they could be performing the same sexual act. This knowledge is made explicit as a warning during sex education lessons in Singaporean schools. Even books such as *And Tango Makes Three* by Parnell and Richardson (2005), which features a pair of gay penguins who had a baby, is removed from the children section of the national library as well as the school library for promoting "the gay agenda." Heteronormativity as a hegemonic culture continues to be normalized (Sumara & Davis, 1999), and such practices continue to marginalize Queers in Singapore. For example, sex education in Singapore, which covers four key aspects of sexual activities—physical, emotional, social, and ethical aspects—portrayed only one school of thought, heteronormativity. Anything that doesn't fall into this heteronormative practice and value as decided by the Singaporean government is rejected and faces marginalization. The social aspect, which includes but is not limited to the exploration of non-conforming identities (lesbian, gay, bisexual, or transgender), would not be allowed to be taught at schools, as this would question societal heteronormative identities of cis-gendered straight men and women. The physical aspect of sex education explicitly teaches students that sex happens only between a man and a woman. Any other coupling combinations such as between two men or two women are not mentioned because they do not exist. Should students raise questions regarding this, the standard response would be to highlight how those thoughts are wrong and illegal as reflected in Penal Code Section 377A (Lim, 2010). As suggested in Allen (2004).

> through text and dialogue, critical educators need to create an environment of dissonance that brings White students to a point of identity crisis. In order for the crisis to result in a race-radical White identity, White students must be shown other ways of being White. (p. 133)

In the context of Singapore's curriculum, heterosexual and homosexual students, and educators must be allowed to get involved in a dialogue that encourages discussions. A Fanonian safe space (Leonardo & Porter, 2010) where engaging conversation is encouraged and allowed is much needed to help create a sexual-radical heterosexual identity. In such safe spaces which can be made possible in classrooms, heterosexuals in Singapore are made aware of other ways to portray their heterosexuality without marginalizing or imposing heteronormativity upon homosexuals. Educators play a critical role in educating the masses through developing a curriculum that engages in critical thinking and positive debates with the goal of learning and informing.

Currently, Queers in Singapore do not enjoy a legal status (Lim, 2010). This is because heteronormativity as a hegemonic culture is an ideology that has been legalized for the past 54 years in Singapore. Queers as a marginalized community continue to be transparent in Singapore society. Their voices of pain expressed through their narratives (counter-stories) continue to remain on the periphery of the social, cultural, and political scenes in Singapore. As an educator, I believe that a critical pedagogy is needed to allow for critical thinking and dialogues in classrooms to transform heternormativity. Such pedagogy does not aim to turn heterosexuals into homosexuals; rather, it is an approach to allow a revolutionary process. This process as Freire (2012) highlighted, is a communicative approach where the oppressed (homosexuals) and the oppressors (heterosexuals) begin to get in dialogue to start the healing process to create a more equal and inclusive society (Phillips, 2013). This ideal society in Singapore would imply that Queer youths can be given the opportunity to explore their identities in a healthy manner at a much younger age, without having to leave the country as I did. Allowing a communicative approach also means that a safe conversation that informs can take place with neither judgement nor guilt. The Pink Dot event held yearly (Tan, 2015) is a positive step towards a communicative approach; however, more work is still needed in our classrooms to help students feel safe in their own skin.

Repositioning Queers and Society through Re-Education

Queers in Singapore are subjected to two extreme microaggressions due to the lack of awareness among dominant members of society. This lack of awareness arises from a colonial curriculum that exerts heteronormativity as a universal norm. The act of tolerance is expressed when Singaporeans are being polite towards Queers. In an alternative scenario, rejection is often the observed treatment towards the already marginalized Queer community (Liang, 2013). Dominant members of society need to be aware that being Queer does not make a Singaporean any less of a human being, any less of a Singaporean; therefore, Queers in Singapore should be extended equal rights to job opportunities, housing, marriage, and adoption rights. Queers should also not be discriminated against at work, and promotion opportunities should be evaluated based on their performance (Singapore Survey Report, 2012). Queers should not be discriminated against because of their identities and/ or perceived identities. The first step to acceptance is to remove the present status of the Penal Code, Section 377A, that currently makes homosexual acts in Singapore illegal. A top down approach is necessary in the context of Singapore where her citizens still hold onto the colonized mentality, in which they still feel the need to be guided in their decisions and choices within society (Memmi, 1992). An accepting government is a step towards building a more accepting society that values equality among her citizens. Acceptance can be expressed through a rigorous change in the sex education curriculum in Singapore.

Another step towards creating a more inclusive society that accepts the Queer community begins with education of the masses in schools, which has been discussed extensively earlier. As highlighted, at present sex education in Singapore schools covers four keys areas. They are the physical, emotional, social, and ethical aspects of sexual activities. The social component plays a pivotal role in shaping re-education of mainstream Singaporeans. This is because the social component looks at how Queers, Singaporeans, and re-education can co-exist in helping to re-shape a positive identity for Queer youths in Singapore.

Social aspects in sex education are defined as sexual norms and behaviors and their legal, cultural, and societal implication. However, this definition only considers heterosexual activities as the norms and fails to provide a safe space for the discussion of homosexual activities (Ministry of Education, 2013). As a result, Queer youths continue to feel marginalized and alienated for being different. Queers are not provided the safe space similar to the one discussed in Leonardo and Porter (2010), where one can openly discuss issues of their sexual orientation. They are constantly being taught that the norm is to be heterosexual. These young Queers may develop what Du Bois (2009) refers to as a double-consciousness.

Du Bois (2009) discussed double-consciousness in his book *The Souls of Black Folk*. He used the example of African Americans feeling rejected because of the African in them trying to fit in with the American, also present in them. This double-consciousness existed because of the struggles of duality within identity that could not merge as one. Du Bois described this as the "sense of looking at one's self through the eyes of others, of measuring one's soul by the tape of a world that looks on in un-amused contempt and pity" (Du Bois, 2009, p. 7). Queers like myself experienced the "double-consciousness" of living in a country where our Queer identities do not enjoy legal status. The need to be Singaporean, a "legal citizen," and at the same time maintain our Queer identities, has been a struggle, but a necessary struggle that needs to be carried on as Queers re-situate ourselves against heteronormativity. Our Singaporean birthrights and the acceptance of the practice of Queer culture are basic human rights that should be granted us.

Besides minimizing the alienation of the Queer minority, it is also important to provide a safe space, as suggested in Leonardo and Porter (2010) for discussion of issues such as sexual orientation. This is to help remove the biased lens through which the majority of mainstream Singaporeans view Queers in Singapore. A safe space also encourages a more multicultural assimilation of Singaporeans from all walks of life.

In the Singapore context, the Fanonian safe space (Leonardo & Porter, 2010) is much needed to humanize both bourgeoisie society and its Others so that they can begin to develop the understanding that homosexuals are as much human beings as heterosexuals. It needs to be relayed that being Queer does not take away one's identity as being human. Therefore, a true humanizing sexuality dialogue is much needed to help begin the transition process of healing, both for the mainstreams as well as the Queers. The present movement of tiptoeing around the issue of legalizing Penal Code, Section 377A has not been effective. Instead, the act of tiptoeing has continued to downplay the importance of acceptance, masking tolerance as the acceptable practice when interacting with the Queer community. Re-education of the masses, which encourages a dialogue on true humanizing sexuality that involves not only Queers but also mainstream Singaporeans, can help to create a rigorous but safe space to discuss pertinent issues.

GLOBAL APPLICATION

Although this critical reflective narrative has focused solely on the Queer community in Singapore, with discussions of their struggles from political, cultural, and social perspectives, its application is global. Singapore is not the only country that hegemonizes heteronormativity. At present, there are only twelve countries and some parts of the United States, Brazil, and Mexico that have begun to legalize same-sex marriages and civil unions (Encyclopedia Britannica, 2013). The experiences of the Queer community in Singapore do not occur in isolation, as these occurrences are observed across the globe. Queers are often a marginalized group because we are the minority within the society in which we live. Being a minority puts us at a disadvantage from social, cultural, and political perspectives. Education of the masses is one of the ways to change the power dynamic and bring about equality in a society. However, for education of the masses to achieve this goal, an effective educational reform needs to be put into practice.

Bowles and Gintis (2011) discuss educational reforms looking at schooling in what they describe as capitalist America. Although their arguments focus mostly on achievement gaps in the United States, the application of educational reforms mirrors capitalist Singapore. Bowles and Gintis describe education of the 20th century as "the new ideology of opportunity" (p. 8). I propose three thoughts on this ideology: 1) Education is an arena for discovering one's talent. 2) Education is to provide equal opportunity to all. 3) There is the underlying notion that those who fail to measure up only have themselves to blame. Supporting the ideology is the myth that schools are the answer for creating equal opportunities and full development for all youths. Like the United States, Singapore too subscribes to this ideology as the government invests $10.6 billion into educating Singaporean youths (Ministry of Education, 2018). However, in all the plans for educational reforms, the essential question is still left unaddressed. How can an education system that aims to create equal opportunity for all and develop full personal potential attempt to include youths, both from dominant and marginalized communities, in this ideology?

CONCLUSION

This critical reflective narrative highlighted how the silencing of the Queer community through heteronormativity has resulted in the continued tolerance of their existence in capitalist-driven societies such as Singapore. It described how Queers in Singapore exist at the periphery of Singaporeans' cultural norms and practices as they continue to survive without being able to exercise their Singaporean birthrights prescribed in the national pledge. "Our Pledge" provided at the beginning of the article and later deconstructed reveals that Queers are excluded altogether from the promise of building a nation based on justice and equality. Queers in Singapore contribute to the thriving economy, but they have not been given the opportunity to vote on pivotal decisions that impact their community. Equality has not been extended to them as a community. Their voices have been minimized with respect to the laws that disregard their existence within society. This is observed in the continued battle to remove Penal Code 377A. This reflective narrative repositions

Queers in Singapore, as I question my positionality as a Singaporean Queer fighting for my birthrights and the birthrights of those like me.

This chapter aims to be one of the many beginning voices of the marginalized Queers in Singapore, as the petition for the removal of Penal Code Section 377A continues to be one of the central debates that argues for gay rights in Singapore. An in-depth study of the Queer community and the relationship they share with mainstream Singaporeans is needed to better position Queers and their "illegal" status with regard to their existence within capitalist Singapore society.

REFERENCES

Allen, R. L. (2004). Whiteness and critical pedagogy. *Educational Philosophy and Theory, 36*(2), 121–136.

Bowles, S., & Gintis, H. (2011). *Schooling in capitalist America: Educational reforms and the contradictions of economic life.* Haymarket Books.

Collins, P. H. (1989). The social construction of Black feminist thought. *Signs: Journal of Women in Culture and Society, 14*(4), 745–773. doi: 10.1086/494543

Du Bois, W. E. B. (2009). *The souls of Black folk.* Paradigm Publishers.

Encyclopaedia Britannica. Same-sex marriage. [Encyclopaedia Britannica]. (n.d.). Retrieved September 26, 2019,from http://www.britannica.com/EBchecked/topic/753687/same-sex-marriage/297960/Same-sex-marriage-around-the-world

Freire, P. (2012). *Pedagogy of the oppressed.* Continuum.

Gramsci, A. (2010). *Prison notebooks* (Vol. 3). International Publishers.

Gutierrez y Muhs, G. (2012). *Presumed incompetent: The intersections of race and class for women in academia.* University Press of Colorado, Utah State University Press.

Hemmings, A. B. (2004). *Coming of age in U.S. high schools: Economics, kinship, religious, and political crosscurrents.* Lawrence Erlbaum Associates.

hooks, b. (1994). *Teaching to transgress: Education as the practice of freedom.* Routledge.

Human Rights Watch. (2013). World Report 2013. Retrieved May 2, 2013, from https://www.hrw.org/world-report/2013

Leonardo, Z., & Porter, R. K. (2010). Pedagogy of fear: Towards a Fanonian theory of "safety" in race dialogue. *Race, Ethnicity and Education, 13*(2), 139–157.

Lewis, A. E. & Manno, M. J. (2012). Inside the K–12 pipeline for Black and Latino students. In Stulberg, L. M. & Weinberg, S. L. (Eds.), *Diversity in American Higher Education* (pp. 43–53). Routledge.

Liang, A. (2013). Court ruling deals blow to gay rights in Singapore. [AFP News]. Retrieved from http://sg.news.yahoo.com/court-ruling-deals-blow-gay-rights-singapore-090604697.html

Lim, L. P. (2010). Penal Code Section 377A. Retrieved from: http://eresources.nlb.gov.sg/infopedia/articles/SIP_1639_2010-01-31.html.

Memmi, A. (1992). *The colonizer and the colonized.* Beacon Press.

MOE. (n.d.). Bringing out the best in every child. [Ministry of Education page]. Retrieved December 26, 2018, from http://www.moe.gov.sg/default-source/document/about/files/moe-corporate-brochure.pdf

MOE. (2013). Sexuality education. [Ministry of Education page]. Retrieved from http://www.moe. gov.sg/education/programmes/social-emotional-learning/sexuality-education/

Parnell, P., & Richardson, J. (2005). *And Tango Makes Three*. Simon and Schuster Children's Publishing.

Phillips, R. (2013). "We aren't really that different": Globe-hopping discourse and queer rights in Singapore. *Journal of Language and Sexuality 2*(1), 122–144. doi: 10.1075/jls.2.1.05phi

Singapore Survey Report: Impact of homophobia and transphobia on LGBTQ individuals in Singapore. (2012). [Oogachaga page]. Retrieved from https://oogachaga.com/impact-of-homophobia-transphobia

Sumara, D., & Davis, B. (1999). Interrupting heteronormativty: Towards a queer curriculum theory. *Curriculum Inquiry, 29*(2), 191–208.

Tan, C. (2015). Pink dot: Cultural and sexual citizenship in gay Singapore. *Anthropological Quarterly, 88*(4), 969–996. doi: 10.1353/anq.2015.0058

Warner, M. (1993). *Fear of a queer planet: Queer politics and social theory*. University of Minnesota Press.

Irdawati Bay Nalls
Nanyang Technological University, Singapore

Chapter Four

A Pedagogy of Resistance: Feminist Service-Learning in
an Urban Middle School

Jennifer L. Martin, Brianna Boehlke, and Courtney Cepec

. . . we still have no name for what happens to women living in a culture that hates them.

—Jessica Valenti

In a climate where movements such as #MeToo, Black Lives Matter, and March for Our Lives are gaining traction to fight against systemic issues such as sexism, racism, and gun violence, students are increasingly becoming aware of their duty to advocate for the betterment of society, and seeking ways they may become participants in the activism they witness. Service-learning can increase empathy and advocacy skills (Scales, 1999), and can thus also provide students with an avenue to create sustainable change within their communities, and to resist school-based oppressions within a pedagogical context.

When service-learning is paired with feminist pedagogy, it can be transformational for students in terms of how they view themselves, and how they view the world and interact within it (Martin, 2017). Ochoa and Pershing (2011) conceptualize a pedagogy of resistance that utilizes Freire's concept of "conscientization": ". . . feminist pedagogy has as its goal the liberation of learners via the development of critical thought. While diminishing the authority of the teacher, feminist pedagogy encourages critical awareness about racism, sexism, oppression, and domination" (p. 24). Encouraging such dialogue can dismantle student notions of how the classroom works. Through this process, students transform from knowledge consumers to knowledge producers (Freire, 1970) as they become engaged in active learning and become social change agents (Ochoa & Pershing, 2011). Feminist pedagogy necessitates an examination of what is taught, and what is not taught, what is voiced, and what is ignored—on behalf of teachers, administrators, and students, including school policies and informal practices.

E. Mikulec, D. Beichner (eds.), Distraction: Girls, School, and Sexuality, 49-65.
© 2021 DIO Press, Inc. All rights reserved.

This chapter focuses on how feminist service-learning pedagogies can play a crucial role in combating school-based oppressions, providing a specific case example of a middle school service-learning project. T.R.U.E. Queens was an afterschool gender studies course for a group of primarily non-hegemonic[2] middle school girls with the purpose of combating microaggressions, sexism, and racism.

SERVICE LEARNING

Service-learning is a pedagogical technique through which students learn to develop academic and social skills by actively participating in self or class generated work for the betterment of school and/or community. These service experiences meet actual community needs; are coordinated by school and community; are integrated with academic curricula; and provide students with opportunities to apply academic and social skills to real life situations. Service-learning experiences must meet the following three criteria: they involve purposeful civic learning, enhance academic learning, and promote relevant and meaningful service with the community (Howard, 2001). Service-learning extends learning beyond the classroom thereby enhancing curricular objectives, helps to facilitate a sense of personal and civic responsibility, and promotes a sense of caring for others (Eyler, Giles, Stenson, & Gray, 2001).

In a summary of service-learning research, Billig (2002a) found that students who participated in service-learning were more positive about school, about themselves, and about their futures and communities. Participants also scored higher on standardized tests in mathematics and reading (Billig, 2002b). Researchers have found that service-learning can improve scores on high-stakes tests while also providing other academic and social benefits (Eyler et al., 2001), heightening students' connection to school, the community, and increasing their sense of self-worth (Catalano et al., 2004; Dymond et al., 2008; Koliba et al., 2006). Service-learning can also promote a reduction of stereotypes, deeper cultural sensitivity, and increased student understanding of socio-political institutions (Eyler et al., 2001; Zimmerman et al., 2009). In addition to its academic benefits, Service-learning can have a lasting positive impact on students; students may feel more personally and socially empowered and more connected to school.

Combining service-learning and feminist pedagogies can be truly powerful in inspiring students to examine the society in which they live. It is only through clear examination and reflection that they can then determine what societal changes are necessary to promote social justice and a more equitable world. Critical reflection on society and one's place within it is powerful for it encourages students to look beyond themselves, to see themselves as members of communities (Deeley, 2010). For some, service-learning is a foray into social activism; when paired with feminist pedagogy, service-learning can lead not only to feminist identification but also to sustained community engagement (Martin, 2016). Teachers can begin to inspire student interest into social activism by explicitly teaching about current social movements.

TEACHING SOCIAL MOVEMENTS

Teaching social movements can do much to inspire students to action. When students understand that small groups of caring people can change and have changed the status quo or an unfair situation, they may become inspired to do the same within their own schools and lives. The following are some current successful social movements that started small, and went viral worldwide, inspiring change and influencing people and policies.

#MeToo

> Though you muffle my voice, I speak./ Though you clip my wings and cage me, I fly./ And though you batter my body,/ commanding me to kneel before you,/ I resist.

> —Samira Ahmed

The #MeToo movement had its beginnings in 2006 when activist Tarana Burke became determined to connect with survivors of sexual harassment and assault. #MeToo turned viral hashtag when actor Alyssa Milano took to Twitter to share her story, and to inspire others to do the same. And many activists are striving to keep the movement intersectional in its focus. According to Vagianos (2017), "The #MeToo movement highlights a common problem: Feminist movements are often Whitewashed when they are brought into mainstream conversations. Women of color are often overlooked and left out of the very conversations they create" (para. 11). Alicia Garza, one of the founders of Black Lives Matter, thanked Burke for bringing the issues of sexual assault and harassment into mainstream parlance—as these issues continue to be a monumental problem.

New York Times reporters indicate that the #MeToo movement has and is dismantling existing power structures in society's most visible businesses (Carlsen et al., 2018). In various industries, over 200 powerful men lost their jobs over charges of sexual misconduct: "Forty-three percent of their replacements were women. Of those, one-third are in news media, one-quarter in government, and one-fifth in entertainment and the arts" (para. 8). According to Carlsen et al., citing law professor Joan Williams (2018), "'We've never seen something like this before. . . . Women have always been seen as risky, because they might do something like have a baby. But men are now being seen as more risky hires'" (para. 4). Through advocacy, the #MeToo movement aims to ensure that perpetrators of sexual misconduct receive their due consequences, such as losing employment and paying damages to victims.

The #MeToo movement continues to be influential, inspiring the recent Lifetime documentary series *Surviving R. Kelly*, prominently featuring Tarana Burke, and advocating that Kelly be brought to justice for decades of abuse upon untold numbers of women of color, the majority of whom were underage when the abuse began. Among the immeasurable troubling aspects revealed in the docuseries, one was ever present: that Black girls do not warrant the same cause for concern as would their White peers. A recent study solidifies this notion. The Georgetown Law Center on Poverty found that ". . . black girls were more likely to be viewed as behaving and seeming older than their stated age," even in girls as young as five (as cited in Green, 2017, para. 2). Additionally, this phenomenon of "adultification" or "age compression" prevents some from seeing children of color as victims of sexual abuse and trauma. These findings echo a 2014 study by Goff, Jackson, Di Leone, Culotta, and DiTomasso where Black and Brown children were perceived to be older than their chronological years, and thus more culpable for their actions (Goff et al., 2014). In both studies, the findings indicate that Black children are not perceived to possess the same level of innocence as their White peers; this has devastating implications for the school-to-prison pipeline.

Startling findings from the U.S. Department of Education Civil Right Data from 2014 include the fact that African American students account for only 18 percent of U.S. pre-K enrollment, but they account for 48 percent of preschoolers with multiple suspensions. African American students are expelled three times more than their White counterparts. African American and Latina/o students account for 40 percent of enrollment at schools offering gifted programs, but only 26 percent of students in said programs. Additionally, Black children are 18 times more likely to be sentenced as adults within the criminal justice system. Morris (2016) argues that Black girls are pushed out of schools for subjective "offenses," such as dress code violations and instances of "disrespect." Black girls, already viewed as guilty, are subject to the policing of their (perceived lack of) innocence and their sexuality, making Black girls more vulnerable and less protected: this places them in a societal double bind that they have no chance of winning. The Lifetime docuseries is a prime example of this. #MeToo is one entity that is bringing these issues to light.

According to Mowatt, French, and Malebranche (2013), "Black female bodies are both invisible and hypervisible, highlighting their deviance from hegemonic norms and beauty and discipline" (p. 647). To translate this trope to the high school environment: the angry Black woman becomes the loud, uncontrollable, and unmanageable Black girl, made acceptable only through strict discipline policies and consequences (Morris, 2016; U.S. Department of Education Office for Civil Rights, 2014). Many young women receive the neo-liberal implicit cultural message that self-interest is the only road to success or empowerment; solidarity does not exist for them. #MeToo is a vehicle through which girls and women can find solidarity—whether it be online or in school.

Black Lives Matter

Black Lives Matter formed in response to the 2013 murder of Trayvon Martin. Trayvon Martin was a seventeen-year-old Black student who was stalked and murdered by George Zimmerman, a neighborhood watch patrolman. Many attributed Zimmerman's heinous crime to his racial profiling of Martin. Despite the crime, George Zimmerman was acquitted of all charges in the case (Bates, 2018).

Black Lives Matter formed from the outcry that followed the Zimmerman ruling. Alicia Garza, Opal Tometi, and Patrisse Khan-Cullors were infuriated by the ruling and, as a result, #BlackLivesMatter was born. Black Lives Matter began as a social media movement to bring attention to problems that people of color face. For example, the Black Lives Matter movement inspired Wil Gaffney (2018), a professor at Brite Divinity School, to include curriculum that challenged her students to confront systemic issues of racism and white supremacy. As Gaffney (2018) writes,

> The killing of Trayvon Martin on 26 February 2012 marked a turning point for me in my understanding of the degree to which Black folk are not regarded as fully—if even at all—human. The ready proffer (and acceptance) of a defense for shooting an unarmed child walking in his neighborhood based on the terror evoked by the mere presence of Black bodies communicated to me that there is a broad acceptance of the anti-Black dehumanizing bigotry of George Zimmerman. (p. 205)

The murder of Trayvon Martin acted as a catalyst for the Black Lives Matter movement, and equipped people of color with a platform to create substantial, sustainable change. And the movement also goes far beyond the social media campaign. It has become a global movement that works to give voice to the concerns of people of color worldwide. Black Lives Matter is split into chapters, which allows for each branch of the movement to focus on specific, local issues. In response to injustices, local chapters can easily and efficiently mobilize into action.

Black Lives Matter also confronts political issues that perpetuate prejudice and racism. Especially during the election season in the United States, Black Lives Matter offers its support to candidates that fight for the rights of all people. The movement also presents critiques on different legislation and works to promote legislation that benefits people of color.

Because Black Lives Matter gained traction on social media, many middle school students are aware of the movement; however, they might not understand all of the intricacies behind the movement. A service project could easily be designed around the movement that encourages research and creative thought. Students might help disseminate petitions or write posts on social media with the hashtag, #BLM. They might design an awareness campaign within the school centered on the movement or create an art piece inspired by the movement. In designing such a project, students became activists committed to the goal of bettering the world. Students become aware of the intersectional potential of service-learning projects and begin to independently work to address issues. Students, no matter their age, no longer feel like voiceless victims to the mandates of adults; they become change-makers. A recent example of students acting as change-makers is the movement March for Our Lives.

March for Our Lives

On February 14, 2018, seventeen high school students at Marjory Stoneman Douglas High School in Parkland, Florida lost their lives while completing the simple and everyday task of attending high school. According to Chuck, Johnson, and Siemaszko (2018), a former student opened fire with a semi-automatic rifle, killing seventeen of his former classmates and injuring fourteen. Nineteen-year-old Nikolas Cruz had recently been expelled from the school and had posted a comment on YouTube stating, "I'm going to be a professional school shooter" (as cited in

Chuck et al., 2018). The survivors of this horrific tragedy, students of Marjory Stoneman Douglas High School, decided that enough was enough—school gun violence needed to come to an end. In March of 2018, March for Our Lives became a national organization with schools all over the world participating in walk-outs and protests. The mission statement is "not one more," as the goal is to ensure not one more child, student, or person falls victim to gun violence.

On March 24, 2018, one month and ten days from the Parkland shooting, students of Marjory Stoneman Douglas High School gathered in Washington, D.C. with millions of supporters to protest the lack of government mandated gun violence prevention. They called this event March for Our Lives, breaking the record for the largest global protest in history. The students of Marjory Stoneman Douglas High School made it their personal goal to ensure what they experienced never happens again.

The overall goal of March for Our Lives is not only to advocate for stricter gun policies, but also to encourage the younger generations to vote "morally just leaders into office." The website includes a button where a visitor can "Register to Vote" in under two minutes, encouraging all of the website viewers to do so. "March for Our Lives" also has a petition to sign with three movement goals, including banning assault weapons, prohibiting the sale of high-capacity magazines, and closing background check loopholes. Once these three tasks are completed, the founders of March for Our Lives believe gun violence argue that these three tasks will contribute to the reduction of gun violence in U. S. schools. The founders will not stop until they believe justice is served. March for our Lives is a prime example of students taking the lead for social justice change. Teaching explicitly about social justice can engage students to look outside of themselves, to issues of justice in the larger world.

TEACHING SOCIAL JUSTICE

Teaching about issues of social justice, or lack thereof, can also do much to inspire students to examine the world around them for issues that may impact their own lives. When students have the opportunity to discuss global, national, or local oppressions that impact people like them, they may be inspired to act. Additionally, teaching students about our neo-liberal milieu can also provide a background on the struggle to make real, lasting, sustainable cultural change. In our current social and political time, the collective good is favored over the individual; privatization and "the market" are viewed by owners of industry and many politicians, as viewed as the ultimate good. Privatization, austerity, and deregulation, all phenomena that serve to remove government spending from the public good, in favor of increasing the private sector within the economy and within the larger society.

It is also important for students to understand the political and cultural context in which they live. Our current neo-liberal political climate influences how social movements and social justice are perceived. For example, in our current neo-liberal milieu, the individual is more valued than the collective. The culture of protest is often now characterized as meaningless, and even unpatriotic, e.g., Trump rallying against Black athletes, kneeling in protest of police brutality (Grunwald, 2018; O'Neal, 2017).

Jennifer L. Martin, Brianna Boehlke, and Courtney Cepec

According to Bay-Cheng (2015), "Neoliberalism. . . . [s]ince the 1990s. . . has also come to permeate popular culture and discourse. . . championing self-interested striving through depoliticized tropes of personal empowerment. . ." (p. 280). According to Weber (2010)

> . . . neoliberalism allows us to see the ways in which postfeminism privileges entrepreneurial success over political solidarity. Neoliberalism disallows systemic injustices (like racism or sexism), arguing instead that in a free market, all players compete on a level playing field and thus rise or fall strictly on the strengths of their merit and effort. . . . (p. 127)

According to Ringrose and Walkerdine (2008), our current "post-feminist moment" involves, ". . . reversals and appropriations of feminism, to stake out new truth claims about universal gender equality and all girls and women having 'made it' in contemporary society" (p. 232). Ringrose and Walkerdine remind us that:

> These various motifs are "postfeminist" fantasies where women and girls are celebrated as benefactors of equal opportunities, who must also retain their femininity. . . while processes of regulation into the neo-liberal economic order are masked within the psychological discourses of individual adaptation and entrepreneurship (p. 232).

Gender-Based Harassment and the Trump Era Effect

Gender-based harassment or violence is defined by Else-Quest and Shibley Hyde (2018) as ". . . forms of violence in which women are the predominant victims and men are the predominant perpetrators; transgender individuals are overrepresented as victims" (p. 409). Gender-based harassment or violence is characterized by targeted acts of violence against women. This can manifest through catcalls, physical altercations, and sexual assault.

Teen dating violence is one manifestation of gender-based violence. Chan (2011) found that though there is little difference between the frequencies of violence among boys and girls in the seventh grade, boys utilized more prolonged and severe methods of dating violence than girls. The motives behind the violence, such as sexism and prejudice, generate a more significant degree of violence between middle school heterosexual couples.

Holt and Espelage (2007) argue that gender-based harassment too often affects middle school girls by focusing on the prevalence of school-based violence and its effects based on gender. The researchers polled 70,600 middle school students in grades seven, nine, and eleven in the state of California. In the survey, the students reported whether they had bullied or sexually harassed another student in the past year, then, if the reason for bullying was a result of the victim's gender, religion, or sexual orientation. The researchers found that victims were teased as a result of their gender twelve percent of the time and physically bullied as a result of their gender seven percent of the time. Additionally, the researchers found that 62 percent of boys admitted to sexually assaulting a peer. Gender-based crimes, such as sexual and dating violence, often affect girls at a higher rate than boys.

Gender-based violence was already prevalent within middle schools; however, the Trump era inspired an increase (Huang & Connell, 2018). The rhetoric of a president who openly confessed to desiring to sexually assault women seemed to have an impact on the perceptions of appropriate behavior, especially in areas representing greater support for Donald Trump (HRC, 2017). The Human Rights Campaign (HRC, 2017) conducted an online survey to gauge the amount of bullying in schools since the 2016 election. In addition, since the 2016 election, 70 percent of students polled said they had witnessed bullying, harassment, and hate messages.

Huang and Cornell (2019) polled 155,000 seventh and eighth grade students between the years of 2013, 2017, and 2017. The goal was to determine if political affiliation would correlate to an increase in bullying within schools. According to Huang and Cornell (2019):

> In localities favoring the Republican candidate, there were higher adjusted rates of students reporting: (1) they had experienced some form of bullying in the past year (18% higher) and (2) "Students in this school are teased or put down because of their race or ethnicity" (9% higher). For these two outcomes, there were no meaningful differences prior to the election. (para 1)

In areas with a high number of Trump voters, students experienced more bullying than in previous years, especially students of color (Huang & Cornell, 2019). In sum, the politics of adults affects the attitudes and behaviors of children (Huang & Cornell, 2019). Because of these unfortunate trends, it is more important than ever to teach students about their civil rights, and the protections they possess.

Title IX[3]

Title IX of the Education Amendments of 1972 established that: "No person in the United States shall, on the basis of sex, be excluded from participation in, be denied the benefits of, or be subjected to discrimination under any education program or activity receiving Federal financial assistance." Title IX was named the Patsy T. Mink Equal Opportunity in Education Act on October 9, 2002. Title IX protects students of all genders and sexual orientations from sex discrimination in schools. Students in federally-funded institutions, public schools, colleges and universities, have a right to an education free from discrimination on the basis of sex; this right includes: equitable access to all academic programs, activities, athletics, course offerings, admissions, recruitment, scholarships; and freedom from harassment (including assault) based upon sex, gender, gender identity and expression (real and perceived)[4], and sexual orientation (real and perceived). Title IX protects students in academic and non-academic activities because of pregnancy, birth, miscarriage, and abortion. Title IX also protects faculty, staff, and whistleblowers from sexual harassment, sex discrimination, and retaliation.[5]

School policies must provide for prompt and equitable investigation and resolution, including timeframes for resolution and an anti-retaliation statement (Title IX prohibits retaliation against those who file complaints). School policies must specifically indicate that sexual assault, even a single incident, is covered under Title IX. Students have the right to file a complaint with the school if their rights under Title IX are violated. Victims may also file a complaint with the Department of Education's Office for Civil Rights if a school's policies or handling of a complaint are not compliant with Title IX. Victims may also recover monetary damages under Title IX if the school shows deliberate indifference in dealing with the discrimination or related retaliation.

Each federally funded institution (school district) must designate a Title IX Coordinator to oversee compliance and grievance procedures. The identity and contact information of the Title IX Coordinator must be made public and be readily available to students, staff, and parents. Ideally, school districts should make the name and contact information of their Title IX Coordinator easily accessible to parents and students; placing this information on district websites is optimal, yet still uncommon. Awareness of Title IX protections is crucial. For example, it is critical that students, parents, teachers, administrators, and district officials understand that LGBTQ+ students are still protected from sexual harassment under Title IX despite the fact that the Trump administration is trying to make those protections less visible.

Rollback of LGBTQ+ Title IX/Civil Rights Protections under Trump

According to Sallee and Diaz (2013), individuals in more vulnerable identity classes, while protected by civil rights laws, are more susceptible to bullying. These individuals include those possessing non-hegemonic identities, such as racial and ethnic minorities, sexual minorities, and women. For example, Lesbian, Gay, Bisexual, Transgender, Queer, and Other Identities (or LGBTQ+) students are the most susceptible group of students to experience bullying and harassment in schools (GLSEN, 2017). LGBTQ+ students have been more exposed to increased harassment since the 2016 election (Turner, 2017), and are also the most vulnerable to suicide (GLSEN, 2017).

According to Parshall (2018), the Trump administration has done much to attempt to dismantle civil rights protections for students in various ways. In 2017, the Trump administration revoked Obama administration guidance detailing school-based obligations to LGBTQ+ students under Title IX. The protections are still there, and students and their families can sue or file a civil rights complaint, but if they do not know their rights, then the situation can become dire. Moreover, removing guidance as to the responsibilities of schools under Title IX to protect LGBTQ+ students serves only to muddy the waters. LGBTQ+ students are still entitled to the legal protections of Title IX. The removal of Title IX guidance language served only to cloud schools' understanding of their obligations to transgender youth—opening them up to potential legal actions. The Department of Education's Office of Civil Rights has frequently dismissed cases of discrimination filed by LBGTQ+ and their families. In September of 2017, education secretary Betsy Devos withdrew Title IX guidance addressing sexual harassment and sexual violence. This action also disproportionately impacts LGBTQ+ students.

In 2014, the U.S. Department of Justice Civil Rights Division and the U.S. Department of Education's Office for Civil Rights issued a joint Letter to Colleagues reiterating that schools are explicitly prohibited from discriminating against students on the basis of race, national origin, sex, religion, or disability, and providing data and guidance on exclusionary discipline policies and practices. In late 2018, Secretary of Education Betsy Devos rescinded this guidance, which was aimed at protecting students from discrimination in school discipline.

Additionally, according to Green, Beener, and Pear (2018), the Trump administration actively worked to define gender more narrowly, as biological, immutable, and defined at birth by genitalia. This is perhaps the most radical of the Trump administration's rollback of LGBTQ+ civil rights, which flies in the face of what the medical community advises. In sum, the Trump administration actively undermined various LGBTQ+ student guidance written under the Obama administration. The rescinding of civil rights protections is collectively concerning because they are clearly intersectional issues. For example, between 2013 and 2017, 86 percent of transgender murder victims were people of color, and are the product of a combination of racism, sexism, and transphobia (Green, Beener, & Pear, 2018). The Trump administration actively undermined non-hegemonic students. Teaching gender-based social issues, such as the Trump administration's attempt to dismantle Title IX protections, and other civil rights protections, can do much to inspire students to act within their own lives.

Case Study: T.R.U.E. Queens[6]

The professor of an undergraduate Gender Studies class at a small Midwestern private university required a service-learning project as a culminating experience for her students. Meanwhile, she learned of an afterschool program at the local middle school in want of programming. She broached the idea to her (mostly) all-female class: "What if you take what you learned in this class, and taught it to middle school girls?"

The professor asked her students at what stage in their lives the information that they had learned in class would be most useful. Most of the college students responded with middle school, for it was a period of transition rife with confusion, ignorance, and insecurity. The professor's class agreed that this would become their culminating service-learning project. However, it was a huge commitment: six weeks, four days per week, 90 minutes per day—a total of 36 hours of programming. Students grouped up around preferred topics and were in charge of leading at least one day of programming. The professor would attend each session and assist when necessary. Students deemed the afterschool class a "crash course in feminism," and named it T.R.U.E. Queens. T.R.U.E. stood for tenacious, respected, united, and educated students. Some of the topics included self-value, microaggressions, discrimination, racism, and feminism. The goal was to inspire the students to engage in any necessary change in their own school.

One of the most powerful lessons was on microaggressions. As defined by Sue (2010), microaggressions are ". . . the brief and commonplace daily verbal, behavioral, and environmental indignities, whether intentional or unintentional, that communicate hostile, derogatory, or negative racial, gender sexual-orientation, and religious slights and insults to target the person of group" (p. 5). The slights work to undermine people, though these insults are sometimes hidden within sugarcoated language. Middle school is a time rife with microaggressions. Bullies often use microaggressions to attack other students in ways that are not always detectable by others. A victim of a microaggression may feel uncomfortable and unimportant after such microaggressions, but they might not be able to articulate the specific reason for the discomfort. It is important for middle school students to be aware of microaggressions so that they can combat the insults as they occur. If middle school students hold one another responsible, such insults may cease to exist.

In the T.R.U.E. Queens course, students were equipped with a verbal mantra to utilize whenever they heard a microaggression. Often, when confronted with an injustice, people do not know how to respond. Too often, people stay silent because they do not think of a response quickly enough. By preparing a statement in advance, the middle school students would be able to quickly and easily respond. Students created the phrase, "That's a microaggression, and that's not okay!" They were chanting the sentence by the time the class concluded.

In the following session, Victoria, a student in the course, reported that she had utilized the mantra in the school hallways. The perpetrator was left perplexed at the use of such a large word, and Victoria felt she triumphed. Perpetrators often engage in microaggressive behaviors within the classroom as well. It is important for the teacher to respond appropriately to microaggressions when they occur. Teachers who allow microaggressions to pass without addressing the issue cause students to feel attacked, or unsupported.

According to Derald Wing Sue (2010), microaggressions, especially racial microaggressions, are common within the classroom. Discrepancies in levels of privilege create an environment of conflict. White students often do not recognize their privilege, and, as a result, assume that their experience within the world aligns with students of color. White students may not understand why their statements offend students of color. Unintentional or not, the microaggressions must be addressed within the classroom. Too often, conversations about race are left unresolved; the teacher may be too timid or ill-equipped to give the issue the response it warrants. If left unresolved, students may internalize the trauma and stereotypes of the comment.

A teacher must turn moments of microaggression into opportunities for learning of systemic issues of racism, sexism, and homophobia. As stated by Sue (2010), "In the hands of a skilled facilitator, difficult dialogues on race can represent a potential learning opportunity for personal growth and understanding, improved communication, and racial harmony" (p. 248). Teachers too often fear losing control of the classroom when discussing race; however, the benefits far outweigh the risks. Having an honest discussion with a class on the realities of microaggressions can turn negative experiences into opportunities for growth. It is crucial for teachers to emphasize with the impact of microaggressions on students.

Another lesson in the T.R.U.E. Queens Course focused on the importance of having strong female role models. Middle school curricula often neglect the histories and contributions of women and people of color. As a result, the college students encouraged the middle school students to pick a female woman of color role model to whom they could write a letter of gratitude so that the students could learn about neglected female heroes. Letter recipients included Malala Yousafzai, Anita Hill, Alice Coachman, and Michelle Obama. A gratitude project works to empower girls through recognizing people who often do not receive their due credit.

While reflecting on the project after its completion, the college students came to the conclusion that they were the ones who were truly the most impacted by the service-learning project. Though the goal had been to educate others, the college students found that they had learned a great deal as well. By taking a stance in the community, advocating for gender equity, and teaching lessons that they wished they had learned while in middle school, the students learned just how much effort it takes to make a difference. Each session with the middle school students had to be meticulously planned, meaningful, and fun. The college students also formed close bonds with one another. They worked together as a team, gaining leadership and social skills. They were able to talk individually with students to discover the students' issues with body image, privilege, microaggressions, and prejudices.

According to exit tickets that the undergraduate students disseminated throughout the program, the middle school students left the T.R.U.E. Queens program with practical skills to change their world. Service-learning pedagogy has the potential to change lives. It empowered both instructor and student, as both work together to create sustainable change. As shown by the experiences of the T.R.U.E. Queens participants, it is crucial for educators to create lessons that take on relevant, sometimes difficult, and real topics, such as racism, homophobia, sexism, and other societal injustices. Service-learning and rigorous content are essential to middle school empowerment and success. It is also crucial that students have a voice within their curriculum, in determining what they study; otherwise, school is a hegemonic proposition, and a predominantly White space. Students know what the school values by what they learn; they understand these hidden messages. This disconnection and alienation can lead to resistance to academics (Kohl, 1994). After this six-week course, students were confronting microaggressions in the hallways, and challenging the racist and sexist comments of their peers. Service-learning has the potential to transform students into advocates and activists.

Educator Suggestions for Student Liberation

> [T]he political struggle for freedom and equality must first of all be a struggle within each person.
>
> —Martha Nussbaum

Teaching Tolerance is the Southern Poverty Law Center's (SPLC) education arm, which provides free resources and curriculum to teachers. See the Teaching Tolerance website https://www.tolerance.org to sign up for resources (e.g., lesson plans, teaching strategies, posters), professional development opportunities (webinars, podcasts, workshops, etc.), grants, and other resources for educators. The mission presented on the Teaching Tolerance website states: "Our mission is to help teachers and schools educate children and youth to be active participants in a diverse democracy." Overall, the SPLC provides educators with the resources they need to be anti-racist, equitable educators for their students and community.

In addition to brave educators inspiring their students to engage in counter-hegemonic service-learning projects, we suggest the following strategies to assist teachers in facilitating hope, equity, and liberation in the hearts and minds of their students:[7]

As indicated previously in the case study, we suggest that educators create, with the leadership of their students, a mantra that they practice and recite that will inspire and assist them in their unique challenges.

We also suggest that educators encourage students to listen to inspiring podcasts. Recommending podcasts to students can lead to learning about hidden figures in history and politics. We recommend: *No Man's Land: Stories for Women with Something to Say and Nothing to Prove* by The Wing: https://www.the-wing.com/nomansland/. In addition, think about having students create and publish their own podcasts.

We recommend the following young adult and children's books to inspire feminism and social justice activism:

Dumplin' by Julie Murphy

Herstory: 50 Women and Girls Who Shook Up the World by Katherine Halligan

History vs. Women: The Defiant Lives that They Don't Want You To Know by Anita Sarkeesian and Ebony Adams

Internment by Samira Ahmed

Milk and Honey by Rupi Kaur

Moxy: A Novel by Jennifer Mathieu

Nowhere Girls by Amy Reed

Rad Women Worldwide: Artists and Athletes, Pirates and Punks, and Other Revolutionaries Who Shaped History by Katie Schatz

She Persisted: 13 American Women Who Changed the World by Chelsea Clinton

The Princess Saves Herself in This One, by Amanda Lovelace

Shout by Laurie Halse Anderson

Today's Lesson: Black Lives Matter by Willie D. Jones

We Should All Be Feminists by Chimamanda Ngozi Adichie

Women of Resistance: Poems for a New Feminism edited by Danielle Barnhart and Iris Mahan

Sharing videos of spoken word poets may inspire students to write their own. We recommend the following: Dominique Christina, "Period Poem": https://www.youtube.com/watch?v=4vu2BsePvoI; and Olivia Gatwood, "When I Say That We Are All Teen Girls": https://www.youtube.com/watch?v=MHaCKwYCFZs

As indicated previously in this chapter, studying current social movements, such as #MeToo and Black Lives Matter, can inspire students to work to make change in their own lives and schools.

CONCLUSION

The above suggestions are just a brief list for educators to get started engaging their students in social justice advocacy work. We suggest that educators continue to devise and test their own strategies, as well as to take guidance and suggestions from their own students. Best educational practice warrants that student engagement will increase when students are actively working toward their own interests and needs. We welcome this important work.

REFERENCES

Bay-Cheng, L. Y. (2015). The agency line: A neoliberal metric for appraising young women's sexuality. *Sex Roles, 73*, 279–291.

Billig, S. H. (2002a). Service-learning. *Research Roundup 19*, 1–4.

Billig, S. H. (2002b). Support for K–12 service-learning practices: A brief review of the research. *Educational Horizons 80*, 184–189.

Billig, S. H. (2000). The effects of service-learning. *School Administrator, 57*, 14–18.The Black Lives Matter Movement (2017). Black lives matter. Retrieved from: https://blacklivesmatter.com/

Carlsen, A., Salam, M., Cain Miller, C., Lu, D., Ngu, A., Patel, J. K., & Wichter, Z. (2018, October 29). #Metoo brought down 201 powerful men: Nearly half of their replacements are women. *New York Times*. Retrieved from: https://www.nytimes.com/interactive/2018/10/23/us/metoo-replacements.html

Chan, K. L. (2011). Gender differences in self-reports of intimate partner violence: A review. *Aggression and Violent Behavior, 16*, 167–175.

Chuck, E., Johnson, A., & Siemaszko, C. (2018, February 15). 17 killed in mass shooting at high school in Parkland, Florida. NBC News. Retrieved from https://www.nbcnews.com/news/us-news/police-respond-shooting-parkland-florida-high-school-n848101

Deeley, S. J. (2010). Service-learning: Thinking outside the box. *Active Learning in Higher Education, 11*(1), 43–53.

Else-Quest, N. M., & Hyde, J. S. (2018). *The psychology of women and gender*. SAGE Publications Inc.

Eyler, J., Giles, D. E., Stenson, C. M., & Gray, C. J. (2001). *At a glance: What we know about the effects of service-learning on college students, faculty, institutions and communities, 1993–2000* (3rd ed.). The Corporation for National Service Learn and Serve America National Service Learning Clearinghouse.

Freire, P. (1970). *Pedagogy of the oppressed*. Seabury Press.

Gafney, W. (2017). A reflection on the Black Lives Matter movement and its impact on my scholarship. *Journal of Biblical Literature, 136*(1), 204–207.

Goff, P. A., Jackson, M. C., Di Leone, B. A., L., Culotta, C. M., & DiTomasso, N. A. (2014). The essence of innocence: Consequences of dehumanizing black children. *Journal of Personality and Social Psychology, 106*(4), 526–545.

Gould, K. A. (2018). Parkland students provide a model for personal and public narratives to say #NeverAgain. *Dimensions of Critical Care Nursing, 37*(4), 199–200.

Green, A. (2017, June 29). How black girls aren't presumed to be innocent. *The Atlantic*. Retrieved from: https://www.theatlantic.com/politics/archive/2017/06/black-girls-innocencegeorgtown/532050/

Green, E. L., Beener, K., & Pear, R. (2018, October 21). "Transgender" could be defined out of existence under Trump administration. *New York Times*. Retrieved from: https://www.nytimes.com/2018/10/21/us/politics/transgender-trump-administration-sex-definition.html

Grunwald, M. (2018, November/December). How everything became the culture war. Politico magazine. Retrieved from: https://www.politico.com/magazine/story/2018/11/02/culture war-liberals-conservatives-trump-2018-222095

Holt, M., & Espelage, D. (2007). A cluster analytic investigation of victimization among high school students: Are profiles differentially associated with psychological symptoms and school belonging? In J. Zins, M. Elias, & C. Maher (Eds.), *Bullying victimization, and peer harassment: A handbook of prevention and intervention* (pp. 85–102). Haworth Press.

Howard, J. (2001). *Service-learning course design workbook*. OCSL Press.

Huang, F. L. & Connell, D. (2018). School teasing and bullying after the presidential election. *Educational Researcher, 48*(2), 69–83.

Human Rights Campaign. (n.d.). Post-election survey of youth. Human Rights Campaign Foundation. Retrieved from https://assets2.hrc.org/files/assets/resources /HRC_PostElectionSurveyofYouth.pdf

Justbeinc. (n.d.). Just be inc. Retrieved from: http://justbeinc.wixsite.com/justbeinc/the-me-too-movement-cmml

Kohl, H. (1994). "I won't learn from you" and other thoughts on creative maladjustment. The New Press.

Koliba, C. (2003). Generating social capital in schools through service-learning. *Academic Exchange, 7*(2), 336–345.

March for Our Lives. (n.d.). Retrieved from: https://marchforourlives.com

March for our Lives Founders. (2018). *Glimmer of hope: How tragedy sparked a movement*. Penguin Random House LLC.

Martin, J. L. (2017). And the danger went away: Speculative pedagogy in the myth of the post-feminist. In J. L. Martin, A. Nickels, & M. L. S. Grier (Eds.), *Feminist pedagogy, practice, and activism: Improving lives for girls and women* (pp. 5–34). Routledge.

Martin, J., & Beese, J. (2016). Girls talk back: Changing school culture through feminist and service-learning pedagogies. *The High School Journal, 99*(3), 211–233.

Morris, M. W. (2016). *Pushout: The criminalization of Black girls in schools*. The New Press.

Mowatt, R. A., French, B. H., & Malebranche, D. A. (2013). Black/Female/Body hypervisibility and invisibility. *Journal of Leisure Research, 45*(5), 644–660.

Ochoa, A., & Pershing, L. (2011). Team teaching with undergraduate students: Feminist pedagogy in a peer education project. *Feminist Teacher, 22*(1), 23–42.

O'Neal, L. (2017, November 16). The message to NFL players: Dance for us, but don't kneel. The Undefeated. Retrieved from: https://theundefeated.com/features/the-message-to-nfl-players-dance-for-us-but-dont-kneel

Parshall, H. (2018, April 26). Three ways Betsy Devos has undermined protections for students. The Human Rights Campaign. Retrieved from https://www.hrc.org/blog/three-ways-betsy-devos-has-undermined-protections-for-students

Ringrose, J., & Walkerdine, V. (2008). Regulating the abject: The TV make-over as site of neo-liberal reinvention toward bourgeois femininity. *Feminist Media Studies, 8*(3), 227–246.

Scales, P. (1999). Increasing service-learning's impact on middle school students. *Middle School Journal, 30*(5), 40–44.

Sue, D. W. (2010). Microaggressions in everyday life: Race, gender, and sexual orientation. John Wiley & Sons, Inc.

Turner, A. (2017). New survey of 50,000+ young people reveals troubling post-election spike in bullying & harassment. The Human Rights Campaign. Retrieved from https://www.hrc.org/blog/new-survey-of-50000-young-people-reveals-troubling-post-election-spike-in-b

U.S. Department of Education Office for Civil Rights. (2014, March). Civil rights data collection data snapshot: School discipline. Retrieved from: http://www2.ed.gov/about/offices/list/ocr/docs/crdc-discipline-snapshot.pdf

Valenti, J. (2016). *Sex object: A memoir*. Harper Collins.

Vagianos, A. (2017, October 17). The "Me Too" campaign was created by a Black woman 10 years ago. *The Huffington Post*. Retrieved from: https://www.huffingtonpost.com/entry/the-me-too-campaign-was-created-by-a-black-woman-10-years-ago_us_59e61a7fe4b02a215b336fee

Weber, B. R. (2010). Teaching popular culture through gender studies: Feminist pedagogy in a post-feminist and neoliberal academy? *Feminist Teacher, 20*(2), 124–138.

Zimmerman, T. S., Krafchick, J. L., & Aberle, J. T. (2009). A university service-learning assignment. *Education, Citizenship, and Social Justice, 4*(3), 195–210.

Jennifer L. Martin
University of Illinois at Springfield

Brianna Boehlke
University of Mount Union

Courtney Cepec
University of Mount Union

FOOTNOTES

2. Non-hegemonic refers to an individual who possesses one or several historically marginalized identity categories, such as those of a non-dominant/privileged race, class, gender, sexuality, religion, ethnicity, disability, etc.

3. This section was developed by Jennifer L. Martin, Ph.D., with help from Wendy Murphy, New England Law, Boston.

4. Bullying, sexual harassment, and sexual assault are often conflated or used interchangeably. Such mislabeling does not alleviate schools from responding properly and enforcing Title IX provisions.

5. Schools may have the authority and responsibility to address sexual harassment even if the behavior occurs off campus, and/or in social media and other cyber venues.

6. The lead author of the chapter is the professor noted in this case study. The second author is a student in the course noted in this case study.

7. Please note that this list is not exhaustive.

Chapter Five

The Power of the Sisterhood: Young Women Coding at the

Middle School Level

Gwendolyn Nuding

As middle school girls grow up in a time in which women are making unprecedented gains in gender equality through political and professional activism, some may wonder what this means for them (Cook Political Report, 2018; Women's Initiative, 2018). Middle school students may see small improvements in the representation of women in what have long been male-dominated sectors, but there still exists a pervasive hole in women's presence in fields like computer science and mathematics. Women make up only 26 percent of the technology workforce. This issue goes even further beyond gender inequity when recognizing that women of color experience underrepresentation at even higher rates (National Center for Women & Information Technology, 2019). Only 32 percent of that 26 percent are Asian women, seven percent are Black women, and five percent are Latinx women. This disparity cannot be taken lightly.

In the past decade, industry leaders have attempted to examine this issue through the design of educational programs that promote technology and engineering fields. This perhaps led to the popularization of the term "STEM education" (Lyons, 2018). STEM programs have been rapidly created and implemented in schools since then; many have placed focus on the interconnectedness between science, technology, engineering, and math and others have utilized their programs as opportunities to advertise their industries to prospective job candidates. Throughout this process, the problem persisted: women were still underrepresented in the job market despite these efforts (Amador & Soule, 2015; Ashcraft, Eger, & Scott, 2017; Simpson, Che, & Bridges, 2016). The programs did not, in fact, create more equitable learning and working spaces for women.

One commonly held belief about the cause of underrepresentation is the undervalued perspective and presence of women in the world of technology and

E. Mikulec, D. Beichner (eds.), Distraction: Girls, School, and Sexuality, 67-82.

engineering (Master, Cheryan, & Meltzoff, 2016; Simon, Wagner, & Killion, 2017). The suppression of inclusivity through gender roles and stereotypes at an early age contributes to the interests and choices of young women as they develop. Due to media portrayal, marketing, and societal norms, many girls grow up with the idea that computer science is impractical or unattainable and that the average scientist, mathematician, or computer programmer is male (Mann et al., 2015). These learned perceptions could amass for years and influence the career and academic choices of women.

When the unique identities and experiences of women involved in coding are unaccounted for a void exists in the greater body of science that stagnates the progression of the discipline (Heybach & Pickup, 2017). The presence of women's voices and faces in computer science, particularly those from historically underrepresented groups, is a necessity. Some researchers and statisticians add that addressing the issue in relation to gender alone is not enough. The intersectionality of identities such as race, socioeconomic status, sexual orientation, and age is a major contributor to life experiences and decision-making (Amador & Soule, 2015; Ashcraft et al., 2017; Mann et al., 2015; Simpson et al., 2016). If young women are not provided with safe and inclusive environments that celebrate personal growth and allow all to feel seen and heard, they may not feel inclined to pursue certain programs.

In 2012, Reshma Saujani decided to act on these findings. She and her team founded Girls Who Code, an organization created with the intent to introduce girls to computer programming in ways that celebrated the contributions of women to the field and also allowed for supported exploration of coding (Girls Who Code, 2018). Now an internationally-known organization, Girls Who Code provides authentic computer programming experiences to interested candidates by encouraging members to use coding as a catalyst to promote positive change in the world. One such portion of their efforts includes a 15-week school club curriculum in which grade school students assemble on a weekly basis and learn about coding through guided tutorials and create a finished project that aligns with a common theme. Their programs have made notable gains toward more equitable environments for women coders. Alumni of Girls Who Code enter the field of computer science at fifteen times the national rate, and their Black and Latina graduates at sixteen times the national rate.

The organization formulated a component within their middle school and high school club curriculum referred to as a "Sisterhood Spotlight" specifically to empower their members through positive representation. During this segment of the lesson, young women learn about women coders from all over the world who utilize coding in their daily lives and careers. They then discuss the characteristics of these women and compare them to their own. The current study will examine these club components and their effectiveness.

The purpose of this study is to research the value of the intentional development of a sisterhood within an all-girls afterschool coding program in promoting confidence, positive supports, and computer science skills among the 15 middle school participants. In the current study, "sisterhood" will be defined as a mutual support system including participants, club facilitators, mentors, and supplemental curriculum materials.

This study may be particularly impactful to those directly familiar with Girls Who Code, but the results of the study could very well also serve as countering evidence to those skeptical of support systems created by and for women at the middle level. Girls Who Code participants and facilitators may be more likely to place emphasis on the Sisterhood Spotlight segments if they positively impact the self-agency of women club participants. Policy makers may be inclined to more intentionally encourage clubs specifically serving young women interested in computer science should the results indicate their effectiveness. The results of this study might also validate the feelings of the club participants in the current study, providing affirmation and evidence of a supportive coding sisterhood.

REVIEW OF LITERATURE

Existing literature revealing gender disparities in representation in computer is plentiful, as many researchers are calling into question the causes and effects of this phenomenon. Most research examines the differences in the likelihood of women and men to pursue STEM work in high school and postsecondary education; this work places emphasis on shifts in interest in STEM subjects due to achievement gaps, exposure to role models, and puberty (Bettinger & Long, 2005; Eccles & Wang, 2016; Ilumoka, Milanovic, & Grant, 2017; Karcher, 2008). Other research links the underrepresentation of women in computer science fields to a lack of confidence and/or access to technology (Hand, Rice, & Greenlee, 2017; Litzler, Samuelson, & Lorah, 2014). Even the physical environment of STEM spaces has been considered a factor (Ridenour & Hassell Hughes, 2016; Legewie & DiPrete, 2014; Simpson et al., 2016; Mann et al., 2015). Such studies indicate differences in interest between women and men in science and mathematics fields due to the presence or lack of traditional classroom materials such as front-facing desks, lined lab tables, and STEM-related décor.

Recent work acknowledges the complexity of the issue by describing its place in relation to intersectionality, discrimination, and lack of representation in curricula, asserting that there is no holistic approach to solving the issue (Ashcraft et al., 2017; Booher-Jennings, J, 2008; Fields, Kafai, Nakajima, Goode, & Margolis, 2018; Grossman & Porche, 2014; Ayres & Leaper, 2013). Gender non-conformity and gender fluidity as they relate to underrepresentation are not widely discussed in the current literature, and this is an area for further research in the future. Because of limitations within this study, the researcher will not pursue this piece of the issue.

The extensive research about the issue paired with the prolongation of the underrepresentation of women in STEM signals the need for continued efforts toward a solution. Efforts to create equity in computer science are critical for all stakeholders.

Underrepresentation of Women in Computer Science Programs and Fields

Countless pieces of literature support the validity of the claim that women are not equitably represented in STEM fields (Karcher, 2018; Levine, Serio, Radaram, Chaudhuri, & Talbert, 2015; Toglia, 2013). Though consciousness of this issue has been prevalent for decades, the percentage of women that hold positions in STEM has steadily dropped since the early 1990s, with percentages of women personnel in computing decreasing from 37 percent to its current standing at 26 percent. (U.S. Department of Labor, 2015; National Science Foundation, 2013). This is problematic on several levels, but perhaps most notably is the effect it creates on the perceived roles of individuals in terms of efficacy. Disparities in computer science demographics can cause impositions of stereotypes and gender norms, and students are prone to feel the pressures of such forces when determining their interests and beliefs (Master et al, 2016; Simon et al., 2017). Popularized representations of scientists, mathematicians, and coders often portray male figures due to the long history of male dominance in such areas. When women pursue courses, colleges, and careers, they may not consider those relating to coding, computer science, or mathematics due to a lack of a sense of belonging in those environments.

Master et al. (2016) formulated a study consisting of two experiments testing these very stereotypes in computer science (CS). The first experiment was conducted with the intention of determining the effects of different classroom environments of girls' interest in computer science courses. Girls and boys were provided the same surveys and were asked to identify their interest in enrolling in a computer science course if it took place in a stereotypical setting or a non-stereotypical setting (one consisting of subject-unspecific décor such as artistic posters, collaborative seating, and access to fiction books). Girls were more likely to express interest in enrolling in the computer science course occurring in the non-stereotypical setting than the stereotypical setting. It was also noted that the interest level of boys did not differ between the two settings, indicating that a shift in classroom environment in order to better serve the needs of young women would not negatively impact the enrollment of boys in such a course. This could have vast implications on curriculum design, as it provides clarity to stakeholders that young women are aware of stereotypes in scientific fields. It also exposes existent stereotypes in the physical classroom space as another potential contributor to underrepresentation.

Heybach and Pickup (2017) echoed these findings and reminded stakeholders that attempts to "paint STEM pink" through the design of programs and products targeted specifically towards girls often reinforce gender stereotypes (p. 681). They argued that the practice of science, ideally, is non-gendered in nature. Efforts to appeal to "girl culture," rather than creating equitable learning spaces, only further ostracize young women as outsiders in computer science and promote deficit-minded thinking (p. 622).

Mirrors, Not Windows

Some researchers have hypothesized that such drastic disparities in computer science can be attributed to the scarcity of positive representation of the experiences of women in computer science curricula and media (Karcher, 2018; Pinkard, Erete, Martin, & McKinney de Royston, 2017). Mentoring relationships have been proven vital in the development of girls and boys alike, as positive and purposeful guidance allows children and adolescents the safety to take risks and celebrate successes (Karcher, 2018). When girls interact with highly engaging content alongside experienced mentors, they are more likely to find success in computer science (Ashcraft et al., 2017; Levine et al., 2015). This confirms that girls feel more confident and competent when figures representative of their own identities are present in academia and career life. The implications of this could potentially be cyclic: girls may feel a more positive self-esteem and competence when they are supported and represented in prospective careers; experiencing a more positive self-esteem and a sense of competence may also lead to increased interest in such fields.

Self-Esteem

Self-esteem is defined by Adams (2010) as a "healthy sense of self-acceptance" (p. 257), that often includes confidence, worth, and belief about one's abilities. Many researchers have studied the impact of confidence and self-esteem on academic achievement and involvement in an attempt to explain the differences in gender representation in STEM-related programs (Adams, Kuhn, & Rhodes, 2006; Kutob, Senf, Crago, & Shisslak, 2010; Simpson et al., 2016). Existing studies provide differing results related to the impact of self-esteem on the likelihood of an individual to pursue specific fields.

One such study by Bayazit (2014) examined an all-girl afterschool club in order to test hypotheses linking recreational activities to improvements in self-esteem. Girls involved with the program demonstrated increases in self-esteem when they enjoyed the activities and felt like they belonged. These findings aligned with similar work that found that a sense of belonging, interest in club happenings, and structured support systems led to higher self-esteem levels and increased interest in STEM fields (Demirdag, 2015; Liang, Lund, Mosseau, & Spencer, 2016; Pinkard et al., 2017). It is evident that voluntary participation in clubs and activities increases self-esteem in women participants; however, self-esteem may not be the only factor that determines involvement and interest. Other research contends that self-esteem is not as closely aligned with interest as other studies insist, but rather societal pressures, life experiences, identity, school environment, previous knowledge, and material advantages or disadvantages play a greater role in the likelihood of students to pursue computer programming (Rhodes, Roffman, Reddy, & Fredriksen, 2004). This brings about the question of whether or not self-esteem is significant in the argument about the causes of underrepresentation of young women in STEM.

Intersectionality

Trends in research are shifting, indicating that considering the issue solely based upon gender differences or lack of access to technology and programs may be rudimentary. Themes in current studies do not target gender as the single contributor to underrepresentation, but rather consider the intersectionality of gender, sex, school environment, socioeconomic status, race, ethnicity, age, and other identities as equally important to consider (Riegle-Crumb, King, Grodsky, & Muller, 2012; Heybach & Pickup, 2017). Intersectionality is defined by McAlear, Scott, Scott, & Weiss (2018) as "the complex interactions between multiple identities and dynamics of power, racism, sexism, and oppression" (p. 2). In addition to sexism, women of color face barriers to a degree that White women do not such as the threat of stereotypes and biases, lack of representative mentors and role models, and access to networking opportunities (p. 3). These barriers exist not only in the workplace, but throughout all of society, including the classroom setting.

Ashcraft, Eger, and Scott (2017) conducted a study involving observations of two groups of middle school and high school girls enrolled in an immersive program called COMPUGIRLS, a computer programming experience designed through the University of Colorado at Denver. The girls and their "mentor teachers" participated in three units focused purposefully on developing identity through social justice projects designed by the researchers (p. 236). Researchers concluded that when the young women were able to celebrate personal identities in a setting in which others were doing the same, the young women were more likely to feel invested in the programming experience. Many participants, regardless of differences in access, prior involvement in an all-girls program, or coding competency, were engaged in the programs when given the opportunity to discuss self-efficacy and use that discussion as motivation to advocate for supports and services.

METHODOLOGY

Design

The present study seeks to fill a gap in the extant research about the perceptions of club participants involved in an explorative, women-centered experience designed intentionally to combat gender inequities in computer science. This action research was designed using a qualitative approach consisting of a survey and a focus group. Survey results provide data about the demographics of the participants and a holistic view of the participants' perceptions. The subsequent focus group allows for more extensive narration on the themes presented in the survey.

Study Participants

The 15 students in this study were voluntary members of a club division of the Girls Who Code computer science program facilitated in a suburban middle school in Illinois. The group was comprised of five sixth grade, two seventh grade, and eight eighth grade students. Participants showed active membership in the club, meaning they attended most or all of the weekly meetings throughout the year.

Instrumentation

Survey. The first stage of data collection involved the distribution of a survey within Qualtrics, containing questions directly pertaining to the participants' club experience. This instrument was selected due to its data collection and analysis capabilities, but also its user-friendly interface. Club members had access to computers at every club meeting and were familiar with survey-style tasks and programs, so online data collection was more appropriate and sensible than physical collection tools. Survey questions and statements were formulated with the intention of revealing trends in the experiences of club members; the survey consisted of multiple-choice, short answer, and subscale responses. Participants received this survey through the provision of a direct link to the Qualtrics site.

Focus group. Three young women were selected to engage in the focus group based on the grade level designation identified through the survey (one sixth, seventh, and eighth grade student). The focus group was conducted in a semi-structured manner to allow the researcher and participants the opportunity to supplement original survey questions with ones that provided an opportunity for a more narrative response. The goal for this line of questioning was to determine the extent to which club components impacted the overall experiences of participants.

Procedures

In December 2018, consent forms were distributed to guardians of eligible participants at the conclusion of the club's regular meeting time and collected during school hours thereafter. The researcher collected assent forms following this consent. All forms and data are held in a secure cabinet at the school site that only the researcher may access.

The survey was distributed mid-January 2019 and was facilitated by another adult supervisor associated with Girls Who Code. During the time that participants engaged in the survey, non-participants continued the work of regularly scheduled meetings. Participants completed the survey during club time and submitted their results at the conclusion of the meeting. After submission, the researcher began the process of data analysis. The researcher allotted two weeks for this process before facilitating the focus group. Consent and assent were revisited prior to engagement in this process as well as a reminder about the presence of a recording device during this session.

The focus group took place during a short piece of the regularly-scheduled club hours. Non-participants continued the club curriculum with another supervisor while this occurred. The researcher began the semi-structured while recording the responses on a password-protected recording app. Upon the conclusion of the focus group, data acquisition ceased, and data analysis began. The recording of the focus group was transcribed personally by the researcher on a digital document and saved on a secure network provided by the school district.

Data Analysis

Data obtained from the survey consisted of gender identity, ethnicity, age of participant, prior experience in an all-women club, and perceptions of self-esteem and sisterhood. The short answer portion was coded based on repeated terms, themes, and perceptions across the data related to sisterhood, self-esteem, or other significant insight. The responses from the focus group were coded similarly with an emphasis on the perception of sisterhood, gender demographics of the club, and representation.

RESULTS

The researcher organized response trends into broader categories using open, axial, and selective coding methods. The researcher analyzed the focus group transcription using the same method, specifically looking for similarities in themes. The subsequent information is outlined based on those themes, using narrative samples from participants to support findings.

Survey

All fifteen participants engaged in the survey portion of the study. The data indicated three clear themes including representation and prospects of the future, participant coding competence, and support systems.

Representation and the future. Seven of the participants identified as Asian, three as Latinx, three as White, and two as Black. Though racial or ethnic identity may play a significant role in the experiences of club members and the overall system of support within the club, differences in racial identity did not clearly correlate to differences in responses. Thirteen out of fifteen participants declared that they knew their own strengths and weaknesses and a few participants disagreed with the notion that they felt more confident in their abilities solely as a result of involvement in Girls Who Code.

The participants were, however, in strong agreement about their satisfaction about the Sisterhood Spotlight. Every participant reported feeling proud to be a woman after discussing the Sisterhood Spotlight. Many used the word "inspired" to describe their attitudes during the segment, but several also used language to denote that their abilities are not yet on par with those highlighted through the Sisterhood Spotlight. An eighth grader said of the professionals, "It makes me feel really happy for them because they are successful, but it makes me feel like I could be doing more." Another said, "It makes me feel like someday I could be just as successful as them." Seven out of 15 responses indicated an attitude that success could only come in the future. Most responses were thematically similar, but sixth grade participants expressed a greater value for coding work time than any other group. They echoed strong desires to spend time coding with friends within the group. Eighth grade participants more often expressed an interest in the sisterhood activities and Sisterhood Spotlight than the other grade level.

Coding competency. Many participants wanted to acknowledge the importance of the organization's coding opportunities in relation to those available to girls in the community as a whole. They felt it necessary to verbalize the need for continued development in this sense. A seventh grade participant excitedly said, "I LOVE that this club is targeted toward girls because right now in this society, girls are known as the gender that cannot do anything targeted toward STEM. And this club shows others that girls can ROCK STEM!" An eighth grader added, "Coding as a skill is very important in the modern world, and I am glad that this generation of girls are getting exposure to it." Three members reflected upon trying to find organizations that provided opportunities for coding practice, and Girls Who Code was the first one that made coding seem "normal" for girls.

Support system. Thirteen of fifteen participants indicated positive connections between the Sisterhood Spotlight segment and an overall feeling of support and acceptance between members. One of the major themes throughout the survey was a clear excitement for sisterhood and a connection between club members. When asked about the level of support that the participants felt during collaborative tasks in club time, all fifteen participants strongly agreed that they felt supported by other members within the sisterhood. Several responses acknowledged appreciation for the gender-homogenous environment. A seventh grader reported:

> I think that it provides a good area for girls who hang out and code together. I'm in algebra and it seems like the girls are always left out in the conversation or are always outshined during classes. I think this provides a special place where girls and their friends can come together and code without feeling pressured by judgment.

Seven other participants responded at length with similar experiences. One survey question asked participants to explain Girls Who Code to non-members. In response to this item, some participants focused in on coding aspects of the club, such as one member who said, "This is a club that empowers woman/girls and where I can become better at coding and it helps me become more confident since everyone at the club becomes your friend and sister." Other participants looked beyond coding, articulating that the club brings something out of its members. One participant described it as ". . . a place where girls can be who they really are. . . ." Another said it is a "safe place to be, a sisterhood, where we have a lot of laughs and where change begins." One even referred to the club as a "sanctuary." Participants repeated this sentiment consistently throughout their responses, revealing a strong presence of a support system within the group.

One survey item led participants to disclose their prior experiences in an all-girls club. The majority of participants have had experience with an all-girls club, but when analyzing this variable alone, there was no significant indication of whether or not their responses differed from those without the same experience.

The researcher analyzed the qualitative data obtained from the initial survey prior to facilitating the focus group in order to identify trends in participant responses and target questions related to those themes. A sixth, seventh, and eighth grade representative from the sample were chosen based on their use of the words "sisterhood" and "self" during the survey. Inadvertently, the three participants represented three different racial groups; however, none of them cited their racial identities as contributors or barriers to underrepresentation in the focus group discussion.

Representation and the future. Focus group participants continuously noted gender underrepresentation in relation to STEM. The eighth grade focus group participant specifically related with Sisterhood Spotlights featuring women that recalled moments in their middle school years when they felt as though they were underestimated by boys, teachers, or parents. The seventh grader agreed, saying that it was nice to see that women could overcome those obstacles. She also added that it was inspiring to see the amount of career options available to girls interested in STEM during the Sisterhood Spotlights.

Coding competency. Participants were eager to discuss the development in the opportunities that have become available to them as they have progressed in their schooling. The seventh grade representative noted:

> Well, I feel really good about myself at Girls Who Code because I get to further my coding understanding. 'Cause, like, I would do it, like, in fifth grade and I didn't really understand most the stuff . . . it kind of helps me get to know the others around me, too. So, like, I was close with the people who are in Girls Who Code before, but not like, very close, so now we get to talk all the time.

She went on to say:

> . . . in 5th grade, it was kind of like a requirement to do the Hour of Code things, and I didn't really like that, but we moved on to Scratch later on, and I liked using that because I could create whatever I wanted to, and I realized that you could re-mix, so in sixth grade I started working with that stuff, but now it's even more fun.

In the participants' district, participation in the nationwide coding initiative "Hour of Code," which features a basic block coding program, is typically a curricular requirement at the elementary level. They are not introduced to Scratch, a more advanced program, until late middle school, if at all. The other focus group participants echoed their enjoyment of the diversity in coding opportunities offered through Girls Who Code. They spoke confidently in their coding abilities and desired more challenging tasks relating to coding. As was consistent with the survey results, the sixth grade participant most valued the segment of club meetings when participants are able to code freely, saying, "My favorite part is probably just going off and coding, because I've always liked to code and stuff, so like, it's fun to just go off and show your friends what you've done." This was not as emphasized by the other two focus group participants.

Support system. Though not initially accounted for in the creation of the focus group questions, the three participants frequently referenced gender homogeneity within the club. The participants often referred to club members as "friends" or "sisters," though this is not how the club sponsor generally addresses the group. They started this conversation by discussing their observations that they are "friends with everyone" in the club, going on to add that even sixth graders and eighth graders co-mingle. The seventh grader broached the subject of club demographics by saying:

> And it's nice to just like, know that girls from every single grade are getting represented by it, and we can just talk and hang out and be ourselves without the fear of getting made fun of or having to get back on task or anything from some of the boys that are in our grades.

The other two participants vehemently agreed. The eighth grade participant added that boys would probably be too embarrassed to join for fear that their friends would think they would be weird for participating in an all-girls club. The seventh grader responded by stating that she would be open to boys joining the club if they were more open to listening to her during math, noting that they sometimes try to outshine her by shouting out answers in class when she raises her hand. The sixth grader weighed in by saying that some boys would be really strong coders but may try to "annoy the girls" if they joined. When the researcher asked the participants if they felt that Girls Who Code could become a co-ed club, the girls were skeptical, fearing that the sense of woman empowerment within the club might be at stake. One thought the power of the Sisterhood Spotlight might be lost, saying of boys that "they might laugh, make fun of them, and say, 'well, a boy could do that, too.'" This sentiment was shared amongst all three participants.

DISCUSSION

While some researchers and practitioners attempt to link gender underrepresentation in STEM to negative self-esteems of women coders, the results of this study show no correlation between the two (Hand et al., 2017; Litzler et al., 2014). The participants showed little need for increases in self-esteem, but more so desires for strong support systems and positive representation. They respect and enjoy coding and are looking for opportunities to improve their skills.

Representation and the Future

Every participant in the sample expressed feelings of positivity and capability as a result of involvement in the Sisterhood Spotlight segment of the club meetings. Recent research suggests a lack of diverse role models as a barrier for women of color in computer science, and while this is necessary in all contexts, the Girls Who Code Sisterhood Spotlight segment offers a targeted opportunity to see and hear from multifaceted coders (McAlear et al., 2018). Several participants idolized the spotlighted women, saying phrases like, "I feel inspired and motivated by them" and "When I see those girls doing awesome things, I think that I can, too." Participants' excitement to learn about the contributions of others is not unusual, as other studies in this context have found that positive representation yields similar results (Ashcraft et al., 2017; Booher-Jennings, J, 2008; Fields et al., 2018; Grossman & Porche, 2014). Some participants displayed hopeful attitudes that they may gradually become just as successful as those in the passages and videos, and others saw the accomplishments of spotlighted women as an opportunity to use their skills in the present to make change.

Coding Competency

Every participant had prior experience with coding before joining Girls Who Code, though their involvements varied in depth and duration. More than half of the participants found the learning process to be challenging and ultimately rewarding. They appreciated the "share out" club segment in which they report their accomplishments, explain their setbacks, and describe their processes for overcoming obstacles. One participant mentioned that she enjoys letting her creativity show and likes to "help others learn skills that I didn't know not too long ago." They desired more information on how to develop new coding skills and share their knowledge.

Support System

The only negative responses from participants were the feelings of disapproval in contexts outside of the club. Participants iterated that they sometimes do not feel supported by some male peers and even adults in their academic efforts in other settings. One participant compared the club setting to that of her core classes, saying, "I wish I felt supported like this during school." This may indicate that fluctuations in self-esteem are not a result of the participants feeling incapable themselves but are rather observations and perceptions that others feel that they are incapable. These feelings could have implications on participants' math and science involvement over time, though this was not observed in the short span of the study. Some studies found that women experience a shift in interest from computer science to humanitarian-centric fields over the span of schooling (Bettinger & Long, 2005; Eccles & Wang, 2016; Ilumoka et al., 2017; Karcher, 2008). This did not present itself in the current study, but this may be because the participants are voluntary members of a club specifically centered on coding and are therefore invested in computer science learning.

Many participants discussed their perceptions of the environment of the club. Several studies in the existing research found that women are more engaged in STEM when learning in environments that contain less stereotypical STEM features (Ridenour & Hassell Hughes, 2016; Legewie & DiPrete, 2014; Simpson et al., 2016; Mann et al., 2015). Though there were not any participants that commented on the physical environment of the English classroom, several noted the intangible culture of support within the room. They valued the ability to converse with club members across grade levels and abilities and articulated feelings of safety, security, and togetherness within the learning environment.

LIMITATIONS

The intersectionality of women coders and its connection to underrepresentation is a major gap in existing research. Data in the current study did not reveal barriers related to race as pervasive problems for coders of color, but this could be due to the fact that the club participants formed a collective group consisting of several racial identities that were acknowledged and celebrated throughout the year. The line of questioning did not explicitly connect racial identity to support, self-esteem, or other themes, and this could have also contributed to this fact.

The limited duration of the study might have impacted the results because the survey occurred only once during the year-long program rather than as a recurring evaluation of the perceptions of sisterhood and self-esteem across the span of the school year. Though this did not lead to data deficiencies, the findings of the study may have been further supported by even more data.

IMPLICATIONS

The data demonstrates that participants involved in this particular program—regardless of prior experience in an all-girls club—are thriving with self-worth, agency, and a desire for equity. Not a single participant expressed feelings of inadequacy or self-loathing in terms of their coding abilities or overall well-being. The supports within the Girls Who Code program focus on each participant's strengths and abilities, and the participants articulated them clearly. This was a common theme in existing research, as well (Riegle-Crumb et al., 2012; Heybach & Pickup, 2017). All 15 participants expressed passion for coding and even more for learning from others.

The existence of environments in which girls can explore and share their interests could be a starting point towards dismantling male-dominance in STEM fields. Even further, it is important that the support of girls interested in STEM transfers into other academic and non-academic settings. The establishment of genuine and continued mentoring relationships between prospective and experienced coders, those that offer guided learning opportunities and personal testimony, may be a more productive use of time than work based in deficit thinking (Karcher, 2018; Pinkard et al., 2017).

This is not only the responsibility of students and teachers. It extends into local and global communities as well. A critical examination into the media representations of women on a larger scale is one step in this systemic process. The development of genuine opportunities for women to network and share their work is another. The need is great, but the stakes are high. The sooner that society shifts attention toward the development of positive systems of support for women, the more attainable equality will become.

CONCLUSION

The results of this study indicate the need for continued efforts to mitigate the underrepresentation of women in STEM fields. Stakeholders in this work are plentiful, but a refinement of the efforts of all involved is nothing short of a necessity (Karcher, 2018; Levine, et al., 2015; Toglia, 2013; U.S. Department of Labor, 2015). The presumption that poor self-esteems of young women keep them from pursuing STEM careers is unfounded and futile. Instead of framing women (those impacted by the oppression) as contributors to their own problem, those looking for ways to encourage girls to pursue STEM should expend their energy by critically examining the systemic flaws in societal foundations in order to offer authentic, fruitful support. The participants in this study long for opportunities to learn from the success of others and hone their own skills in unique ways. They are disheartened when feeling that their work is not valued and celebrated in ways that their male counterparts' may, and this is the case across the nation (Master et al., 2016; Simon et al., 2017). With focused and purposeful supports, women can celebrate success in enriching coding opportunities that align with their interests and goals. It is the duty of all stakeholders to ensure that young women are given access to supportive and inclusive communities that allow them to explore their interests, pursue their dreams, and share their stories along the way.

REFERENCES

Adams, P. E. (2010). Understanding the different realities, experience, and use of self-esteem between Black and White adolescent girls. *Journal of Black Psychology, 36*(3), 255–276. doi: 10.1177/0095798410361454

Adams, S. K., Kuhn, J., & Rhodes, J. (2006). Self-esteem changes in the middle school years: A study of ethnic and gender groups. *RMLE Online, 296*, 1–9, doi: 10.1080/19404476.2006.11462029

Amador, J. M., & Soule, T. (2015). Girls build excitement for math from scratch. *Mathematics Teaching in the Middle School, 20*(7), 408–415. doi:10.5951/mathteacmiddscho.20.7.0408

Ashcraft, C., Eger, E. K., & Scott, K. A. (2017). Becoming technosocial change agents: Intersectionality and culturally responsive pedagogies as vital resources for increasing girls' participation in computing. *Anthropology & Education Quarterly, 48*(3), 233–251. doi: 10.1111/aeq.12197

Ayres, M. M., & Leaper, C. (2013). Adolescent girls' experiences of discrimination: An examination of coping strategies, social support, and self-esteem. *Journal of Adolescent Research, 28*(4), 479–508. doi: 10.1177/0743558412457817

Bayazit, B. (2014). The effect of recreational activities on self-esteem development of girls in adolescence. *Educational Research and Reviews, 9*(20), 920–924.

Bettinger, E., & Long, B. (2005). Do faculty serve as role models? The impact of instructor gender on female students. *American Economic Review, 95*, 152–157. doi: 10.1257/000282805774670149.

Booher-Jennings, J. (2008). Learning to label: Socialisation, gender, and the hidden curriculum of high-stakes testing. *British Journal of Sociology of Education, 29*(2), 149–160. doi:10.1080/01425690701837513

Cook Political Report. (2018). 2018 House race ratings. Cook Political Report. Retrieved from https://www.cookpolitical.com/ratings/house-race-ratings

Demirdag, S. (2015). Classroom management and students' self-esteem: Creating positive classrooms. *Educational Research and Reviews, 10*(2), 191–197.

Eccles, J. S., & Wang, M.-T. (2016). What motivates females and males to pursue careers in mathematics and science? *International Journal of Behavioral Development, 40*(2), 100–106. doi: 10.1177/0165025415616201

Fields, D. A., Kafai, Y., Nakajima, T., Goode, J., & Margolis, J. (2018). Putting making into high school computer science classrooms: Promoting equity in teaching and learning with electronic textiles in "exploring computer science." *Equity & Excellence in Education, 51*(1), 21–35. doi: 10.1080/10665684.2018.1436998

Girls Who Code (2018). Girls Who Code: Join the Girls Who Code movement. Girls Who Code. Retrieved from https://girlswhocode.com

Grossman, J. M., & Porche, M. V. (2014). Perceived gender and racial/ethnic barriers to STEM success. *Urban Education, 49*(6), 698–727. doi: 10.1177/0042085913481364

Hand, S., Rice, L., & Greenlee, E. (2017). Exploring teachers' and students' gender role bias and students' confidence in STEM fields. *Social Psychology of Education: An International Journal, 20*(4), 929–945. doi: 10.1007/s11218-017-9408-8

Heybach, J., & Pickup, A. (2017). Whose STEM? Disrupting the gender crisis within STEM. *Educational Studies: Journal of the American Educational Studies Association, 53*(6), 614–627. doi: 10.1080/00131946.2017.1369085

Ilumoka, A., Milanovic, I., & Grant, N. (2017). An effective industry-based mentoring approach for the recruitment of women and minorities in engineering. *Journal of STEM Education: Innovations and Research, 18*(3), 13–19.

Karcher, M. J. (2008). The cross-age mentoring program: A developmental intervention for promoting students' connectedness across grade levels. *Professional School Counseling, 12*(2), 137–143.

Kutob, R. M., Senf, J. H., Crago, M., & Shisslak, C. M. (2010). Concurrent and longitudinal predictors of self-esteem in elementary and middle school girls. *Journal of School Health, 80*(5), 240–248. doi: 10.1111/j.1746-1561.2010.00496.x

Legewie, J., & DiPrete, T. A. (2014). The high school environment and the gender gap in science and engineering. *Sociology of Education, 87*(4), 259–280. doi: 10.1177/0038040714547770

Levine, M., Serio, N., Radaram, B., Chaudhuri, S., & Talbert, W. (2015). Addressing the STEM gender gap by designing and implementing an educational outreach chemistry camp for middle school girls. *Journal of Chemical Education, 92*(10), 1639–1644. doi: 10.1021/ed500945g

Liang, B., Lund, T. J., Mousseau, A. M. D., & Spencer, R. (2016). The mediating role of engagement in mentoring relationships and self-esteem among affluent adolescent girls. *Psychology in the Schools, 53*(8), 848–860. doi: 10.1002/pits.21949

Litzler, E., Samuelson, C. C., & Lorah, J. A. (2014). Breaking it down: Engineering student STEM confidence at the intersection of race/ethnicity and gender. *Research in Higher Education, 55*(8), 810–832. doi: 10.1007/s11162-014-9333-z

Lyons, T. (2018). Helping students make sense of STEM. *Teaching Science: The Journal of the Australian Science Teachers Association, 64*(3), 37.

Mann, M. J., Smith, M. L., & Kristjansson, A. L. (2015). Improving academic self-efficacy, school connectedness, and identity in struggling middle school girls: A preliminary study of the "REAL Girls" program. *Health Education & Behavior, 42*(1), 117–126. doi:10.1177/1090198114543005

Master, A., Cheryan, S., & Meltzoff, A. N. (2016). Computing whether she belongs: Stereotypes undermine girls' interest and sense of belonging in computer science. *Journal of Educational Psychology, 108*(3), 424–437. doi:10.1037/edu0000061

McAlear, F., Scott, A., Scott, K. & Weiss, S. (2018). Data brief: Women of color in computing. Kapor Center/ASU CGEST. Retrieved from https://www.wocincomputing.org/wp-content/uploads/2018/08/WOCinComputingDataBrief.pdf

National Center for Women & Information Technology (2019). By the numbers. Retrieved from https://www.ncwit.org/resources/numbers

National Science Foundation. (2013). Bachelor's degrees awarded, by sex and field: 2001–2010. Division of Science Resources Statistics. Retrieved from http://www.nsf.gov/statistics/wmpd/2013/sex.cfm

Pinkard, N., Erete, S., Martin, C. K., & McKinney de Royston, M. (2017). Digital youth divas: Exploring narrative-driven curriculum to spark middle school girls' interest in computational activities. *Journal of the Learning Sciences, 26*(3), 477–516. doi: 10.1080/10508406.2017.1307199

Rhodes, J., Roffman, J., Reddy, R., & Fredriksen, K. (2004). Changes in self-esteem during the middle school years: A latent growth curve study of individual and contextual influences. *Journal of School Psychology, 42*(3), 243–261. doi: 10.1016/j.jsp.2004.04.001

Ridenour, C. S., & Hassell Hughes, S. (2016). Girl talk: A qualitative study of girls talking about the meaning of their lives in an urban single-sex elementary school. *Teacher Educator, 51*(2), 97–114. doi: 10.1080/08878730.2016.1150753

Riegle-Crumb, C., King, B., Grodsky, E., & Muller, C. (2012). The more things change, the more they stay the same? Prior achievement fails to explain gender inequality in entry into STEM college majors over time. *American Educational Research Journal, 49*(6), 1048–1073. doi: 10.3102/0002831211435229

Simon, R. M., Wagner, A., & Killion, B. (2017). Gender and choosing a STEM major in college: Femininity, masculinity, chilly climate, and occupational values. *Journal of Research in Science Teaching, 54*(3), 299–323. doi: 10.1002/tea.21345

Simpson, A., Che, S. M., & Bridges, W. C., Jr. (2016). Girls' and boys' academic self-concept in science in single-sex and coeducational classes. *International Journal of Science and Mathematics Education, 14*(8), 1407–1418. doi:10.1007/s10763-015-9676-8

Toglia, T. V. (2013). Gender equity issues in CTE and STEM education: Economic and social implications. *Tech Directions, 72*(7), 14–17.

U.S. Department of Labor. (2015). Current population survey: Detailed occupations by sex and race. Washington, DC: U.S. Department of Labor.

Women's Initiative. (2018). Gender matters. Center for American Progress. Retrieved from https://www.americanprogress.org/issues/women/news/2018/08/06/454376/gender-matters/

Gwendolyn Nuding
Chiddix Junior High School

Chapter Six

The Experience of Vocational Girls' Schools in Turkey and How It Reflects on Working Life

Tülay Kaya

Ralph Tyler's definition of education as "a process of changing behavior patterns of people" (1950, p. 4) is one of the main references in Turkish literature on education (Ertürk, 1997; Sönmez, 1986). However, the agenda of critical pedagogues also includes the question of who the beneficiary of these desired changes of behavior is. At the core of this question, power elites, such as the state and corporations, are blamed for using school education as an instrument for maintaining their prevailing status quo (Kaya, 2016). This is because those who are vulnerable in the current system can only maintain their current positions through bringing up each new generation as individuals who adopt their social status without questioning it at all (Althusser, 2014; Apple, 2012; İnal, 2008; McLaren, 2015). As women's work has become a cheap and abundant source of labor since the 19th century, the indoctrination of gender roles has become particularly important. In these terms, one anchor of criticism made about schools in terms of maintaining the prevailing status quo is their function in the reproduction of gender roles.

From the moment of birth, parents prepare girls and boys for their place and prospective professions in society through the choice of toys, through hair length and style, and through color of clothing (Vatandaş, 2007). However, in the process of socialization, children are shaped by factors other than parents. School and school culture are amongst the most important of these. Schools are crucial platforms where stereotype gender roles which have already been established at home—such as the "quiet and emotional girl" or the "strong and brave boy"—are reproduced. Stereotypes related to gender roles are reinforced through various channels, such as educational programs, the content of books, curriculum, school uniforms, spatial layouts of classrooms and playgrounds, gender-based disciplinary punishments, formation and distribution of tasks assigned to students, plus the way teachers attend to them during classroom activities (Esen, 2013; Meredyth

E. Mikulec, D. Beichner (eds.), Distraction: Girls, School, and Sexuality, 83-97.

& Tyler, 1993; Tan, 2008; Thorne, 1993). Within the school climate, student re-production of gender-role stereotypes, with a gender bias that persists in society later in their lives, would be natural outcomes. Thus the social and cultural climate experienced at schools becomes visible in various gender-based responsibilities. Keeping house, cooking, and taking care of younger siblings are seen as women's duties, and are confined to the home, whereas men's duties take place in the outside world: representing the family, being successful, and earning a living.

Vocational and technical high schools in girls' education stand out among various school types in supporting the reproduction of traditional gender roles, while providing training and skilled labor. In Turkey, vocational training as part of a highly centralized education system is conducted at the upper-secondary school level through various institutional structures and options. According to the Ministry of National Education [MoNE], the number of vocational schools at the upper-secondary level in Turkey totals 3,636. Vocational training lasts for four years and constitutes the final stage (from ninth to twelfth grades) of a 12-year compulsory education, which must be completed in order to continue on to university studies. Apart from the limited number of vocational and technical high schools, the majority of upper-secondary vocational institutions have no selective requirement and are open to both young women and men. As of the 2017–2018 school year, among the 1,642,635 students who continued their formal education at vocational upper-secondary schools, 864,591 (56.%) were boys and 677,008 (44%) were girls (MoNE, 2018a).

The purpose of vocational training is to educate young people in skills and competencies required by industry, such as commerce, carpentry, construction, mechanics, information technology, and other service areas. In addition to their contribution to industry, vocational and technical high schools also provide an opportunity for challenging traditional gender roles, which, in the long run, may help to eliminate bias in employment process. However, girls are still encouraged to prepare for certain occupational fields that are in accordance with traditional gender roles, such as fashion, design, illustration, child development, communication, and health (MoNE, 2018a). The allocation of training fields at vocational and technical high schools also results in the reinforcement of existing gender roles, which further restricts their employment prospects (Kelly & Nihlen, 1982).

Turkey provides an excellent environment to study how girls are sexualized through school practices at vocational and technical high schools. In this context, this chapter will examine how even though the content of girls' vocational training has changed over time, these schools have served as genderizing spaces that reinforce societal norms and expectations for girls and young women in Turkey. To that end, the Ottoman Empire experience in girls' vocational training will be taken into account, since its history began with the Empire's moves to westernize and modernize in the late 19th century. Tracing from the history of vocational training for girls, there are certain patterns which are still prevalent in Turkey these days.

In order to give a detailed description of the recent state of girls' vocational training and its implications for working life, a historical analysis will be applied, along with a broad literature review of various research, plus articles on girls' vocational education and strategy and policy master documents provided by NGOs and state institutions in Turkey. Becoming familiar with the experience in Turkey will contribute to theoretical and practical studies for determining the scope and extent of sexism in education.

HISTORICAL HIGHLIGHTS OF GIRLS' VOCATIONAL TRAINING IN TURKEY

The Ottoman Empire saw vocational education as a tool to prepare men for the labor force according to the changing dynamics of the late 19th century, with the purpose of catching up on industrial developments in the West. Therefore, vocational and technical education had become a priority and new schools were established, because in this new era the percentage of qualified manpower was an indicator of the level of development (İnal, 2011; Kaya, 2018).

Among the schools that were opened in the 19th century, the foundation of inas rüşdiyye (women's middle schools) in 1858 was particularly significant, since sıbyan mektepleri (primary schools) had been the only option for girls before this period (Somel, 2000). These new schools "would teach women about religion and worldly issues in order to provide their husbands comfort in domestic matters and to preserve their own chastity" (Somel, 2001, p. 57). The Cevri Kalfa Inas Rüşdiyye is considered the beginning of vocational education for girls because of the handicraft courses organized at that school (Sakaoğlu, 1991); whereas, the institutions that highlighted vocational education for girls would be the Islahhanes (vocational orphanages).

An Islahhane was kind of a factory-school for vagrant, orphaned, destitute, and poor city children between the ages of five and thirteen (Maksudyan, 2011). The first Islahhane, named Kız Sanayi Mektebi (Girls' Industrial School), was established in 1865, and orphaned girls were trained there as seamstresses by sewing military uniforms for officers and men. Other girls' industrial schools were established soon after, mainly in Istanbul. Even though the original reason for the foundation of these schools was to prepare girls for industry, in 1900 "industry" meant handicrafts such as needlework, embroidery, housewifery (i.e., housekeeping), flower making, carpet weaving, cookery, piano, and music as a way of focusing on solidifying the housewife role (Akşit, 2004; Demir, 2017). However, with the foundation of the Turkish Republic in 1923, these schools were soon replaced by Girls' Institutes to train future housewives and mothers. As the new republic was established on the principal of achieving "modern" nation statehood, a critical role was assigned to women; to shape the new ideal society by becoming potential mothers of the forthcoming generation (Gök, 2007).

Girls' Institutes were single-sex educational establishments at the high school level, with a curriculum that included subjects such as child development, embroidery, painting, sewing, pastry baking, nutrition, and home economics (Toktas & Cindoglu, 2006). Special emphasis was placed on the objective of training girls in housework, childcare, health, etc. to help them perform their duties as women and mothers in an ideal way, thus contributing to the ideal of Turkey becoming a modern country (Demir, 2017). With such a stance it can be said that these schools were in line with the objectives of U.S. schools at the same period. As argued by early U.S. advocates of women's education, it was necessary to educate women to become better wives and mothers and thus contribute to the raising of future citizens (Childress, 2008). Taken from this perspective, while the function of motherhood would be to raise citizens for the state according to the priorities of the Republic, the function of housekeeping would be to establish the modernized lifestyle. Modernization was seen as keeping up with the West in terms of technological development, with the easy importation and adoption of Western advancements while not harming national values and traditions. Even though the graduates of these schools were not in the first instance expected to form part of the labor force, they were expected to contribute to the formation of the nation state and its ideals of modernization through domestic work. As role models for a whole society, they were expected to disseminate Republican reforms in the public sphere.

Girls' Institutes were more popular among high socioeconomic status (SES) families as the materials used in these schools were costly and needed a higher income family background. The instrumental appeal of the Institutes to families was that they provided daughters with the titles "educated" and "good housewife and mother" (Toktas & Cindoglu, 2006). In these terms, Girls' Institutions targeted the elite and middle classes; whereas the target groups of Islahhane-rooted girls' industrial schools were vagrants and orphans with very low income, and who would work as cheap labor (Durakbaşa & Karapehlivan, 2018).

Over time, the school structure for the construction of the "new Turkish woman" as a homemaker/nationmaker was found to be insufficiently functional to meet society's new needs, especially during the economic expansion of 1960–1980. Also, its outcomes were unsatisfactory when compared with international norms in the same period (Cecen, Dogruel, & Dogruel, 1994). In this new economic climate, Girls' Institutes were transformed into Girls' Vocational High Schools in 1974 with the purpose of bringing up qualified personnel to be employed in the industrial and service sectors (Gökşen, Yükseker, Alnıaçık & Zenginobuz, 2012). In other words, a new dimension—that of "worker"—was added to the duties of being housewife and mother.

CURRENT STATE OF GIRLS VOCATIONAL TRAINING

Today vocational training at upper-secondary level is provided through three types of schools: Vocational and technical high schools, multi-program high schools, and vocational training centers. The differences between these types of schooling are more on structural schema. Other than that, they share the same purpose of preparing individuals to enter labor markets by training them in occupational skills. Vocational and technical high schools provide students with academic courses along with occupational courses. Multi-program high schools are schools in less densely populated areas that offer vocational and general education programs under one roof. Their students are awarded diplomas according to the type of school program (whether vocational or general) they go through (MONE, 2018a). In comparison with vocational and technical high schools, vocational training centers have a non-academic vocational career path. Vocational training centers admit students without age limit, provided they have completed their eight years of basic education; and then prepare them in line with their skills and sector demands, through apprenticeship, journeyman, and mastership training (MoNE, 2014). There are 3,636 vocational institutions at the upper-secondary school level in Turkey currently. Of these institutions, 2,552 (70.21%) are vocational and technical high schools, 762 (20.93%) are multi-program high schools, and 322 (8.86%) are vocational training centers (MoNE, 2018a). The majority of students can enroll in any of these vocational upper-secondary training institutions without selective requirements apart from proving, by their home address, that they live in the neighborhood of the school they wish to attend. Only 449 vocational and technical high schools require a national placement exam result for enrollment (MoNE, 2018b).

A common curriculum is applied in the 9th grade. However, from the 10th grade onwards, students can choose their occupational training according to their own wishes, interests and abilities from amongst 54 fields, including: Child Development and Training, Information Technologies, Electric/Electronic Technology and Clothing Production Technologies at vocational and technical high schools (see the Appendix for a full list of occupational fields of training at vocational and technical high schools). In the 11th and 12th grades, students study their chosen branch amongst 199 options—from apparel to olive technology—developing competency in the various professions. Branch studies involve the on-the-job training stage, with two days theoretical (school training), and three days practical (in-company training). In the 12th grade, students who have completed the procedures are qualified for the diploma and become entitled to Europass certificates as technicians (MoNE, 2018a). Moreover, if graduates of these schools wish to pursue higher education, they may.

However, the number of students who go on to attend university is quite limited, and the primary purpose of vocational high schools is to prepare students to get into subordinate economic roles rather than preparing them for higher education as in general high schools. The immediate result of this structure is the students' reduced chance of gaining entry to socially desirable occupations and other high-prestige professions. In addition, vocational high schools are less selective and the least prestigious of high school options. This also leaves students feeling undervalued from the beginning of their secondary education and can affect their aspirations for the future in a negative way, limiting future socioeconomic mobility (Kaya, 2018). An even larger issue in the long run is the reproduction of inequality across generations as these students are likely coming from lower SES families. Research has shown that secondary education pupils in Turkey tend to go to schools and types of school according to their families' SES. In this context, Serdar Polat (2009) in his study shows that most of the students at vocational high schools come from lower SES families; and what is especially of note in this context is that the level of education of vocation school parents is lower than that of parents whose children go to more prestigious establishments, such as science high schools. Another study, made in 2014, shows that whereas 51% of the students of science high schools come from higher SES families, 23% of the vocational high school students come from the bottom 20% of SES (Oral & McGivney, 2014). Under these circumstances, the role of the vocational and technical high schools that lower SES students attend becomes more important in overcoming gender clichés and transforming the existing disadvantageous positions of girls in the labor market.

THE ROLE OF VOCATIONAL TRAINING IN OVERCOMING GENDER CLICHÉS

Since school environments are crucial for enriching social and cultural capital, vocational high schools can be a platform to widen women's opportunities. But it is doubtful whether these schools achieve their full potential to overcome perceptions created in the early stages of life regarding the assignment of occupations as "masculine" and "feminine." First, whereas in these schools both sexes are legally eligible for all occupational fields, the data indicates that girls still tend to be clustered in near single-sex programs. For instance, MoNE statistics for the 2010–2011 academic year (MoNE, 2011, cited in Gökşen, et al., 2012) show that Child Development and Training is the most preferred program (36.3%) among the training fields offered, whereas Information Technologies is the second (13.3%) and Clothing Production Technologies is the third (12%). Although only Information Technologies appear to be an innovative training field for the vocational education of girls, this field is associated with secretarial work and office staff jobs. Although equally well qualified as boys, having been taught in the same classroom and with the same curriculum (including the use of computer equipment and processes for the creation, storage and exchange of all forms of electronic data, etc.), girls still tend to limit their occupational abilities to clerical jobs because secretarial work is considered more suitable for women, and because the working conditions and office hours would not harm their roles at home. This indicates that students remain within the boundaries of given gender roles in their choice of profession, casting doubt on the schools' functionalities (Gökşen et al., 2012).

Despite the occupational field diversity offered at vocational and technical high schools, MoNE statistics also indicate a concentration of girls in fields related to traditional gender roles. Between 2008 and 2014, more than 90% of graduates in the areas of Metal Technology, Climate and Ventilation Technologies, Motor Vehicle Technology, Electric-Electronic Technologies, Aircraft Maintenance, Furniture and Interior Design, Shipbuilding, Mechanical Technology, Industrial Automation Technology, Maritime, and Agriculture were male. Whereas 90% of graduates in the areas of Child Development and Training, Handicrafts Technology, Family and Consumer Services, Beauty and Hair Care Services, Clothing Production Technology, and Graphics and Photography were female (MoNE, 2018a).

The research paper "Gender Equality at Vocational Schools: The Examples of Ümraniye and Şişli Vocational and Technical High Schools" (Eğitimde Reform Girişimi [ERG], Çelikel Eğitim Vakfı & Friedrich Ebert Stiftung, 2015), which discusses the quality and status of vocational and technical high schools in terms of gender equality, showed similar findings. According to the results of this research, vocational and technical high schools have been coded as either boys' schools or girls' schools because of the programs they offer. For example, while there isn't a single female student in the Metal Technology field at the sample schools, the number of girls studying in fields such as Construction Technology, Information Technology, Motor Vehicle Technology, and Mechanical Technology is highly limited, as these fields are considered male occupations. Gender-based distribution by field is also observed in the higher education programs. According to statistics provided by higher education for the 2018–2019 academic year, technical sciences were mostly preferred by male students compared to female students. For example, while the total number of male students registered at the faculty of mechanical engineering is 4,768, the number of female students is 841. While the number of male students at the faculty of education is 72,256, the number of female students is 143,759 (Council of Higher Education, 2019).

On the other hand, the research paper Vocational School Students' Views and Attitudes Towards Gender Based Choice of Profession (Ankara University Women's Problems Research and Implementation Centre, 2017, cited in Özkazanç, Sayılan & Akşit, 2018) shows that girls consider it an advantage, rather than a disadvantage, to be in lower numbers than boys on study programs which are traditionally identified as male. In fact, it is stated that girls are actually happy being fewer in number as they think the exclusivity helps them gain self-reliance and gives the chance of becoming in a pioneer in their field. However, another significant finding from the data was the concern female students showed that the profession they had selected was not viewed as suitable for women. Even though many students who were interviewed expressed the view that more girls should choose the fields that are associated with male occupations, most of them would still abide to the idea that "women are better at social fields and men are at technical ones." In this context, it has been observed that many of the girls interviewed would discriminate based on the physical differences between genders, citing jobs such as driving heavy goods vehicles or doing manual labor as opposed to desk-based jobs. Therefore, even though female students at vocational and technical high schools receive education in fields which are typically preferred by male students, the positions they envisage themselves doing in their future working lives for companies of this nature do not require driving heavy vehicles or doing manual labor, but rather taking "desk jobs" that would involve them in administrative functions (Özkazanç et al., 2018, p. 160).

Efforts have been made in vocational training to eliminate genderized divisions. For instance, Turkey has become party to international agreements such as the Convention on the Elimination of all Forms of Discrimination Against Women (CEDAW), and the Beijing Declaration, with the aim of fulfilling gender equality by creating training programs/curricula and opportunities that allow women to go beyond traditional gender roles (Özkazanç et al., 2018; Tan, 2007). To abolish gender discrimination, a vast number of initiatives, projects and campaigns launched in collaboration with MoNE, national and international NGOs, the European Union, and World Bank. For instance, Turkey's Engineer Girls Project (2016–2020) targets female students to become role models in their profession. Similarly, The Forewomen Painters Project (2016–2017) was put into practice to provide women with occupational knowledge in different sectors. I Exist/Challenge, Too Project

(2014–2017) on the subject of social gender equality, participation in life, and employment was carried out with teachers and students of girls' vocational and technical high schools and the students' families (General Directorate on the Status of Women [GDSW], 2019).

Nationwide administrative steps have been taken, such as the approval of standard curricula and co-education. Most recently, boys' vocational schools and girls' vocational schools were united under the name of Vocational and Technical Anatolian High Schools in Turkey in 2014 (Durnalı, 2015). Despite these efforts, as can be seen from the various studies presented here, traditional gender distribution has not changed to a great extent and vocational education in Turkey still retains a gender-based structure. Female students are still concentrated in occupational training fields in accordance with traditional gender roles such as fashion, illustration, child development, and communication, with reference to some personality traits: for instance, that women are more compassionate, sensitive, and innately nurturing. More importantly, these fields are assumed to allow young women, as prospective wives and mothers, to spend more time at home and with their children after graduation. Thus, they will be able to fulfill the gender roles expected by the current social order, even if they work after graduation (Kaplan, 2015). Therefore, although girls seem to be able to make their own occupational field choices, they continue to make choices within the limits determined by society. In other words, cultural values and pre-existing gender roles still determine their vision regarding prospective occupations that would not paralyze established gender roles. Among those factors which cause this cycle to continue, the most important is the cultural climate in schools; while in addition, there is the fact that vocational fields are subject to discrimination because of gender biases in schools.

Genderized Practices in Vocational Training

In-school processes are as effective in building students' gender roles as their out-of-school equivalents. The experiences students acquire in being schooled have certain effects on their prospective positions in society. First of all, they internalize their place in society, and then this internalization determines a mindset regarding what the prospects to which their working lives may be limited. Vocational and technical high schools could have been instrumental in challenging and overcoming the widely accepted gender roles in society, since at the secondary school level, students are at an age when they become more aware of what is socially appropriate for their gender (Dumais, 2002). However, besides female students' concentrations at school in areas that correspond to traditional gender role patterns, the fact is that they live in a cultural environment that confirms the gender-based separation of vocational training programs at schools. Research shows that, in Turkey too, girls are under the sway of a culture that involves sexist role patterns and practices that have implicitly or explicitly been reinforced via hidden curriculum such as educational materials, practices and attitudes, in addition to the behavior of teachers in schools (Deniz, 2014; ERG et al., 2015; Gökşen et al., 2012; Sayılan, 2012; Tan, 2008).

In this context, teachers as both role models and authority figures have a critical position in the classroom. In other words, teachers are not only in the classroom to import academic knowledge to the students, they also have a crucial potential in challenging the already settled gender beliefs of the students with their discourse and behavior. The reason for this is that, although students come to school with their own previously established opinions, they also observe their teachers from all dimensions, from their style of dress to their use of language. Most importantly, at the same time, students learn what kind reaction will gain approval. In this respect, students can easily detect their teachers' stereotyping behavior, which reinforces the gender stereotypes in the classroom, acknowledging it to be as concrete as the behavior they have observed outside of school (Cullingford, 1993).

Sexist attitudes of teachers vary from interfering with students' appearance and dress to putting pressure on opposite-sex friendships, to the categorizing of course content, to arranging classroom seating along gender lines (Tan, 2008). Sexist behavior in teachers becomes especially visible in classroom management. For example, female and male students are assigned different responsibilities for maintaining order in the classroom, such as assigning workshop arrangement and cleaning to female students (Deniz, 2014). Members of each gender may have different disciplinary punishments imposed based on different types of disorderliness, and with regard to stereotypical images such as "nice, quiet, and successful girl" and "harsh, rebellious, and brave boy" (Sayılan, 2012, p.14).

Sexist attitudes of teachers at schools are also manifested via daily routines in the control of girls' appearance in terms of dress, hair, and makeup; and also in the expectation that the way they should talk is "appropriate for a girl" (Deniz, 2014, p. 160). It is worth mentioning that nowadays such reactions are not identical to practices in the early days of the Republic at the Girls' Institutes, where any indication of the student sexuality was supposed to be suppressed. That was why students were required to wear a black uniform with a white collar, black stockings, and black shoes. The rules were not only restricted to appearance. Students were expected to have certain behavior patterns: having boyfriends, wearing makeup, smoking and having long nails were all strictly prohibited (Gök, 2007). Of significance here is that the fact that these expectations and controls over sexuality still continue to be seen in the vocational and technical high schools of Turkey.

Reflections on Employment

The gender role pattern ascribed to women has been transformed since the employment rate of women became a tangible indicator, fulfilling a basic requirement in the evolution of a modern 20th century state (Almaçık, Gökşen & Yükseker, 2019). In these terms, girls' vocational training has stood at the intersection between the increase of women's educational attainment and employment levels in Turkey. However, the employment rate of female graduates of vocational and technical high schools is still lower than male graduates. According to the Ministry of Industry and Technology's Industrial Requirements for Labor Force Qualifications Report data, while 82.2% of the male graduates of vocational and technical high schools joined the labor force in 2017 and 82.3% in 2018, this ratio was 41.0% for girls in 2017 and 42.3% in 2018 (MoNE, 2018a).

Although there is no gender discrimination in high profile professional areas such as law, medicine, dentistry, architecture, pharmaceutics, or academia (Vatandaş, 2007), gender discrimination still remains in sectors where semi-qualified vocational school graduates are employed. The sector where women are most prominently employed is in the service sector, which is stated to be accepted throughout society as "areas proper for women." Although women employees are preferred in labor-intensive branches of industry, such as textiles and food, industrial sectors, especially manufacturing industry, are where women's employment is highly limited. An echo of the attitude in social life that separates jobs and professions into "men's work" and "women's work" is the concentration of women in limited areas that are thought to be peculiar to women, and their obligation to accept working there at low-status and low-paying jobs (GDSW, 2011).

Given that vocational training for women in Turkey is a gendered and gendering process, with a curriculum that echoes the cultural norms about women's role in society, graduates already continue to seek pathways into the labor market within this framework (Almaçık et al., 2019). Because of the gender-based awareness they acquire through their education, girls and young women evaluate their future job opportunities in a kind of self-censored way. If they wish to continue in the fields where they have been educated, working at desk-bound or customer-related jobs seems to be one of the limited number of options that are considered "appropriate for women." For example, those girls who graduated from the motor vehicle technologies field are employed in the automotive companies as customer relations representatives, with job descriptions including phone communications, e-mailing, making appointments, informing customers about the status of their cars, etc. At the same companies, jobs like wheel balancing, gearbox replacement, etc., are still done by men. Therefore, the reason why young female vocational and technical high school graduates naturally seek employment elsewhere is the lack opportunity to work in the areas they were trained for (ERG et al., 2015).

CONCLUSION

Sexist approaches encountered in different layers of life are certainly closely related to established stereotypes. The question is how effective we are in using the existing channels to transform those stereotypes. Research frequently emphasizes the fact that women's access to education opportunities and employment are functional channels in the struggle against sexist approaches. Vocational and technical high schools, being ascribed the mission of training individuals to gain the skills and qualifications required by industry, outshine other school categories in their potential to contribute to the education and employment of women. These schools' principal relationships with industry, by definition, also point to their potential capacity in terms of women's employment. They also serve as a robust platform that allows women to raise their awareness, so that they realize they can go beyond the traditional gender roles in their choice of profession. Again, if education is—as asserted—the process of ensuring desired changes in individuals' acts and attitudes, vocational schools in particular can be utilized to overcome sexist approaches, and to increase the employment rate of women. However, despite this potential of vocational and technical high schools, there is a question as to what extent they have managed to transform the mission of preparing female students for "women's work" and, in the background, "the gender roles" as was the case at the beginning of the 20th century.

Within the process, the content of girls' education in Turkey has changed. Education, especially vocational training, has added working woman to the roles of housewife and mother. However, as can be seen from following the history of these short insights into the vocational education of girls in Turkey, vocational and technical education has still been differentiated by gender. Despite transformational actions described in the research, vocational and technical high schools maintain their features as institutions where traditional gender roles are reproduced. Although it is both a right and an option for female students to have education in vocational areas known as "male-specific," the number of girls choosing areas that are male-specific is still limited. Today, gender-based differentiation is still observed at vocational and technical high schools; and the fact that male and female graduates continue to make career choices in accordance with gender-role related expectations indicates that, despite the changing conditions, sexist coding is still consequential.

The fact that vocational schools—whose program distributions comply with sexist divisions of labor and which exist in a sexist cultural atmosphere—are institutions reinforcing gender roles instead of transforming them can be seen early on when young female graduates get their first jobs. From the very beginning, female students get stuck in career choices by their selection of study areas at vocational schools where they study to raise their employability. Therefore, though it is important to be party to gender equality protocols both on national and international platforms, this by itself is still inadequate. The decisions taken must also be supported by the education process and culture at the schools. Thus, one of the determinants in this process is the educators. By their practice in the classroom and the way they treat female and male students, teachers structure students' thoughts and attitudes towards gender roles; and such gender disparities are deeply internalized by the students. Consequently, despite vocational schools, and also through their contribution, sexist approaches still continue to be a problem area to overcome.

In Turkey, which has been on the road to becoming a modern industrialized society since the middle of the 19th century, there has been no hesitation to define a mission for women, starting with the first vocational schools for girls. Nevertheless, sexist attitudes have been reproduced at vocational and technical high schools, and the "women's work/men's work" stratification continues to be maintained. Also, the consequence of this loop in daily life is the fact that women cannot take advantage of social resources equally with men. In other words, as long as these schools are not used as platforms to develop attitudes towards gender equality, ensuring women's access to education alone fails to achieve equality. For this reason, these schools should not be perceived as a ticket to second-class status, but rather to challenge the given status of women and help them to take a full part in the life of work.

REFERENCES

Akşit, E. E. (2004). *Girls' education and the paradoxes of modernity and nationalism in the late Ottoman Empire and the early Turkish Republic* (Doctoral dissertation). Retrieved from ProQuest Dissertations and Thesis database. (UMI No. 3139156).

Almaçık, A., Gökşen, F., & Yükseker, D. (2019). School to work or school to home? An analysis of women's vocational education in Turkey as a path to employment. *Gender and Education, 31*(8), 1040–1056.

Althusser, L. (2014). On the reproduction of capitalism: Ideology and ideological state apparatuses. Verso.

Apple, W. M. (2012). *Education and Power.* Routledge.

Cecen, A. A., Dogruel, A. S., & Dogruel, F. (1994). Economic growth and structural change in Turkey 1960–88. *International Journal of Middle East Studies, 26*(1), 37–56.

Childress, F. J. (2008). Creating the 'new woman' in early republican Turkey: The contributions of the American collegiate institute and the American college for girls. *Middle Eastern Studies, 44*(4), 553–569.

Council of Higher Education. (2019). 2018–2019 öğretim yılı yükseköğretim istatistikleri [Higher education statistics for the 2018–2019 academic year]. Retrieved from https://istatistik.yok.gov.tr/

Cullingford, C. (1993). Children's views on gender issues in school. *British Educational Research Journal, 19*(5), 555–563.

Demir, M. (2017). Tanzimat'tan Cumhuriyet'in ilk yıllarına Türkiye'de ev kadınlarının eğitimi: İdare-I beytiye [Education of housewives in Turkey from the Tanzimat period to the early years of the Republic: Housewifery]. *Bartın Üniversitesi Çeşm-i Cihan Tarih Kültür ve Sanat Araştırmaları e-Dergisi, 4*(1), 108–120.

Deniz, E. E. (2014). *Kız meslek lisesi öğrencilerinin toplumsal cinsiyet rol ve kimliklerinin inşasına yol açan süreçlerin analizi: Ankara ili Mamak ilçesinde bir Anadolu meslek ve kız meslek lisesiörneği* [Analysis of the processes which cause the construction of gender roles and identities for the vocational girls' high school students: Case of an Anatolian vocational high school and a vocational girls' high school in Mamak, Ankara]. Retrieved from the National Thesis Center of the Turkish Council of Higher Education. (Accession No. 354790).

Dumais, S. A. (2002). Cultural capital, gender, and school success: The role of habitus. *Sociology of Education, 75*(1), 44–68.

Durakbaşa, A., & Karapehlivan, F. (2018). Progress and pitfalls in women's education in Turkey (1839–2017). *Encounters, 19*, 70–89.

Durnalı, M. (2015). Mesleki eğitim finansmanı [Financing the vocational education]. *International Journal of Social Sciences and Education Research, 1*(2), 572–583.

Eğitimde Reform Girişimi, Çelikel Eğitim Vakfı & Friedrich Ebert Stiftung. (2015). Meslek liselerindetoplumsal cinsiyet eşitliği: Ümraniye ve Şişli mesleki ve teknik Anadolu liseleri örneği [Gender equality at vocational schools: The examples of Ümraniye and Şişli vocational and technical Anatolian high schools]. Istanbul, Turkey: Education Reform Initiative.

Ertürk, S. (1997). Eğitimde program geliştirme [Program development in education]. Ankara, Turkey: Meteksan.

Esen, Y. (2013). Hizmet öncesi öğretmen eğitiminde toplumsal cinsiyet duyarlılığını geliştirme amaçlı bir çalışma [A study for developing gender sensitivity in pre-service teacher education]. *Eğitim ve Bilim, 38*(169), 280–295.

General Directorate on the Status of Women. (2011). Türkiye'de kadının durumu [The status of women in Turkey]. Ankara, Turkey: Republic of Turkey Ministry of Family, Labor and Social Services.

General Directorate on the Status of Women. (2019). Women in Turkey. Ankara, Turkey: Republic of Turkey Ministry of Family, Labor and Social Services.

Gök, F. (2007). The girls' institutes in the early period of the Turkish Republic. In M. Carlson, A. Rabo, & F. Gök (Eds.), *Education in "Multicultural" Societies – Turkish and Swedish Perspectives* (vol. 18, pp. 93–105). Istanbul, Turkey: Swedish Research Institute.

Gökşen, F., Yükseker, D., Almaçık, A., & Zenginobuz, Ü. (2012). Kız teknik ve meslek liseleri kapsamlı değerlendirme notu [A comprehensive assessment note on technical and vocational girls' high schools] (Working Paper 2012/06). Istanbul, Turkey: Boğaziçi University.

İnal, K. (2008). Eğitim ve ideoloji [Education and Ideology]. Ankara, Turkey: Kalkedon.

İnal, V. (2011). The eighteenth and nineteenth century Ottoman attempts to catch up with Europe. *Middle Eastern Studies, 47*(5), 725–756.

Kaplan, S. P. (2015). *Eğitim sendikalarında toplumsal cinsiyet politikaları: Kadın öğretmenlerde toplumsal cinsiyet.* [Gender policies in the education trade unions: The Gender awareness of female teachers] (Master's thesis, Istanbul University, Turkey). Retrieved from the National Thesis Center of the Turkish Council of Higher Education. (Accession No. 422343).

Kaya, T. (2016). Eğitim ve aktivizm: Özgür okullar örneği [Education and activism: The case of free schools]. In N. Y. Sert (Ed.), Aktivizm: Toplumsal değişimin yeni yüzü (Activism: The new face of social change] (pp. 109–132). Istanbul, Turkey: Değişim.

Kaya, T. (2018). Vocational education in Turkey: Past and present. In U. Gaulee (Ed.), *Global adaptations of community college infrastructure* (pp. 94–109). Hershey, PA: IGI Global.

Kelly, G., & Nihlen, A. (1982). Schooling and the reproduction of patriarchy: Unequal workloads, unequal rewards. In M. W. Apple (Ed.), *Cultural and economic reproduction in education: Essays on class, ideology and the State* (pp. 162–180). Routledge & Kegan Paul.

Maksudyan, N. (2011). Orphans, cities, and the state: Vocational orphanages ("Islahhanes") and reform in the late Ottoman urban space. *International Journal of Middle East Studies, 43*(3), 493–511.

McLaren, P. (2015). Life in schools: An introduction to critical pedagogy in the foundation of education. Routledge.

Meredyth, D., & Tyler, D., Eds. (1993). *Child and citizen: Genealogies of schooling and subjectivity.* Brisbane, Australia: Institute for Cultural Policy Studies, Griffith University.

Ministry of National Education. (2014). Vocational and technical education strategy paper and action plan 2014–2018. Ankara, Turkey.

Ministry of National Education. (2018a). Eğitim analiz ve değerlendirme raporları serisi No: 1. Türkiye'de mesleki ve teknik eğitimin görünümü [Education analysis and evaluation report series No. 1. A view of vocational and technical education in Turkey]. Ankara, Turkey: Author.

Ministry of National Education (2018b). Sınavla öğrenci alacak ortaöğretim kurumlarına ilişkin merkezi sınav başvuru ve uygulama kılavuzu [Central exam application guide for the secondary education institutions].

Oral, I., & McGivney, E. J. (2014). Türkiye eğitim sisteminde eşitlik ve akademik başarı, araştırma raporu ve analiz [Equality and academic achievement in Turkey's education system, research report and analysis]. Istanbul, Turkey: Sabancı University.

Özkazanç, A., Sayılan, F., & Akşit, E. E. (2018). Toplumsal cinsiyet ve mesleki eğitim: Mesleki Teknik lise kız öğrencileri üzerine bir araştırma. [Gender and education: A study on female students of technical vocational schools]. *Fe Dergi 10*(2), 150–164.

Polat, S. (2009). Türkiye'de eğitim politikalarının fırsat eşitsizliği üzerindeki etkileri. [The impacts of education policies on educational inequalities of opportunity in Turkey] (Planning Expertise Thesis, State Planning Organization, Ankara, Turkey).

Sakaoğlu, N. (1991). Osmanlı eğitim tarihi [History of Ottoman education]. Istanbul, Turkey: İletişim.

Sayılan, F. (2012). Toplumsal cinsiyet ve eğitim [Gender and education]. In F. Sayılan (Ed.), *Toplumsal Cinsiyet ve Eğitim: Olanaklar ve Sınırlar [Gender and education: Opportunities and limitations]* (pp. 13–67). Ankara, Turkey: Dipnot.

Somel, S. A. (2000). Osmanlı modernleşme döneminde kız eğitimi [Girls' education in the Ottoman modernization period]. *Kebikeç, 10*, 223–238.

Somel, S. A. (2001). *The Modernization of public education in the Ottoman Empire, 1839–1908: Islamization, autocracy, and discipline.* Leiden, the Netherlands: Brill

Sönmez, V. (1986). Türkiye'de eğitimin kalitesi ve geleceği [The future and quality of education in Turkey]. *Eğitim Fakültesi Dergisi, 1*, 49–63.

Tan, M. G. (2007). Women, education and development in Turkey. In M. Carlson, A. Rabo & F. Gök (Eds.), *Education in "Multicultural" Societies – Turkish and Swedish Perspectives* (vol. 18, pp. 107–122). Istanbul, Turkey: Swedish Research Institute.

Tan, M. (2008). Eğitim [Education]. In M. Tan, Y. Ecevit, S. S. Üşür, & S. Acuner (Eds.), *Türkiye'de toplumsal cinsiyet eşitsizliği: Sorunlar, öncelikler ve çözüm önerileri [Gender inequality in Turkey: Issues, priorities and ssuggestions]* (p. 27–112). Istanbul, Turkey: TUSIAD - KAGIDER.

Thorne, B. (1993). *Gender play: Girls and boys in school.* Rutgers, NJ: Rutgers University Press.

Toktas, Ş., & Cindoglu, D. (2006). Modernization and gender: A history of girls' technical education in Turkey since 1927. *Women's History Review, 15*(5), 737–749.

Tyler, R. W. (1950). *Basic principles of curriculum and instruction.* Chicago, IL: University of Chicago Press.

Vatandaş, C. (2007). Toplumsal cinsiyet ve cinsiyet rollerinin algılanışı [Gender and the perception of gender roles]. *Sosyoloji Konferansları Dergisi, 2*(35), 29–56.

APPENDIX

List of Occupational Fields of Training at Vocational and Technical High Schools: Accommodation and Travel Services; Accounting and Finance; Agriculture; Aircraft Maintenance; Animal Husbandry and Health Care; Art and Design; Beauty and Hair Care Services; Biomedical Devices Technology; Cartography-Land Surveying; Ceramics and Glass Technology; Chemical Technology; Child Development and Training; Civil Aviation; Construction Technology; Design Technology; Electric/Electronic Technology; Entertainment Services; Family and Consumer Services; Fashion Design Technology; Firefighting and Fire Protection; Food and Beverage Services; Food Technology; Footwear and Leathercraft Technology; Furniture and Interior Design; Graphics and Photography; Handicraft Technology; Health Services; Industrial Automation Technology; Information Technologies; Installation Technology and Air Conditioning; Jewelry Technology; Journalism; Justice; Laboratory Services; Maritime; Marketing and Retail; Mechanical Technology; Metal Technology; Metallurgical Technology; Meteorology; Mining Technology; Motor Vehicles Technology; Musical Instrument Making; Office Management; Patient and Gerontological Services; Plastic Technology; Printing Technology; Public Relations and Organization Services; Radio and Television; Rail Systems Technology; Renewable Energy Technologies; Shipbuilding; Textile Technology; Transportation Services (MoNE, 2018a).

Tülay Kaya
Istanbul University

Chapter Seven

Forgotten, but Not Lost: The Effects of Exclusionary School
   Policies and Practices on Black Girls

Abiola Farinde-Wu, Davonna Graham, and Stephanie Jones-Fosu

Black girls are consistently disciplined more harshly than their White counterparts (Crenshaw, 2015). In fact, they are five times more likely to be suspended than White girls and twice as likely to be suspended as White boys (Epstein, Blake, & González, 2017). Simply put, they are being pushed out of schools (Morris, 2016), potentially precluding their academic development and trajectory.

When Black female students are compared to their Black male counterparts, Black girls are often perceived as "doing well" (Rollock, 2007). However, many Black girls are suffering in silence, negotiating a school system influenced by teachers' implicit biases and cultural perceptions of Blackness and gender (Farinde & Allen, 2013; Morris, 2007). This dominating viewpoint that negatively labels many Black female students as deviants because of their unwillingness to conform to hegemonic, White-American ideals of gender (Richardson, 2009) prevents a nurturing school environment of academic possibilities. Considering that involvement in school discipline sanctions may engender detrimental consequences, such as poor academic performance, school dropout, and negative life outcome (Rocque, 2010), greater attention must be given to Black female students' disciplinary experiences.

In examining the sequence of events that led to a major school fight between approximately 30 Black female students, we ask: What school policies and practices influenced Black female students' schooling experiences, and how did these policies and practices impact these girls' gendered racial identities? The purpose of these questions is not to condemn the school or its personnel; rather, this exploration is meant to shine a light on the school's actions in hopes of improving the educational experiences and identity development of Black girls.

E. Mikulec, D. Beichner (eds.), Distraction: Girls, School, and Sexuality, 99-119.

Beginning, we provide a brief overview of the literature on Black female students' school experiences. Next, through the lenses of intersectionality (Crenshaw, 1989, 1991) and Black feminism (Collins, 2000; Lorde, 1984), we draw from data from a three-year ethnographic study to explore the implicit, explicit, and null school policies and practices that may have influenced the identity development of Black girls who participated in a major school fight. Through an examination of this physical altercation, Black female students' contextual experiences are placed at the center of analysis. Concluding, we offer policy and practice recommendations for educators.

THEORETICAL FRAMEWORK

This study employs intersectionality (Crenshaw, 1989, 1991) and Black feminism (Collins, 2000; Lorde, 1984) as theoretical lenses. It is imperative that we consider the intersectionality of race and gender as it relates to exclusionary discipline policies and practices. In this case, an intersectional perspective examines the nuanced experiences of Black female students as they are neither only Black *or* female at any given time (Crenshaw, 1989). Intersectional theory acknowledges that "modes of inequality, such as race, class, and gender, can combine in ways that alter the meaning and effects of one another" (Morris, 2007, p. 491).

Complementing intersectionality, Black feminism was derived from the marginality present in the feminist movement (hooks, 1981; Lorde, 1984) due to its singular focus on gender and frequent omission of race (Collins, 2000). Collins (1986), extending the works and ideas of Black feminist scholars, coined Black feminist thought (BFT) and defined three characteristic themes of the thought: 1) the meaning of self-definition and self-valuation, 2) the interlocking nature of oppression, and 3) the importance of Afro-American women's culture. BFT advocates for a self-defined image of Black womanhood, seeks to clarify the lives of Black women, and centralizes the experiences and ideas of Black women (Collins, 1986). Moreover, Collins notes that the ideas in BFT were created by and for Black women. Although diversity within class, religion, age, ethnicity, sexual orientation, and region shape the lives of individual Black women, resulting in different expressions, BFT posits commonalities in perception and outlook among Black women's experiences through a shared race and gender identity (Collins, 2000). Because of their race and gender, Black women as a group experience a different reality and a different world than those belonging to other racial or gender groups (Collins, 2000).

Within Black feminism, sexism, gender identity, class oppression, and racism collide. Lorde (1984) captures her contempt for racism by stating, "My response to racism is anger.... the anger of exclusion, of unquestioned privilege, of racial distortions, of silence, ill-use, stereotyping, defensiveness, misnaming, betrayal, and co-optation" (p. 124). For Lorde, anger is used as a tool for critical external evaluation and internal growth. In this examination, race, gender, and class are intersecting features, shaping the schooling experiences of Black girls (Crenshaw, 1989) as they experienced neglect from school officials and subsequently encounter violence from law enforcement (Crenshaw, 1991). In validating the experiences of Black girls, this exploration uses the "lived experiences as a criterion of meaning" concept, which substantiates the epistemological foundation of BFT (Collins, 2000). This concept affirms the validity of "concrete experiences as a criterion for credibility… when making knowledge claims" (Collins, 2000, p. 276), legitimizing Black female students' lived experiences.

Schools play a vital role in the overall development of students. Hence, the implicit, explicit, and null curricula of schools may promote or hinder students' positive identity development. Acknowledging schools' visible and hidden curricula, Eisner (1994) outlines forms of curricula: (a) the implicit curriculum captures messages or practices that are not stated or written down but influence students' opportunities to learn; (b) the explicit curriculum describes student-learning opportunities that are outwardly inculcated and stated or printed in texts (e.g., policies, documents, student, parent-student handbook, etc.); and (c) the null curriculum reveals what is wholly absent from students' learning. A combination of the implicit, explicit, and null curricula, though perceived as innocuous, may obstruct students' positive identity development, engendering negative school experiences for Black female students.

Implicit Curriculum: The Race Gap in Schools

During the 2015–16 school year, 80 percent of public-school classrooms were headed by White teachers (Mcfarland et al., 2018). Latinx and Asian teachers and teachers possessing two or more racial identifications made up approximately 13 percent, so that only seven percent of public school teachers were Black (Mcfarland et al., 2018). These data suggest that there is an implicit curriculum in the teacher demographics of U.S. public schools. Indeed, the underrepresentation of teachers of color sends a subtle message to students about who is and should be in positions of authority and whose pedagogy is valued in classrooms.

In contrast to the U.S. teacher demographics, the National Center for Education Statistics (NCES, 2017) reports that children of color continue to make up the larger proportion of the national student population. Furthermore, the NCES (2017) also predicts that by the year 2027, students of color will make up 55% of the student population, surpassing their White peers who are expected to decline in number by at least five percent from 49 percent to 45 percent nationally. Figures 1 and 2 illustrate this racial/ethnic gap between teachers and students.

Figure 1. Racial Makeup of Teachers During the 2015–16 School Year
Source. Adapted from McFarland et al., 2018.

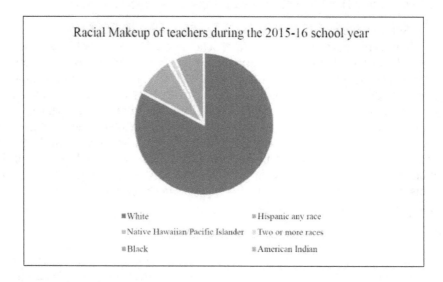

Figure 2. Public School Enrollment by Race in the 2015–16 School Year
Source. Adapted from National Center for Education Statistics, 2017.

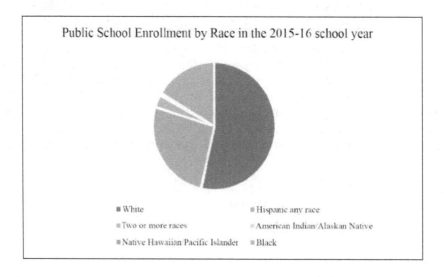

Black Teachers

These changing demographics are of concern because research, although limited, has demonstrated that students benefit academically from being taught by teachers who share their same racial, ethnic, and cultural background (Easton-Brooks, Lewis, & Zhang, 2009). Research on the effects of Black teachers on the academic achievement of Black students is mixed. On one hand, Gershenson, Hart, Lindsay, and Papageorge's (2017) study shows that the "drop out" rate decreases by 29 percent for students who have been taught by at least one Black teacher, particularly in grades 3–5. Even more compelling, for low-income Black boys, the "drop out" rate was decreased by 39 percent, with 18 percent of this group expressing interest in college (Gershenson et al., 2017). Moreover, scholars point to high expectations as one predictor of such success, both on the part of the teacher and the student (Gershenson, Holt & Papageorge, 2015). On the other hand, research is lacking in the examination of ethnic-matching along with gender, socioeconomic status, and in schools with majority students and teachers of color (Easton-Brooks, et al., 2009). Some studies of ethnic-matching have shown little in the way of academic achievement, and their results have been less than reliable, due to faulty design.

Of those widely referenced, however, findings suggest that having exposure to a Black teacher, particular one with high expectations, can yield valuable results for Black students (Dee, 2004; Dee, 2005; Easton-Brooks, 2009). In their study of reading scores over time as influenced by teacher-student ethnic matching, Easton-Brooks et al. (2009) investigate the outcomes of Black students who received instruction from White and Black teachers. They found that Black students who were taught by at least one Black teacher scored 1.50 points higher in reading assessments than those who did not have a Black teacher. Further, Black female students performed 2.31 points better in reading than their male peers at the kindergarten level. Easton-Brooks and colleagues (2009) argue that no exposure to a Black teacher was represented by the highest percentage of variance in the reading scores between kindergarten and fifth grade, though having a Black teacher accounted for positive variances in reading scores. This type of finding is consistent across other studies (Dee, 2004; Dee, 2005) that have demonstrated the influence Black teachers can have on the academic performance of their students.

Teachers of color, particularly Black teachers, tend to value a social justice framework and a challenging curriculum as ways to motivate and prepare their students (Phillip, 2011). Black teachers have reported that they have distinctive goals, pedagogical styles, and decision-making processes that demonstrate empathy, not pity, for their students (Acosta, Foster, & Houchen, 2018; Phillip, 2011). This shared racial and cultural knowledge may provide opportunity for relationship building and deeper understanding of students' lives outside of school. In many cases, Black teachers have been able to connect with students in urban environments because they acknowledged that students' behaviors were often a result of their out-of-school experiences (Milner, Murray, Farinde, & Delale-O'Connor, 2015). Rather than pitying students or perceiving students negatively, Black teachers empathize with students' circumstances, often times because they have shared those same circumstances (Farinde-Wu, 2018).

Teacher perception and student outcomes. Extant literature points to teacher perception as a meaningful and statistically significant factor in student achievement and behavior (Dee, 2004). Using data from the National Education Longitudinal Study of 1988, Dee (2005) finds that 8th grade students who were perceived as disruptive were less likely to enroll in advanced placement courses in the next two proceeding grade levels. Previous research (Ehrenberg, Goldhaber, & Brewer, 1995; Ferguson, 2003) also indicates that the subjective perceptions and evaluations made by teachers are more likely to be higher when they share the same ethnic background of their students. In fact, White teachers are more likely to have negative views of Black students than those of Black teachers (Gershenson, Holt & Papageorge, 2015). To be clear, this is not to suggest that teachers who teach students of a different ethnic background are flatly unable to be "fair" with their students, but that implicit biases often predict the way teachers view and interact with their students. Students who are viewed in a pejorative manner may be less likely to achieve at higher levels.

In addition, language styles, such as grammar and behavioral norms, tend to positively reinforce the interactions between students and teachers of the same ethnicity (Delpit, 2006). Perhaps influenced by these differences, Rimm-Kaufman and Pianta (2000) suggest that White teachers often viewed their non-White students as having difficulty following instructions and behaving immaturely. Rimm-Kaufman and colleagues (2000) finds that teachers of color did not possess this perspective when interacting with their non-White students. Using odds-ratios to interpret teacher perspective, Dee's (2005) study also finds that a student is 1.36 times more likely to be seen as disruptive when they differ in race from their teacher. Findings illustrate that both White and non-White students have a greater likelihood of being viewed more negatively in general by a teacher who does not share their race or ethnicity (Dee, 2005). Furthermore, researchers (Ehrenberg et al., 1995; Ferguson, 2003; Gershenson, Holt, & Papageorge, 2015) posit that the academic performance of Black students tends to be viewed more poorly by White teachers than by non-White teachers.

Social conflicts between students' home cultures and school norms have also been linked to teachers' negative perceptions of students of color and those of a lower socioeconomic status (Fenning & Rose, 2007). Data from Dee (2005) shows that living in poverty compounded the lower expectations of non-racially matched teachers and their students with lower socioeconomic status. White teachers who believe that they understand the "disadvantaged" backgrounds from which many of their students come, may opt to grant what Ladson-Billings (2002) references to as a "permission to fail." This "permission" may be granted especially when teachers factor in the complex situations that students face outside of school. Furthermore, a 2014 report from the Center for American Progress declares that an overwhelmingly White teaching force believes that Black students were 47 percent less likely than White students to graduate from college (Baron, 2014). So, being both Black and poor has tended not to bode well for students taught in racially incongruent classrooms. This finding is in direct contrast to the high expectations set forth by many Black educators who express their commitment to ensuring their students' academic success (Milner, 2006).

Explicit Curriculum: Exclusionary Discipline Policies and Practices

Very often, discussions of school conflict, chaos, and punishment seems to center on urban environments. Sweeping and expensive reform models are frequently packaged and sold to urban schools as a "quick fix" for their problems with student behavior. Movies like *Dangerous Minds*[8] and *Cooley High*[9] depict students in urban schools as disruptive, violent, and uneducable—illustrating exaggerated imagery of the "dangers" of the inner-city. The reality of urban education is that school leadership and corresponding policies and practices tend to prioritize concerns of conflict and disruption over actual academic instruction (Crenshaw, 2015; Mayes Pane, Rocco, Miller, & Salmon, 2014). It appears that few studies unpack the dynamics of social classroom interactions as they influence exclusionary discipline practices.

Exclusionary discipline (i.e., the explicit curriculum) refers to the policies and practices used in classrooms that ultimately eliminate the presence of minoritized students at a rate greater than that of their racial and gendered counterparts (Crenshaw, 2015; Skiba, Arredondo, & Williams, 2014). These policies push out particular students from classrooms for subjective behaviors (Crenshaw, 2015; Morris, 2016; Skiba et al., 2014). A startling gap in disciplinary practices exists between students of color and White students. Black students, in particular, are removed from their classrooms for subjective behaviors, often described as loud, aggressive, disruptive, or disobedient. Most often, White students are referred for objective actions, those infractions that clearly break a school policy such as skipping class or smoking (Skiba, 2001). The outcomes of such subjective punishment may mean that 1) students are unable to identify the specific behaviors that result in discipline; 2) expectations for appropriate behaviors may differ from one teacher to another; or 3) ambiguity involved in identifying inappropriate behavior allows some students to be punished while others are not. Subsequently, perceived problematic students are disproportionately referred, suspended, and expelled (Crenshaw, 2015; Skiba, 2001; Skiba et al., 2014). This pattern of disparity ultimately leaves Black girls with less instruction time, fosters poor or even negative relationships with teachers and peers, and perpetuates damaging stereotypes.

Black girls pushed out. Black girls have historically been described as talkative, loud, aggressive, and violent (Crenshaw, 2015; Morris, 2016). In many instances, the act of speaking up for oneself, using illustrative body language, or overlapping speech are perceived as disrespectful and may result in an office referral or suspension, even when these actions are not intended to be harmful (Morris, 2007; Morris, 2016). In his study of an urban high school's classroom dynamics, Morris (2007) finds that White teachers seemed to focus their attention on the social decorum and physical comportment of Black girls rather than their academic achievement, making reference to girls behaving "unladylike," implying a set of prescribed traits expected of young women. Black female students were regarded as "mature," though this was not seen as a desirable attribute, and more culpable of their teenage indiscretions (Morris, 2007).

While Black boys experience exclusionary practices at the highest rate of all groups, the relative rate of suspension between Black boys and White boys is half that of Black girls and White girls (Crenshaw, 2015). Black girls are five times more likely to be suspended than their White female peers for very similar behaviors (Crenshaw, 2015; Epstein et al., 2017). In other words, the often-innocuous actions of Black female students may be interpreted as "disrespectful" or "aggressive," while those of their White peers are regarded as playful. Moreover, Black girls receive harsher sentences in the juvenile justice system when compared to any other subgroup of girls. Even with evidence of discipline disparity (Crenshaw, 2015; Morris, 2016), few studies exist that explore the long-term outcomes of the Black girl push out effects.

Null Curriculum: Black Girls' Gendered Racial Identity Development

The gendered racial identities of Black girls are often omitted (null) from school curricula, sending additional messages that the identities of these young girls are not important in academic spaces as well as in the learning process. The literature that explores the topic of Black girls gendered racial identity development in recent years has exposed the intricate layers in which Black girls exist in the United States. Based on the Tajfel's social identity theory (Tajfel, 2010), Black girls must assimilate messages they receive from multiple environments, including schools, into their own lived experiences (Thomas, Hoxha, & Hacker, 2013). Racial identity researchers have proposed that internal viewpoints of racial group affiliation in addition to public perceptions to the racial group are significant elements of identity development (Sellers, Smith, Shelton, Rowley, & Chavous, 1998). For Black girls, their context of identity development is laced with oppression and discrimination by being both Black and female, two undervalued identities (Thomas et al., 2013) that can influence trajectory and life outcome.

The remnant of slavery has also influenced the identity perceptions of Black girls to include stereotypes of Mammy, Jezebel, and Sapphire (Thomas et al., 2013). These racist images highlight the restricted roles Black women confront in society. They include Mammy, who was the slave nanny and housekeeper; Jezebel, a sensual sex addict; and Sapphire, who is portrayed as a controlling, loud, argumentative woman. Contemporary and collective versions of these images are presented in mainstream media (Lindsay-Dennis, 2015). Modern versions of these stereotypes include: Black women as superheroes or the strong Black woman, which scholars have noted as influencing the identity development of Black American girls (Jerald, Cole, Ward, & Avery, 2017). Societal images and stereotypes have the capacity to negatively shape the identities of Black girls, which can be detrimental to their overall gendered racial identity development (Townsend, Thomas, Neilands, & Jackson, 2010).

Townsend and colleagues (2010) note that teachers were often the cause of trauma toward Black girls and instrumental in perpetuating the stereotypes that hinder Black girls' development of positive self-identity. The Black girl participants in this study frequently felt battered by teachers and school staff. Furthermore, the participants faced uncooperative teachers and dangerous classrooms, which impacted their self-image and academic success. However, the girls in this study reported a positive view of their intellect and rejected colorism. Black female participants also reported a high sense of belonging and connection to their ethnicities, which positively influenced their self-image and academic self-concept.

Research suggests that identity is connected to motivation, especially as it pertains to achievement (Oyserman, 2009). Previous studies have explored the relationships between racial identity, academic beliefs, and academic performance among African American students. For instance, Chavous and colleagues (2003) find that the racial identity beliefs of students were reinforced by their academic achievement. This research indicates that racial identity encourages academic achievement for adolescence students. In addition, Chavous, Rivas-Drake, Smalls, Griffin, and Cogburn's (2008) study posits that resilient racial identity beliefs shielded students from the harmful effects of a racially unsupportive school environment. Within this study, Black girls recounted additional school-based discrimination, which placed them at an academic disadvantage. However, this study also indicates that Black girls with a sturdier awareness of their racial identity were less likely to be impacted academically by racial discrimination.

Butler-Barnes and colleagues (2017) study also show that Black girls improve academically in a racially safe environment with compassionate teachers. This study affirms that when Black girls feel that they belong in their school environments, they are more academically engaged. Moreover, these environments encourage academic achievement without diminishing Black girl's racial identity beliefs. Many of these studies assert that racial identity development may impact Black girls' academic progress; that is, racial identity may promote higher achievement motivation beliefs among Black girls (Butler-Barnes et al., 2017). With that said, the importance of nurturing Black girls' identity development should not be minimized, especially in schools.

BACKGROUND

In exploring the schooling experiences of Black girls who participated in a major school fight and the preceding and subsequent actions of the school, data from a three-year (2014–2017), ethnographic study (Creswell, 2013) conducted at M. M. Prep (a pseudonym, as all names in this chapter) is referenced in this theory-to-practice chapter to provide context and inform the identity development of Black female students.

The lead researcher collected the majority of the data, and this chapter was derived from her field work with school stakeholders at an urban school site. Ethnographic data from these encounters that are relevant to this discussion consist of observations and formal and informal interviews. Formal, audio recorded interviews were guided by open-ended, semi-structured interview questions. These interviews were later transcribed. Informal interviews consisted of everyday conversations with stakeholders. These verbal exchanges were not transcribed but were documented in the lead researcher's spiral notebook.

School Context

M. M. Prep is a grade 6 through 12 magnet school located in a working-class, historically Black urban neighborhood. M. M. Prep possesses a small student enrollment, serving approximately 500 students. M. M. Prep is state identified as a Title I school with high teacher turnover, discipline, and absentee rates. State standardized test scores outline below proficiency ratings in core content areas. Also, while the faculty is predominately White, the school has a majority-minoritized student population with over 90 percent African American students and more than 80 percent of students eligible for free or reduced lunch. When reflecting on the racial mismatch between teachers and students and student behavior, Ms. Lane, a middle school science teacher, acknowledged that tensions exhibited in her classroom may derive from cultural dissonance between herself and her students. She observed:

> I would say a lot of the behaviors I see and a lot of the things that make my job difficult and stressful everyday are just clashes in cultures, whether or not we are talking about gender or we are talking about race or we are talking about socioeconomic backgrounds. A lot of the ways in which [me and my students] are clashing and not connecting do make my job more difficult.

The clash to which Ms. Lane is referring stems from the dichotomous existence between a majority White faculty and a predominately Black student enrollment. Such a clash often influenced student behavior, classroom instruction, and school climate. "Students may have acted out because they did not see themselves reflected in the teaching faculty and curricula.".

The Fight

Depending on the source, different explanations were offered as to why a fight erupted between approximately 30 Black female students on school grounds. The media reported the existence of long-standing neighborhood and gang feuds that had spilled onto school campus. Despite conflicting accounts about the motivation of the fight, many agreed that the fight was a product of fractured female bonds and friendships. Consequently, on a Monday morning around 9:45 AM, one Black female student was "jumped" in the hallway by a group of girls, initiating numerous smaller fights that engulfed both students and teachers alike. During this chaotic scene, many students sustained physical injuries. The hallway echoed with cries and screams as students emerged from the fight with blood stained clothes and faces. As the fight escalated, the school executed lock down procedures. Ms. Frank, the school's band teacher, captured the event through her vivid description:

> It seems like the entire high school was up there (fourth floor) like just a swarm of bees. And they were moving to different parts of the hallway because the fights were traveling.... And so, I saw another teacher and she said, 'I'm calling 911.' And I was like, 'Is it that bad?' And she was like, there are three teachers in there right now who can't even get out'. And, she said, 'there's blood everywhere'.

In an attempt to restrain the students, armed uniformed police were immediately called to regain school order. Unfortunately, additional physical violence was administered to many young, Black bodies. Black female students were forcibly pushed to the ground, handcuffed, and subsequently arrested.

The fight was reported on numerous local area news stations and newspapers. Once the incident was disseminated via formal and informal outlets, parents, community members, and social justice activists were outraged and deeply concerned. The district and school personnel (e.g., administration and teachers) received immense pressure to ameliorate the current schooling experiences of students at M. M. Prep and ensure that such an incident would never occur again.

Community members viewed the incident as a direct manifestation of sociopolitical issues occurring in the historically Black, urban community. Kofi Usal, a former city councilman, freedom rider, and life-long civil rights activist, provided his analysis of the major school fight. He believed that the fight stemmed from decades of victimization and broken promises to the community. Essentially, institutionalized racism coupled with poverty engendered a petri dish of destruction. He explained:

> Unfortunately, the community is to some extent a victim of years and decades of oppression, and one of the byproducts of years of poverty and oppression is self-loathing, self-hatred. And the anger of the conditions of race and racism and poverty, coupled with self-loathing make it a tinderbox for anger and fighting to turn on ourselves. And so, instead of fighting against poverty and fighting against racism and fighting against the system, we fight with each other sometimes.

Mr. Usal's words capture the conditions Black female students often encounter when obtaining an education and attempting to progress through their PreK–12 experiences. Through no fault of their own, institutionalized and systemic racism can negatively shape students of self and academic trajectory.

Black Girl Identity

The gendered racial identities of Black girls attending M. M. Prep developed amidst a predominately White school faculty. Although the school offered two peer-mentoring enrichment programs (e.g., Girls Circle and FACE) to Black female students that focused on self-confidence and self-image and was led by Black women community members, the time spent in these programs was limited, compared to daily encounters and engagements with faculty and administration who did not often affirm Blackness or Black womanhood. Dee Wilson, a community activist and a participant of one of the school's peer-mentoring enrichment program for girls, explained the strengths and shortcomings of the programs:

> They were hoping to kind of work through some of these issues of femininity and womanhood and sisterhood in particular. But before that, I don't believe there were any girl-specific programs in the building. Again, our program could only reach a couple students at a time.

While enrichment programs tried to promote positive racial and gender identities among the Black female students, Ms. Wakes, a gym teacher, confirmed the disconnect between Black female students and some of the teachers at M. M. Prep, when she conveyed her lack of knowledge about why the Black girls are so angry. She stated, "I just don't know why it seems like the girls are so angry. I don't know if it's—I, I really don't know." Expressing similar sentiments, Ms. Kerry, a ninth-grade civics teacher, explained, "And it is heartbreaking because you wonder, 'what in the world has driven them to get that upset over something that really isn't that big of a deal?' Ms. Wakes and Ms. Kerry's remarks are examples of how the exclusion of issues related to identity, race, gender, and class within an educational context of a predominately White faculty serving majority students of color can engender confusion, misunderstanding, and division between students and teachers.

In addition to the disconnect experienced between many teachers and Black female students in the school, Tracey, an in-class, near-peer college mentor, recounted a conversation with her mentee about her mentee's perception of race and its impact on academic trajectory. Tracey explained that Shana, her mentee, believed that she would not succeed in higher education because of her race, broadly insinuating that Black people do not excel in academic contexts. Tracey explained this exchange:

> On Monday, the girls and I talked a great deal about college plans, during which [Shana] implied that she would probably not do well in college because [she is] Black. She seemed to be referring to and feeding into the systemic racist structures that cause teachers to have lower expectations for minority students, impeding them from reaching their full potential.

Shana's assumption of her own low academic performance because of her racial identification is disconcerting. Based on her thought process, one can infer that she possesses a negative gendered racial identity, one that has not been nurtured by her academic schooling experiences.

The voices of Black female students are pertinent in order to capture their true self-defined identities. After the fight, media outlets depicted an unruly and brutal fight between "troubled" young Black girls. Black female students were never interviewed, nor were they given the opportunity to communicate with the community about their reasons and motivations for fighting. Encountering similar treatment in school, these Black female students were silenced; they were not given a voice to both acknowledge and express their lived, day-to-day experiences. Direct field observation suggested that many Black female students often felt powerless, policed and restricted by a regimented school structure embedded with racist, exclusionary disciplinary policies and practices, and as a consequence, these young girls both protected themselves and displayed their frustrations about their school life through physical altercations with each other. An interview with Robyn, a ninth-grade student, actually revealed students' disdain for fighting. She explained the emotional and social dimensions of fighting by stating,

I don't even be ready to fight, but when I feel like somebody has more power over me, and they're using their power to try to crash down on me, and I'm like 'I'm not worried about you; I'm not trying to fight.' But then, I feel like, okay, now I have to protect my reputation, defend myself, and show people that I'm not going to take it, and I fight. If you let one person run over you that one time, and one person sees that happen, or they can go tell other people, it's over. The whole school will run over you. It can't be you against the whole school. So, you got to stop it at the source.

Robyn described how fighting was inevitable in order to defend and protect one's self. Reclaiming a sense of power and control and mitigating physical assault and ridicule from peers, Black female students felt compelled to fight in an unsafe, school environment in which explicit, implicit, and null policies and practices dictated student behavior. After the lead researcher's interview with Robyn, she escorted Robyn back to her advisory class.[10] The lead researcher then proceeded to the next participant's classroom. On the way back to the interview room, the lead researcher heard and observed an altercation between Robyn and another Black female student. The field note below captured the incident:

Fieldnote, 3/25/16, Dropped Robyn off at her class. Walked by her class and heard her arguing with a Black female student. She cries and said, 'Why do I always have to deal with this in school?' She was angry about a derogatory word that was used against her by her classmate. Robyn was eventually removed from her educational environment—the classroom.

This field note demonstrates how conflict between students is a common occurrence both outside of the classroom at M. M. Prep. Rather than focusing on their academic proficiency and mastery, Black female students navigated a hostile school environment. Their attention and energy were redirected away from developing content skills and competencies as they are often removed from the classroom for discipline infractions, mainly arguing and fighting. Despite the fact that there is a need for curricula and instruction that nurture and promote positive identity development among Black girls, acknowledging and infusing the gendered racial identities of students into curricula was not considered as a medium of instruction by faculty.

Although approximately thirty Black female students engaged in the school fight, many of these same girls did not want to fight at all. Dee Wilson explained how after that fight many of the girls communicated their unwilling involvement in the fight. She recounted,

The girls that were involved in the fighting, we actually heard from a good number. There were a good number of those girls that were like, 'I didn't want to fight her, but my cousin was involved, or my sister was involved, and I didn't want to fight. I don't want to fight anymore.'

Expressing their true motivations (family and friend obligations and loyalties), many of the Black female students loathed the action of previously fighting and fighting in the future.

Considering some of the Black female students' silenced; they were not of self and participation in a large-scale fight despite their reservations, what explicit policies and practices are shaping their identities? What implicit messages are being inculcated in students when those in authority are majority White? And what null messages are communicated about Black identity through the absence of Black epistemologies and representation in classroom lessons and textbooks? These subtle messages may infiltrate Black female students' identity development, obstructing positive self-images and reinforcing societal stereotypes.

Implicit, Explicit, and Null School Policies and Practices

The school's implicit, explicit, and null policies and practices may have influenced the identity development, as well as the positive self-concept of young Black girls involved in a major fight. Although the school initiated mediation after the large fight between opposing girl groups, instead of implementing research-based practices that engender positive results for student progress and achievement, the school increased zero-tolerance practices to student discipline. The school suspended and expelled many of the Black female students, engaged in hyper in-school surveillance, and positioned armed, uniformed police officers in hallways to monitor and control students. When reflecting on possible interventions that could have been implemented for Black female students, Ms. Walker, an administrative assistant, explained how girls were often overlooked and more focus was placed on young Black boys in general. She stated, "That seems to be the trend in high schools, period. The focus is on men, young men and not the young women and teaching them about their own femininity and their own womanhood and the beauty of it." Ms. Walker's interview reflection implied that more could have been done for the Black female students in order to mitigate the events that led to the fight.

After the fight, a reintegration plan was executed. It included violent and punitive language, such as physical assault (rather than fight) and pressing charges (rather than suspension). Students and parents were required to sign a "safety plan" that outlined the legal recourse that would be pursued if students were involved in a number of identified behaviors, such as a verbal or physical altercation. In addition, community stakeholders hosted a community meeting at the school following the fight. A police officer shared that the language used in this reintegration plan read almost verbatim to that of "orientation" manuals given to people being acclimated to the county jail. These examples demonstrate that before and after the fight, exclusionary and punitive policies and practices were implemented within the school's day-to-day structure.

Focusing on detrimental intervention strategies, the school's policies and practices may have caused more harm than good. Mr. Frank, a middle school social studies teacher, acknowledged the need for alternative interventions when combating poor student behavior. He explained,

> I don't know how much [the administration] tried to get parents involved in the mediation process or what consequences other than suspension, which some students might consider a reward they employed. I don't know what consequences

were given out. Perhaps, community service efforts should have been made. I don't think anyone should have been locked up or, you know, gone to jail.

Mr. Frank's suggestions may have produced better results for students' academic progress. Unfortunately, the interventions that were executed removed students from educational environments, expelling them from school grounds for weeks. Those who did return to school lagged behind academically, due to their prolonged absence.

DISCUSSION

Many Black female students are perceived as loud, outspoken, assertive, and "too grown" (Evans-Winters & Esposito, 2010; Morris, 2007). In addition, similar to their Black male counterparts, continued research needs to be conducted on the schooling and disciplining experiences of Black girls, and how these factors influence their identity development and academic progress. Master narratives often depict Black girls as aggressive and, only after being properly socialized, are suitable for classrooms. Their dual nature, possessing two socially assigned and constructed features (race and gender), can produce academic disadvantage. And in addition, social class further influences progress and public perception. As Black girls attempt to uncover their true identities, they combat numerous impediments, such as inaccurate media portrayals, gender and racial stereotypes, traditional gender roles, and implicit biases. Moreover, as they are often absent from positive mainstream images, Black girls are forced to reconcile society's views against their own views of themselves. Within this school context, Black girls carried the weight of race and gender. Indeed, few social groups can comprehend this burden: race amplified by racism, gender defined by gender roles, and both restricting mobility and access. These features, though unique, may alter interactions with society, outwardly displaying differences for all to critique.

Recommendations for Practice

When examining this study, one must consider the question of how so many Black female students were able to orchestrate and participate in a fight of such magnitude during the school day, considering all of the school personnel who were present and who have worked and interacted with these students. Educators must not overlook these girls because Black girls face the same risks as, if not greater risks than, other student groups (Wallace, Goodkind, Wallace, & Bachman, 2008). Indeed, the fight should call educators to question and reevaluate their perceptions, interactions, and treatment of these Black girls. In learning from this experience, we encourage educators to be reflective of their role preceding, during, and after the fight and to engage in open group dialogue about what they could have done differently, individually and as a collective faculty, to circumvent the events that transpired between their Black female students.

Additionally, regardless of students' gender and racial-ethnic backgrounds and classroom behaviors, opportunities to learn should be guaranteed. Rather than issuing exclusionary discipline sanctions, teachers must enact relationship-centered teaching (Farinde-Wu, Glover, & Williams, 2017; Milner, 2018), which will assist in seeing Black female students' behavior outside of a White, Eurocentric feminine lens.

With relationships in mind, focus is redirected from Black female students' behavior to their academic needs. Black female students' unique learning styles, strengths, and weaknesses begin to guide instruction and alter the learning environment. In adopting these young girls' realities, their behavior is re-conceptualized, seen and understood through a sociopolitical lens. From this viewpoint, punitive disciplinary sanctions are acknowledged as hindrances to academic progress.

According to Milner (2018), "In relationship-centered teaching, students and teachers co-build a classroom ethos that considers the evolving and conflicting nature of relationships as real and central to the curriculum" (p. 61). The emergence of an authentic teacher-student relationship can essentially aid White, middle-class teachers in better meeting the needs of their Black female students and promote positive racial and gender identities among their Black girls. No longer will one view of femininity dominate and dictate behavior. This transformation is imperative if Black female students are to have the same educational opportunities that are afforded to their White counterparts. Without relationship-centered teaching, many Black female students, who do not conform to traditional White standards of femininity, will be subjected to inequitable disciple practices that will surely stunt their academic progress. Those that resist, unable or unwilling to conform to White ideals of femininity, will be labeled the problem as they accumulate endless discipline referrals and are pushed out of classrooms. White, middle class teachers that grasp the importance of relationships in understanding students' identities may bridge teaching and gender and racial issues in the classroom. They may not only obstruct the school-to-prison pipeline, but possibly reverse it, nurturing positive outcomes for Black girls.

Recommendations for Policy

This incident is perhaps a cautionary tale of what may transpire when we neglect Black girls' gendered and racial identity development and label them as doing well when compared to their Black male counterparts. From an equity perspective, we must reevaluate our engagement with Black girls, implementing more support programs and resources to ensure that our young Black girls are not forgotten.

The conclusion in extant literature has remained relatively consistent over time; students of color—particularly Black and Brown students—and those from lower socioeconomic backgrounds still disproportionately experience harsher exclusionary practices (see, for instance, Skiba et al., 2011). And for Black girls, the interlocking oppression of race and gender frame this disproportionality. In rectifying this issue, zero tolerance, exclusionary discipline policies and practices are not the answer. In fact, these policies exacerbate the school-to-prison pipeline, contributing to low academic performance. Educational stakeholders should consider discipline policies that affirm the humanity of the student—policies that keep students in schools and provide opportunities for continued learning.

Beyond Teacher Recruitment as a Solution

When examining the racial mismatch in schools between teachers and students nationally, school districts continue to struggle toward an equitable racial and ethnic makeup of educators. Given the dramatic and historical decline in the number of teachers from "minoritized" backgrounds, particularly Black teachers, Milner (2006) recommends that researchers pay close attention to the knowledge, skill, and practices of Black teachers in order to help train White teachers to be successful in their work with Black students. Easton-Brooks and colleagues (2009) propose that, while training White teachers to teach Black students using similar models used by Black teachers is a viable strategy, working toward increasing (and retaining) the number of Black teachers to benefit both students and school systems is ideal. However, Dee (2004) proclaims that, though ethnic and gender match between students and teachers do indeed have large effects on teacher perceptions of student performance and actual student behavior, recruitment of teachers of color may not be a simple panacea. With such dismal percentages of teachers of color in U.S. public classrooms, recruitment is a noble but incomplete solution. In the meantime, both better preparation and vetting of all teachers is vital. With such dismal percentages of teachers of color in U.S. public classrooms, recruitment is a noble but an incomplete solution. In the meantime, both better teacher preparation and vetting of all prospective teachers is vital. Therefore, aiming to admit teacher candidates in teacher preparation programs with beliefs, perceptions, and values that align with racial equity in education, in addition to their demographic makeup may lead to more positive outcomes for students of color.

CONCLUSION

Engaging in a fight does not negate these girls' abilities to learn. Moreover, being perceived as an adult is far different from actually being an adult (Epstein et al., 2017), meaning that Black female students are not adults and are in greater need of nurturing, protection, support, and comfort. Giving a voice to the often overlooked, untold, and misinterpreted experiences of Black female students, this chapter shows how school policies and practices influenced by race and/or gender affect young Black girls' school experiences. It is our hope that with more discourse and action associated with the schooling and disciplining of Black female students, these girls will not be forgotten and will be offered more pathways to success.

REFERENCES

Acosta, M. M., Foster, M., & Houchen, D. F. (2018). "Why seek the living among the dead?" African American pedagogical excellence: Exemplar practice for teacher education. *Journal of Teacher Education, 69*(4), 341–353.

Butler-Barnes, S. T., Leath, S., Williams, A., Byrd, C., Carter, R., & Chavous, T. M. (2017). Promoting resilience among African American girls: Racial identity as a protective factor. *Child Development*, 1–20.

Baron, S. (2014). Local momentum for change to cut poverty and end inequality. Center for American Progress State of the States Report. Retrieved from https://cdn.americanprogress.org/wpcontent/uploads/2014/12/StateofStates2014-report.pdf

Chavous, T. M., Bernat, D. H., Schmeelk-Cone, K., Caldwell, C. H., Kohn-Wood, L., & Zimmerman, M. A. (2003). Racial identity and academic attainment among African American adolescent. *Child Development, 74*, 1076–1090.

Chavous, T. M., Rivas-Drake, D., Smalls, C., Griffin, T., & Cogburn, C. (2008). Gender matters, too: The influences of school racial discrimination and racial identity on academic engagement outcomes among African American adolescents. *Developmental Psychology, 44*(3), 637–654.

Collins, P. H. (2000). Black feminist thought: Knowledge, consciousness, and the politics of empowerment. Routledge.

Collins, P. H. (1986). Learning from the outsider within: The sociological significance of Black feminist thought. *Social Problems, 33*(6), 14–32.

Crenshaw, K. (1989). Demarginalizing the intersection of race and sex: A Black feminist critique of antidiscrimination doctrine, feminist theory, and antiracist politics. *University of Chicago Legal Forum, 14*, 538–54.

Crenshaw, K. (1991). Mapping the margins: Intersectionality, identity politics, and violence against women of color. *Stanford Law Review, 43*(6), 1241–99.

Crenshaw, K. (2015). Black girls matter. *Ms., 25*(2), 26–29.

Creswell, J. W. (2013). *Qualitative inquiry and research design: Choosing among five approaches.* Sage.

Dee, T. S. (2005). A teacher like me: Does race, ethnicity, or gender matter? *American Economic Review, 95*(2), 158–165.

Dee, T. S. (2004). Teachers, race, and student achievement in a randomized experiment. *Review of Economics and Statistics, 86*(1), 195–210.

Delpit, L. (2006). *Other people's children: Cultural conflict in the classroom.* The New Press.

Easton-Brooks, D., Lewis, C. W., Zang, Y. (2009). Ethnic matching: The influence of African American teachers on the reading scores of African American students. *The National Journal of Urban Education & Practice, 3*(1), 230–243.

Ehrenberg, R. G., Goldhaber, D. D., & Brewer, D. D. (1995). Do teachers' race, gender and ethnicity matter? Evidence from the national educational longitudinal study of 1988. *Industrial and Labor Relations Review, 48*, 547–561

Eisner, E. W. (1994). *The educational imagination: On the design and evaluation of school programs.* MacMillan College Publishing Company.

Epstein, R., Blake, J. J., & González, T. (2017). Girlhood interrupted: The erasure of Black girls' childhood. Georgetown Law Center on Poverty and Inequality.

Evans-Winters, V., & Esposito, J. (2010). Other people's daughters: Critical race feminism and Black girls' education. *Educational Foundations, 24*(1-2), 11–24.

Farinde-Wu, A. (2018). #Blackwomenatwork: Teaching and retention in urban schools. *The Urban Review, 50*(2), 247–266.

Farinde, A., & Allen, A. (2013). Cultural dissonance: Exploring the relationship between White female teachers' perceptions and urban Black female students' disciplinary infractions. *National Journal of Urban Education and Practice, 7*(2), 142–155.

Farinde-Wu, A., Glover, C., & Williams, N. (2017). "It's not hard work; it's heart work": Strategies of effective, award-winning culturally responsive teachers. *The Urban Review, 49*(2), 279–299.

Fenning, P., & Rose, J. (2007). Overrepresentation of African American students in exclusionary discipline: The role of school policy. *Urban Education, 42*, 536–559.

Ferguson, R. F. (2003). Teachers' perception and expectations and the Black-White test score gap. *Urban Education, 38*, 460–507.

Gershenson, S., Hart, C. M. D., Lindsay, C. A., & Papageorge, N. W. (2017). The long-run impacts of same-race teachers. IZA Discussion Papers, No. 10630, Institute of Labor Economics (IZA), Bonn.

Gershenson, S., Holt, S. B., Papgeorge, N. W. (2015). Who believes in me? The effect of student-teacher demographic match on teacher expectations. IZA Discussion Papers, No. 9202, Institute for the Study of Labor (IZA), Bonn

hooks, b. (1981). *Ain't I a woman: Black women and feminism.* South End.

Jerald, M. C., Cole, E. R., Ward, L. M., & Avery, L. R. (2017). Controlling images: How awareness of group stereotypes affects black women's well-being. *Journal of Counseling Psychology, 64*, 487–499.

Ladson-Billings, G. J. (2002). I ain't writin' nuttin': Permission to fail and demands to success in urban classrooms. In L. Delpit (Ed.), *The skin that we speak: Thoughts on language and culture in the classroom* (pp. 107–120). The New Press.

Lindsay-Dennis, L. (2015). Black feminist-womanist research paradigm: Toward a culturally relevant research model focused on African American girls. *Journal of Black Studies, 46*, 506–520.

Lorde, A. (1984). *Sister outsider.* The Crossing Press.

Mayes Pane, D., Rocco, S., Miller, L., & Salmon, A. (2014). How teachers use power in the classroom to avoid or support exclusionary school discipline practices. *Urban Education, 49*(3), 297–328

McFarland, J., Hussar, B., Wang, X., Zhang, J., Wang, K., Rathbun, A., Barmer, A., Forrest Cataldi, E., & Bullock Mann, F. (2018). The Condition of Education 2018 (NCES 2018-144). U.S. Department of Education. Washington, DC: National Center for Education Statistics. Retrieved [5-29-2019] from https://nces.ed.gov/pubs2018/2018144.pdf

Milner, H. R. (2006). The promise of Black teachers' success with Black students. *Educational Foundations, 20*, 89–104

Milner IV, H. R. (2018). Relationship-centered teaching: Addressing racial tensions in classrooms. *Kappa Delta Pi Record, 54*(2), 60–66.

Milner, H. R., Murray, I., E., Farinde, A., & Delale-O'Connor, L. (2015). Outside of school matters: What we need to know in urban environments. *Equity & Excellence in Education, 48*(4), 529–548.

Morris, E. W. (2007). "Ladies" or "loudies"?: Perceptions and experiences of Black girls in the classroom. *Youth Society, 38*, 490–515.

Morris, M. W. (2016). *Pushout: The criminalization of Black girls in schools.* The New Press.

National Center for Education Statistics. (2017). Common Core of Data (CCD), "State Nonfiscal Survey of Public Elementary and Secondary Education," 2000–01 and 2015–16; and National Elementary and Secondary Enrollment Projection Model, 1972 through 2027.

Oyserman, D. (2009). Identity-based motivation: Implications for action-readiness, procedural-readiness, and consumer behavior. *Journal of Consumer Psychology, 19*(3), 250–260.

Phillip, T. M. (2011). Moving beyond our progressive lenses: Recognizing and building on the strengths of teachers of color. *Journal of Teacher Education, 62*(4), 356–366.

Richardson, E. (2009). My illiteracy narrative: Growing up Black, po, and a girl, in the hood. *Gender and Education, 21*(6), 753–767.

Rimm-Kaufman, S. E., & Pianta, R. C. (2000). An ecological perspective on the transition to kindergarten: A theoretical framework to guide empirical research. *Journal of Applied Developmental Psychology, 21*, 491–511.

Rocque, M. (2010). Office discipline and student behavior: Does race matter? *American Journal of Education, 116*(4), 557–581.

Rollock, N. (2007). Black girls don't matter: Exploring how race and gender shape academic success in the inner-city school. *Support for Learning, 22*(4), 197–202.

Sellers, R., Smith, M., Shelton, J., Rowley, S., & Chavous, T. (1998). Multidimensional model of racial identity: A reconceptualization of African American racial identity. *Personality and Social Psychology Review, 2*(1), 18–39.

Skiba, R. (2001). When is disproportionality discrimination? The overrepresentation of black students in school suspension. In W. Ayers, B. Dohrn & R. Ayers (Eds.), *Zero tolerance: Resisting the drive for punishment in our schools* (pp. 176–187). New Press.

Skiba, R. J., Horner, R. H., Chung, C. G., Rausch, M. K., May, S. L., & Tobin, T. (2011). Race is not neutral: A national investigation of African American and Latino disproportionality in school discipline. *School Psychology Review, 40*(1), 85–107.

Skiba, R. J., Arredondo, M. I., & Williams, N. T. (2014). More than a metaphor: The contribution of exclusionary discipline to a school-to-prison pipeline. *Equity & Excellence in Education, 47*(4), 546–564.

Tajfel, H. (2010). Social identity and intergroup relations. Cambridge University Press.

Thomas, A. J., Hoxha, D., & Hacker, J. D. (2013). Contextual influences on gendered racial identity development of African American young women. *The Journal of Black Psychology, 39*(1), 8–101

Townsend, T. G., Thomas, A. J., Neilands, T. B., & Jackson, T. R. (2010). I'm no jezebel; I am young, gifted, and Black: Identity, sexuality, and Black girls. *Psychology of Women Quarterly, 34*(3), 273–285.

Wallace Jr., J. M., Goodkind, S., Wallace, C. M., & Bachman, J. G. (2008). Racial, ethnic, and gender differences in school discipline among US high school students: 1991–2005. *The Negro Educational Review, 59*(1–2), 47.

Abiola Farinde-Wu
University of Massachusetts Boston

DaVonna Graham
University of Pittsburgh

Stephanie Jones-Fosu
University of North Carolina Charlotte

FOOTNOTES

8. A 1995 American drama film about a retired U.S. Marine who accepts a teaching position in an underserved, urban high school in California that serves Black and Brown students.

9. A 1975 American film that follows the narrative of high school seniors and best friends in Chicago, Illinois.

10. Classroom session in which a teacher records attendance and makes announcements.

Chapter Eight

Schools as Sites for Reconceptualizing the Identity of School-Age Mother

Abigail Kindelsperger and Heidi Hallman

"STIGMA STORY"

"High school prom brings a bit of normalcy to young moms," announced the headline of a *Denver Post* article on January 22, 2012, describing the planning and preparations for Florence Crittenton High School's first prom. Crittenton, a high school for pregnant and parenting students established in 1984 was also the setting of TLC's reality show *High School Moms*, which aired in 2012. The newspaper article lauds the school and the hard-working students, depicting the prom as a way to boost the students' enjoyment of school and celebrate their resilience. However, not all readers shared the reporter's sentiment. In a talking-head clip from the second episode of *High School Moms*, the school's principal mentions the *Post* article and its response:

> There has been negative comments made from people out in the community, going, 'Why are their girls getting a Prom? They should just be focusing on their education.' They forget that they're teenagers, and they should have fun things in their lives. (Douglas, 2012)

The argument against holding a prom for school-age mothers at Crittenton High School stems from viewing the students' status as school-age mothers as a "distraction" to their education, requiring them to redirect their "focus" in ways not expected of their non-parenting peers. Furthermore, this pushback from community members highlights the stigmatization that school-age mothers frequently face. As Kelly (2000) asserts, adolescent pregnant bodies are highly publicized sites of critique. Not only do pregnant bodies visibly diverge from what is considered a "normal" path of development, as directly referenced by the *Post* article's title, but there is also the link with teenage sexuality, a subject that consistently garners

E. Mikulec, D. Beichner (eds.), *Distraction: Girls, School, and Sexuality, 121-133.*

fascination and excitement (Kaplan, 1997). From film and television series centering on teenage romance to public outcry and controversy over sexual education, adolescent bodies attract attention.

FRAME FOR CONSIDERING SCHOOL-AGE MOTHERHOOD

Like the young women featured on *High School Moms*, school-age mothers around the country continue to pursue high school diplomas, despite the limiting scripts society places upon them. This chapter illuminates curricular choices at two programs that educate school-age mothers, Westside Alternative Center and Eastview School for Pregnant and Parenting Teens,[11] two schools that challenge the dominant portrait of schooling for this population of students. In these settings, rather than a "distraction" to education, parenthood becomes an experience to draw from in reading, writing, and classroom talk.

While the rate of births to adolescent parents has been steadily decreasing for the past sixty years, media attention—particularly in the form of films and reality television shows—on this population has increased significantly in recent decades. *High School Moms* only lasted one season and received little critical attention, but the more popular MTV shows *16 and Pregnant* and *Teen Mom* (along with all their follow-up series) continue to reach millions of viewers (Guglielmo, 2013). Intended as a form of "edutainment," and created as a partnership between MTV, the Kaiser Family Foundation, and the National Campaign to Prevent Teen and Unplanned Pregnancy, these reality shows craft cautionary tales of how school-age pregnancy disrupts teenage life and future academic or career goals (Guglielmo, 2013). In fact, on the very first episode of *16 and Pregnant*, the young woman featured explains that she switched to an accelerated school to graduate before giving birth; she is the only pregnant student and states that she knows her "belly is a distraction" (Freem, et al., 2009). This stigma of distracting other students is directly referenced on the first episode of *High School Moms* as well, when the School Nurse tells the camera that at Florence Crittenton, school-age mothers "can come here and not be judged and not be looked at negatively" (Douglas, 2012). Two simultaneous discourses of distraction are present in these examples from television—pregnant bodies as a distraction to peers and the stigma of motherhood as a distraction to education. Westside and Eastview, the focal schools of this chapter, attempt to resist and reconfigure this discursive world.

There has been criticism of schools that serve school-age mothers from researchers (Kelly, 2000; Luttrell, 2003; Pillow, 2004) who have studied this population of students, as some claim that curriculum at these schools has tended to reside in a "basic skills" model of curriculum. Westside and Eastview, the schools depicted in this chapter, push back on this characterization as they emphasize drawing from students' lives and experiences, rather than only drawing on a remedial-type of instruction. The term basic skills is used broadly to refer to remedial-type instruction for both students and adults (Carnevale, Gainer, & Meltzer, 1990; Chisman, 1989). A curriculum founded on basic skills typically stresses a deficit view of individuals who are placed "at-risk," aiming to remediate these individuals through skill-driven teaching and learning techniques rather than through meaningful engagement with material or other learners. A "transmission" model of teaching and learning typically characterizes remedial instruction, as a whole, and such a model views knowledge as something to impart on students; often such knowledge remains decontextualized. This chapter views a curriculum that builds on students' strengths and skills as one that is opposed to a transmission model. A curriculum built on students' strengths and skills stresses interaction and knowl-edge-in-action over particular static models of instruction. This chapter discusses curriculum at Westside and Eastview in conversation with macro-level discourses about teen pregnancy. This conversation is one that needs further consideration in the study of curriculum and schooling for this population of students. To con-textualize the research study of classrooms at Westside and Eastview, the chapter next offers an abbreviated overview of the history of schooling of the school-age mothers.

A BRIEF HISTORY OF SCHOOLING FOR SCHOOL-AGE MOTHERS

High School Moms, in its focus on a school designed for pregnant and parenting students, represents one of the schooling options for this population. Kelly (2000) describes the two primary models for school-age mothers as "ghettoizing" versus "mainstreaming" (p. 11–12). Kelly explains that schools either view pregnancy as an incurable disease requiring a separate program (ghettoizing), or as a short-term illness that requires no special treatment (mainstreaming). As separate programs, Florence Crittenton and one focal school of this chapter, Eastview, fall into the ghettoizing category. Burdell (1998) notes that, following Title IX legislation in 1972 that ended discrimination against pregnant students attending school, be-tween 1972 and 1979, more than 1,000 community-based programs for pregnant and parenting students emerged in the United States. The prototype for such pro-grams was the Webster School in Washington, D.C., a program established in re-sponse to the tension between wanting to educate pregnant teens and fear that such students might "corrupt the morals of other students" or "distract" from the learning environment (Luttrell, 2003, p. 16). Separate school programs tend to position students as mothers first and students second, with an emphasis on par-enting classes and vocational training (Zellman, 1981; Pillow, 2004). However, as the staff on *High School Moms* states, such settings may also cater to the specific needs of pregnant and parenting students and allow the students to focus on their education with fewer distractions and barriers.

Focal school Westside, on the other hand, is an example of mainstreaming because, at this school, mothers are educated alongside non-parenting peers. In recent years, increasing numbers of separate programs have been closed due to budget constraints, so a majority of school-age mothers now attend mainstream settings. For example, the highly regarded Catherine Ferguson Academy in Detroit closed in 2014, despite high graduation and college acceptance rates and national advocacy from organizations and individuals, including Rachel Maddow (Wells, 2014). The amount of parenting supports in mainstream schools can vary greatly. At Westside, no formal parenting program is in place, but in some semesters a group of teachers hosted a lunch discussion group for parents. The school social worker often supports students in finding daycare placements, as the school—similar to most mainstream settings—does not offer on-site childcare. Little academic research to date has focused on such setting, with the exception of Kelly's (2000) study of a "pull-out program" in a larger high school, which found that teachers set lower academic expectations for parents and focused on remediation, regardless of students' actual academic level.

In her studies of segregating settings, Burdell (1998) theorizes that four hidden curricula shape the school experiences, which she names "concealment" (p. 211), "domination," (p. 214), "protection" (p. 215), and "redemption" (p. 217). The segregation of pregnant students into specific schools or programs conceal the realities of students' lives and further stigmatizes them. Male domination is furthered by programs or classes that emphasize gendered and limited conceptions of success are often devalued within a larger school system, suffering cuts in funding and lacking the resources of other classes. On the other hand, focusing solely on creating a "therapeutic haven" (Kelly, 2000), a curriculum of protection, is characterized by teachers who desire to protect their students from undue stress or stigma by creating a nurturing environment. This is the primary hidden curriculum shown on *High School Moms*, as the students and teachers discuss the significant level of support the school offers. In episode five, a teacher voices a potential concern with this model, asking, "If you can't make it here with the immense amount of support that this school provides, how are you going to make it out there?" (Douglas, 2012). A student on the show, Carla, even states that she does not want to graduate and leave because of the supportive environment. This praise hints at a potential problem with the therapeutic haven approach, in that students may rely too much on the supports and struggle on their own. The emphasis on success stories and hard work on the show also connect with a curriculum of redemption, encouraging young mothers to "turn their lives around."

Kelly (2000) established a framework for understanding the stigma discourses surrounding school-age motherhood. The most traditional, the "wrong-girl" frame, blames the individual girl for making poor choices that result in parenthood. The "wrong-family" frame locates the "problem" in family structures and parental choices that allow adolescents to become unwed mothers. The "wrong society" frame, which argues that social inequalities shape individual choices, and "stigma-is-wrong" frame, which resist moral judgment, exist as counter-narratives to the "problem" of school-age motherhood. These counter-narratives have been the subject of recent social movements, such as #noteenshame and public outrage over teen pregnancy prevention campaigns that rely on stigma (Ronan, 2015). Linking back to the opening example, when the Prom storyline on *High School Moms* received public criticism, the school's principal and students pushed back on the stigma. In a later episode of the series, a graduating student proclaims, "They think we won't make it because we're teen moms, but I think I wouldn't have made it otherwise," a profound counter-narrative to pervasive stigma discourses.

Such frames reinforce that education, including education at Westside and Eastview, always intersects with larger, macro-level, discourses about school-age

Abigail Kindelsperger and Heidi Hallman

motherhood. This chapter focuses on the back-and-forth between these larger discourses and the more concrete literacy practices at Westside and Eastview, building on previous studies that look specifically at the literacy of school-age mothers.

STUDYING THE LITERACY OF SCHOOL-AGE MOTHERS

Although it is more common to study literacies of school-age parents in the contexts of intervention programs and outcomes for their children, a few key contemporary researchers have previously explored the literate identities of school-age mothers. In summary, existing research has found that school-age mothers employ literacy practices for a variety of purposes. Coffel's (2011) research documents the organization of a book club for three school-age mothers from an alternative high school. In this book club, students focused on reading young adult texts about teen parenthood. After the book club, school-age mothers in Coffel's study reflected on reading more outside of school since becoming mothers; they also noted that the reasons for reading included self-improvement and interest in improving their child's chances of success. The school-age mothers in Coffel's study also described that they used reading and writing for social purposes, and read books and articles with a husband, or wrote letters to a father in jail. The mothers in Coffel's study were described as "conventional" readers. The term "conventional" contrasts with "critical," as conventional readers are those who read uncritically and focus on personal points of connection with characters in the texts.

Lycke's (2010) study, similar to Coffel's, describes two school-age mothers, who noted that their home literacy practices and identities both changed after becoming mothers. In her study, Lycke found a "critical reciprocal relationship between teen mothers' literacy practices and children's emergence into literacy" (p. 80). Mothers in the study described participating in literacy activities with their children, therefore showing that they valued education and their literate lives outside of school. The lives they found themselves now living were often viewed as enhanced as a result of having a child. The school-age mothers' literacy practices, in Lycke's study, correspond with the identity shift to "mother." Considering themselves now adults, school-age mothers were more focused on practical matters and used literacy for self-advocacy.

In this study of literacy practices in schools for school-age mothers, the researchers aimed to bring more robust understanding to what literacy looks like in these spaces. What characterizes students' reading and writing practices at such schools? Do students at the schools experience the same development in terms of their literacy as the school-age mothers in Coffel (2011) and Lycke's (2010) studies? This chapter next moves into both school sites and present an example of reading and writing practices at these sites. These examples function as "telling cases" (Ellen, 1984) that bring life to what is happening in these schools that serve school-age mothers. With the focus on the "micro" of the classroom, this chapter features "counterstories" to the stigma discourses that frame so much of how teen parents are considered as students.

The term "counterstories" is drawn from Yosso's (2006) work. Yosso (2006) describes the purpose of counterstories as the following: to "build community with those at the margins," to "challenge the perceived wisdom of those at society's center," to "nurture community wealth, memory, and resistance," and to "facilitate transformation in education" (pp. 14–15). The examples detailed throughout this chapter feature a counterstory that moves the education of school-age mothers to a space where the school-age mothers themselves negotiate and embrace the identities they wished to assume. In the next section, a portrait of Westside Alternative Center and the counterstories of reading practices at this school showcase how motherhood can enrich reading.

LITERACY PRACTICES AT SCHOOLS FOR SCHOOL-AGE MOTHERS

Westside Alternative Center

Westside is one of 20 campuses of a large umbrella of alternative charter schools in a major Midwestern city. Officially considered "dropout recovery," Westside enrolls students who are 17 to 21 years old with at least eight high school credits (approximately one year of high school). The student population is constantly in flux, with students graduating every semester and new students enrolling every quarter. Some students attend for just one semester and graduate; others enroll with few credits and spend two or more years taking classes. The demographic background of students who attend Westside is approximately 98% African American and 2% Latinx. The percentage of school-age mothers varies per semester, but the school social worker estimated that around 25% of students enrolled during the study were parents. The semester-long data collection at Westside included a collection of artifacts related to students' literacy learning, interviews with the students, and field notes. Abby, the researcher who collected data at Westside was neither an "insider" or "outsider" at the school, as she was a former teacher at Westside. This insider knowledge meant that she knew the school's curriculum and its goals for the students. She was also familiar with the school's surrounding community.

Reading at Westside: Informed by Lived Experience

The first counterstory, that of literacy practices focused on reading, is from one particular language arts class at Westside. Rather than grade or ability levels, all of Westside's English classes are mixed-ability and mixed-credit level electives organized around themes. This class was entitled, "Power and Identity," and focused on core texts *Guardian* by Julius Lester (2008) and *Coldest Winter Ever* by Sister Souljah (1999). In the semester in which the research took place, four of the 20 students enrolled the course were school-age mothers. These four students were the most active contributors to class discussions, particularly about literature.

Ms. Price, the English teacher of "Power and Identity," encouraged her students to respond personally to literature. Ms. Price's goal for the semester was for her students "to walk away with knowing a sense of who they are and have some kind of direction towards where they're going," which she stated would be reached through their experiences with course texts. This invitation to connect their lives to literature aligns with Reader Response, or transactional theory, as articulated by Rosenblatt (1978; 1993). For Rosenblatt and Ms. Price, meaning relies on the transaction between reader and text. Readers bring knowledge and personal experiences to texts and select what to be attuned to, based on their purpose for reading (Rosenblatt 1978; 1993). For the school-age mothers in Ms. Price's class, this approach means that experiences as a mother can function as a starting point for meaning-making.

For example, Gloria Jones, an eighteen-year-old mother of an infant, projected future selves of her son onto characters from *The Coldest Winter Ever*. When reading a passage about a character refusing to talk to authorities, Gloria exclaimed in class discussion, "That's how I want my son to be!" Later, on the final exam, which consisted of short-answer questions about *The Coldest Winter Ever*, Gloria selected the character Midnight to analyze for one of the questions. She wrote, "He [*sic*] the kind of man I hope my son become someday, strong, wise, and about his business." Both of the characters Gloria selected were complex, making choices that readers may ethically criticize, such as involvement in the drug trade. Ms. Price allowed for the consideration of that complexity, choosing not to chastize Gloria's connections, but rather accepting Gloria's specific focus on the characters' strengths. While most may see literary analysis as teacher-directed, Gloria illustrates the analytical position she takes in regard to the characters in the text. In commenting on qualities of particular characters and knowing that she would like to see these same characteristics in her son, she does more than make a text-to-self connection; she relates her reading to her world and the context in which she lives.

Twenty-one-year-old mother of two, Candace Dean, also connected her life to situations in the text. On the same final exam question, she chose Santiaga, the protagonist's father, to analyze. She responded, "Santiaga is a hustler, devoted dad, and serious. Santiaga always made sure his girls were straight money-wise, and he made sure they know how to be strong, smart, and about business. He was a businessman and a hustler, but at the same time he was a family man." When focusing on this father, Candace purposefully draws a contrast with the father of her children, who she frequently stated, "don't want to do nothing for his kids" and did not provide for their family. Candace sees, in the text, that a man could embody multiple identities and perhaps this makes her more attuned to analyzing the circumstances of her own life.

In both of these examples, meaning of a text is being constructed through active transactions between text and lived experience related to motherhood (as a mother, as a co-parent). Gloria and Candace selectively attune to the sons and fathers in the text because of their own relationships with sons and children's fathers. Rather than distracting from their understanding of the novel, motherhood functions as a potential asset or "fund of knowledge" to draw from (Moll & Greenberg, 1990). Both examples of character analysis showcase careful consideration of character behaviors, going beyond the surface of the plot to evaluate the characters, resisting basic skills approaches to teaching reading through recall or plot basics. Through encouraging students to read with their lives, Ms. Price's model reminds us of the value of transactional approaches to literacy education, which unfortunately are often pushed aside in classrooms focused on basic "workplace" readiness skills and de-valued by the high stakes testing era of schooling.

Rather than pushing students' lives and experiences aside, Ms. Price was able to leverage those aspects of students' knowledge to create new understandings. Similarly, Eastview teacher Bob Schaefer drew upon students' lives as mothers in the writing assignments students completed for his class. The chapter now turns to Eastview's language arts class and features students' writing.

Eastview School for Pregnant and Parenting Teens

The second school, Eastview School for Pregnant and Parenting Teens, is a separate school for school-age mothers and is housed within a larger alternative school. School-age mothers may enroll at Eastview when pregnant or when parenting a child less than a year old. Young women who attend Eastview are typically between ages 12 and 19, and the demographic background of students who attend Eastview is approximately 60% Black, 20% White, 10% Latina and 10% other, which include Hmong and Vietnamese students.

The eighteen months of data collection at Eastview included the collection of essays, assignments, and artifacts that school-age mothers produced as related to their literacy learning. Data collection also included field notes that documented field trips that Heidi, the researcher who collected data at Eastview, took with the students and teachers. Heidi, as an "outsider" to the school, spent the first semester at the school getting to know the students and teachers, as well as the aims of the school.

Writing at Eastview: Forward-Looking

The second counterstory, that of literacy practices focused on writing, is from the language arts class at Eastview. In this case, the act of writing became a forum for students to negotiate their present selves as well as imagine future selves. Referring to the act of writing as "rhetoric of the future," this counterstory describes how students responded to and refuted societal discourses of teen motherhood through their writing, often seeking to challenge future perceptions of what the term "teen mother" meant. A characterization of Eastview students' writing as rhetoric of the future has important implications for considering the link between writing and identity for students most "at-risk" of school failure.

The teacher, Bob Schaefer, introduced an assignment called the "Letter Poem." This assignment asked students to write a letter to someone in a poetic form. Figure 1 features the assignment guidelines.

Figure 1: Letter Poem Handout

You will be writing drafts of two letters that will not be for exchang-ing news, making plans, or asking for something. You're writing to say something interesting, and to say it in a non-prose way.

Step One: Come up with the names of interesting people. Now think of some "thing" or "force" that interests you (wind, dolphin, shadow, etc.) and write down four or five of these.

Now, look at the names you've written down. If you could only write to one of those persons or things, which would it be?

Step Two: Draft a letter to that name.

Begin:

Dear _____.

In your letter, tell _____ who you are and what's on your mind. Do you want advice? Do you want to ask questions about the life or sit-uation of _____? Do you want to straighten _____ out on a few matters?

Silly or serious?
Distanced or intimate?
Up to You

This should be the "real you" talking. Get close to "real feeling" if you can.

Sign your real name at the bottom.

Work on your draft. Squeeze the draft. Cut extra words out. Replace long with short.

At a point or two where you have the language you like, say more.

Are the parts of your draft in the best order? Read it to check. Make moves if needed.

Read aloud and listen/ look for places to end lines. Look for rhythm and even rhyme (including partial rhymes).

At first, many students expected there to be specifications concerning the person to whom their letter was addressed. Did it have to be someone famous? Did it have to be a living person? Bob told the students that there were no particular specifica-tions concerning to whom the letter was addressed; it really could be a letter to a person of their choice.

Jessi Martin followed the lead of some of her classmates and wrote a letter to her son, one-month-old Marco (Figure 2).

Figure 2: Letter to Marco

Dear Marco,

You are here and are already a month old! Man, how the time seemed to go slow when I was pregnant with you. So many changes happened so fast in my life. Even though things fell apart with me and my parents, I won't let that happen to us. You, your dad, and I and your dad's family are a family now and you have lots of people who love you.

I'm also staying in school and am going to graduate from [Eastview] this year. I thought about going the easy way and getting my GED but I'm going to stick it out and be a good role model for you. Yes, I may be a teen parent but I'm not going to be a statistic and I'm going to get my diploma.

I'll be honest. I've felt sad a lot of times about how life's shown me a lot of ups and downs. I've felt like sometimes people aren't here for you when you need them most. But that's not who I am for you. I gonna be here for you, Marco.

Love, Your mom

Although all texts respond to other utterances, according to philosopher Bakhtin (1981, 1986), Jessi's letter to her unborn son exhibited a dialogue between her, her child, and the larger society. Jessi's letter engages with the frames of teen motherhood that Kelly (2000) writes about and specifically invokes the stigma-is-wrong frame, a counter-narrative to the frames that typically constitute negative images of teen mothers. Jessi talks back through this discourse, asserting the qualities that led her to what she considers to be a responsible choice. Her statement, "Yes, I may be a teen parent but I'm not going to be a statistic and I'm going to get my diploma" articulates Jessi's counterstory to typical representations of teen mothers and her desire to look ahead to change things as they relate to her child's life presents her awareness of how her actions will influence her future.

In the case of writing assignments presented at Eastview, Bob Schaefer, the teacher, played a large role in facilitating curriculum that built on students' lives and experiences. Bob understood the goal of his students' literacy learning as a goal that extended beyond learning discrete skills; instead, he saw literacy learning as making meaning, despite what contextual constraints might be placed in the lives of students. Bob recognized school-age motherhood as both a constraint and an opportunity, saying, "motherhood won't stop them because now it's part of their lives. It's where they are living their lives. Are there challenges? Yes. But, there's a place here at school where we can help them use that to make their lives better." Bob's statement begins by not denying motherhood in the lives of the students who attend Eastview. Though his statement, "It's where they are living their lives," Bob does not juxtapose school-age mother and student, something to which schools, despite their best intentions, might be susceptible to. Instead, Bob's facilitation of literacy practices within the space of motherhood present students with a holistic look at who they are as both mothers and students at once. Such a view prompts us to re-think the characterization of school-age mothers in schools today.

SCHOOL-AGE MOTHERS "AT-PROMISE" RATHER THAN "AT-RISK"

Throughout the presentation of literacy practices at Westside and Eastview, counterstories stand as important sites from which to think about the possibilities for curriculum and instruction for school-age mothers. In the presentations of reading and writing at these schools, authentic literacy practices that allowed students to read with their bodies and lives were permitted. It should remain a concern of advocates that school-age mothers who experience more remedial approaches to instruction may not fare as well, for remedial models are premised on a deficit-based stance, much like the label of at-risk that has typically been used to characterize school-age mothers as students. Instead of "building on students' strengths and interests," as Bob Schaefer, the English teacher at Eastview noted, schools that stress remediation are "primarily skill-driven…lots of basic reading instruction with comprehension tested through skill and drill and worksheets." Though Bob discussed Eastview as starting in the 1970s with a remedial focus, he documented its change over the years. And, it is at this crux of change—a change from a skills-based/ remedial approach to approaches that recognize curriculum and instruction that values students' experiences and lives so that school-age mothers' literacy is able to change and grow. Rather than distract from their reading, writing, and critical thinking abilities, motherhood can add another layer of richness to students' capabilities. Like their literacy, school-age mothers can be viewed as at-promise, as opposed to at-risk.

Lee and Neal (1992/1993) use the term "at-promise" to describe a middle school student who struggled with reading. In their work with this student, they noted that at-promise became an apt description for him, for he had "strong interpersonal skills, excellent home and school support and a willingness to focus…" (p. 276). Yet, Lee and Neal note that this student would never have been labeled as at-promise through a single measure of his reading achievement; instead, he would have been labeled at-risk. There are many parallels to how students at Westside and Eastview are characterized, for being a school-age mother immediately casts students into an at-risk category. Several researchers (Brindis, 1993; Ladner, 1987; Luker, 1996) have documented results that appear contradictory to the early pregnancy/ lack of success model so frequently assumed by the American public, and this can be viewed through the presentation of curriculum and instruction that meets the needs of school-age mothers and pushes them toward expanding in their learning and future possibilities.

Re-thinking curricular choices for school-age mothers is done, in part, by acknowledging that curriculum has never been a neutral series of lessons that fit into classrooms, but rather a process that involves the enactments of teaching and learning, highlighting the possibilities for how subject matter is taken up in classrooms. Stressing the literacy learning of school-age mothers points to the possibilities for change and movement within a model of curriculum for secondary students. Instead of a model that enforces the role of curriculum as a static, uni-dimensional force in classrooms for youth labeled at-risk of school failure and seen as a distraction, curriculum can be a site for growth and change for those at-promise for school success.

Note: Excerpts from this chapter have been previously published in Hallman, H. L. and Kindelsperger, A. (2019). *Reconceptualizing curriculum, literacy, and learning for school-age mothers*. Routledge. Reprinted with permission.

REFERENCES

Bakhtin, M. (1981). *The dialogic imagination*. University of Texas Press.

Bakhtin, M. (1986). *Speech genres & other late essays*. (V. W. McGee, Trans.; C. Emerson & M. Holquist, Eds.). University of Texas Press.

Brindis, C. (1993). Antecedents and consequences: The need for diverse strategies in adolescent pregnancy prevention. In A. Lawson & D. Rhodes (Eds.), *The politics of pregnancy: Adolescent sexuality and public policy* (pp. 257–283). Yale University Press.

Burdell, P. (1998). Young mothers as high school students: Moving toward a new century. *Education and Urban Society, 30*(2), 207–223.

Carnevale, A., Gainer, L., & Meltzer, A.S. (1990). *Workplace basics: The essential skills employers want*. Jossey-Bass.

Chisman, F. (1989). Jump start, the federal role in adult literacy, final report on the project of adult literacy. Southport, CT: Southport Institute for Policy Analysis.

Coffel, C. M. (2011). *Thinking themselves free: Research on the literacy of teen mothers*. Peter Lang.

Douglas, W. (Producer). (2012). *High School Moms*. Denver, CO: Rize USA.

Ellen, R. F. (1984). *Ethnographic research: A guide to general conduct*. London: Academic.

Freem, M. J., Savage, D. S., Dolgen, L., Zalkind, J., Portnoy, A., Cohen, S., & Dutton, J. (Producers). (2009). *16 and Pregnant* [Television series]. Hollywood, CA: MTV.

Guglielmo, L. (2013). Introduction: Teen moms and babydaddies: Interrupting the conversation on teen pregnancy. In L. Guglielmo (Ed.) *MTV and teenage pregnancy: Critical essays on* 16 and Pregnant *and Teen Mom* (pp. vii–xii). Rowman and Littlefield.

Kaplan, E. B. (1997). *Not our kind of girl: Unravelling the myths of black teenage motherhood*. University of California Press.

Kelly, D. M. (2000). *Pregnant with meaning: Teen mothers and the politics of inclusive schooling*. Peter Lang.

Ladner, J. (1987). Black teenage pregnancy: A challenge for educators. *Journal of Negro Education, 56*, 53–63.

Lee, N. G. & Neal, J. C. (1992/1993). Reading rescue: Intervention for a student "at promise." *Journal of Reading, 36*, 276–282.

Lester, J. (2008). *Guardian*. HarperCollins.

Luker, K. (1996). *Dubious conceptions: The politics of teenage pregnancy*. Harvard University Press.

Luttrell, W. (2003). *Pregnant bodies fertile minds: Gender, race, and the schooling of pregnant teens*. Routledge.

Lycke, K. L. (2010). Reading and writing teenage motherhood: Changing literacy practices and developing identities. In L. MacGillvray (Ed). *Literacy in times of crisis: Practices and Perspectives*. Routledge.

Moll, L. C. & Greenberg, J. (1990). Creating zones of possibilities: Combining social contexts for instruction. In L. C. Moll (Ed.), *Vygotsky and education* (pp. 319–348). Cambridge University Press.

Murphy, C. (2012, January 22). Murphy: High school prom brings bit of normalcy to young moms. Retrieved from https://www.denverpost.com/2012/01/22/murphy-high-school-prom-brings-bit-of-normalcy-to-young-moms-2/.

Pillow, W. S. (2004). *Unfit subjects: Education policy and the teen mother*. Routledge Falmer.

Ronan, A. (2015). Teen moms need support, not shame. The Cut. Retrieved from http://thecut.com.

Rosenblatt, L. M. (1978). *The reader, the text, the poem: The transactional theory of the literary work*. Southern Illinois University Press.

Rosenblatt, L. M. (1993). The transactional theory: Against dualisms. *College English, 55*(4), 377–386.

Souljah, S. (1999). *Coldest winter ever*. Washington Square Books.

Wells, K. (2014, June 5). Detroit high school for pregnant teens is closing—this time or real. Michigan Radio. Retrieved from http://michiganradio.org/post/detroit-high-school-pregnant-teens-closing-time-real#stream/0.

Yosso, T. (2006). *Critical race counterstories along the Chicana/Chicano educational pipeline*. Routledge.

Zellman, G. (1981). A title IX perspective on the schools' response to teenage pregnancy and parenthood. Santa Monica, CA: Rand.

Abigail Kindelsperger
University of Illinois-Chicago

Heidi L. Hallman
University of Kansas

FOOTNOTE

11. Names of people and places used in this chapter are pseudonyms.

Chapter Nine

Hard to Conquer, Easy to Love: One Teen's Writings on
Identity, Sexuality, and Agency in the Juvenile Justice System

Judith Dunkerly-Bean, Julia Morris, and Tom Bean

This chapter centers on the experiences of an adolescent girl named Tia (all names
and locations are pseudonyms) who is involved in the juvenile justice system in
the Southeastern region of the United States. Drawn from a larger critical ethnography exploring the literacy practices of justice system involved youth, this
chapter focuses on the ways in which Tia utilized multimodal narratives such as
songs/raps, drawings and poetry to examine and share her experiences as well as
those of other incarcerated youth. Using a bricolage approach (Steinberg, 2012;
Kincheloe & Berry, 2004) that acknowledges that all understandings are created in
a contextualized space, this study seeks to disrupt the narrative that pathologizes
the experiences of youth in the school-to prison-pipeline (Annamma, 2018).

Before going further, however, and in keeping with the hermeneutic notion that the nature of meaning is tentative, situated, and contextual (Steinberg,
2018), it is vital to address our own positionality. All research team members are
White and from middle class backgrounds. Two members are literacy faculty in a
department of teaching and learning whose research has focused on youth experiences at the intersection of social justice and literacy practices, who have both had
family members—or close friends—involved in the criminal justice system. The
third member of the research team is a White female doctoral student who quickly
became a favorite at the site because the residents (co-researchers) felt comfortable
confiding in her.

In the context of the larger study, co-researchers, including Tia, were invited to engage in "alternative" literacy practices such as song-writing and trans-me-
diation of text to image, as well as drawing and collage. Data for this subset of
the study includes Tia's drawings, sketchbooks, spoken word poetry, hip-hop and
R&B songs that that she recorded using Garage Band and other royalty-free music

E. Mikulec, D. Beichner (eds.), *Distraction: Girls, School, and Sexuality*, 135-147.

loops. Data collection also includes semi-structured interviews and conversations with Tia as well as researcher field notes, and photographs or copies of her works.

In sharing Tia's work, and thus her story, the researchers are mindful of the risks of hegemony in speaking for her and will "step back" so that her words can be heard as they were originally heard. Thus, the term "co-researcher" (Steinberg, 2018) is mindfully utilized rather than "participant" in order to acknowledge the centrality of the youth involved in this study and to honor their voices. The caveat to utilizing a co-researcher model, however, is that the length of time spent with the teens involved in the juvenile justice system, including Tia, could be unpredictable given court dates, sentencing, etc.; thus, frequent and on-going discussions were cultivated about the intended meanings and themes of the co-researchers' creations, in lieu of traditional member checks at the point of analysis. Additionally, the teens drove the focus and determined what would be addressed or discussed each week.

This position is also reflected in Brown's (2008) examination of Black girlhood, where she argues, "Adults working with girls in creative capacities who do feel compelled to share girls work have not just a responsibility but an obligation to declare how they themselves were changed in the process" (cited in Winn, 2011, p. 70). In addition, Maisha Winn's (2011) work is also pivotal to this project, in particular her work with incarcerated girls and her use of Peterson's (1995) notion of liminality among marginalized Black women to also ask whether, "it is possible to imagine a scenario whereby the incarcerated could escape, or even return, the gaze of their wardens; undo the dominant culture's definitions of such binary oppositions as order/disorder, normal/abnormal, harmless/dangerous" (Peterson, 1995, p. 8).

In attempting to understand the complexities present in Tia's writings, specific emphasis is placed on the nuanced intersectionality (Cho, Crenshaw, & McCall, 2013) that contributed to their production. For Tia, writing poems, stories, and songs was a means of chronicling the ways in which adolescent girls shared, shielded, and embodied their identities, including sexual identities. Her topics ranged from thoughts on love and relationships to the value of women both within and out of the justice system. While some of her writing was autobiographical, other efforts focused on what she termed "doing research on other kid's lives." During her stays in more restrictive detention centers, she would observe and interview other girls, and then turn their stories into songs or poems. In these writings, Tia shares the stories of other girls and the way their identities, including their sexual identities, replicate or resist examples they have from parents, other family members, and society writ large.

Findings indicate that as Tia employed ethnographic and auto-ethnographic methods instinctively in her writing, she created a "troubled space" where girls' sexual identities are mediated by the system, yet are also places of resilience and resistance to single story narratives, racist stereotypes, and dominant societal positioning. However, in creating a troubled space, Tia and her peers in the juvenile justice system are doing so in a societal construct with a long history of demonizing the sexualities, the relationships, and the bodies of the Girls—especially those of color—in its care (Pasko, 2010; Willingham, 2011). Thus, a brief historical overview is presented of the treatment of girls in the United States juvenile justice system, and how that has influenced, genderized, and pathologized views of girls' sexuality in dominant society. Then, recent scholarship is presented on the adultification (Epstein, Blake, & Gonzalez, 2017) of Black girls to contextualize Tia's experiences and her writings. Although the term adultification has been used in the past to describe children who individually find themselves taking on adult responsibilities by virtue of family or economic circumstance, our use of it here is consistent with recent research that applies it collectively to the phenomenon of the misperception of Black children as more mature, chronologically older, and experienced than their White counterparts. Tia's writings provide a counter-narrative and resist three stereotypical caricatures assigned to Black women by systemic racism as described by Epstein and colleagues (2017) namely, "Jezebel," "Sapphire," and "Mammy." Throughout the chapter, Tia's writings are highlighted and how these writings speak to the issues faced by girls moving through gendered, stereotyped, and repressive spaces.

Take a Walk in My Shoes: Girls in the Juvenile Justice System

> Don't ever ask me why I do what I do. Cause you can never taken one step in my shoes. You don't know what I seen, ain't nothing like it seems. It wasn't a choice—it was the life I was given.
>
> —Excerpt from "Walk in My Shoes"

Historically, the juvenile justice system has sought to restrain and rebuke the sexuality of girls in general, and girls of color in particular. Research into the convictions and sentencing of female offenders often centered on "lewd acts," which could range from something as simple as presumed promiscuity to public displays of affection or actual sexual activity. In general, many young women were arrested for moral, rather than criminal, offenses that resulted in incarceration (Pasko, 2010):

> ...although the first juvenile court originally defined "delinquent" as those under sixteen who had violated a city ordinance or law, when the definition was applied to girls, the court included incorrigibility, associations with immoral persons, vagrancy, frequent attendance at pool halls or saloons, other debauched conduct, and use of profane language in its definition. Perhaps foreshadowing the stereotypes projected on Black girls today, young women subjected to the U.S. juvenile court system of the mid 1800- early 1900s, were seen either as feeble-minded or blatantly promiscuous. It is not surprising then, that men who may have coerced young women into these supposedly lewd or immoral acts, were rarely, if ever punished. This was especially true, if the "crime" involved immigrants or young women of color. (Pasko, 2010, p. 1110)

In an analysis of sentencing of young women in Chicago between 1904 and 1927, Knupfer (2001) found that nearly 70 percent of girls incarcerated, institutionalized, or placed on probation were charged with incorrigibility, sexual delinquency, or other "wayward" behavior. It is important to note, that even in cases of sexual assault, the courts would frequently construct the incident as almost entirely due to lascivious behavior of the girls in question. One noted psychiatrist of the day blamed the influences of "immigrant and disordered families, in need of visiting by Christian women, receiving food or money and coming to the rescue in times of crisis" (Thomas, 1923, p. 151).

Without the saving grace of such intervention, other juvenile justice authorities, such as New York State Girls' Reformatory Superintendent Katherine Davis, believed that the lack of economic security in girls' lives produced "defective" girls who became unwed mothers, used "drink or drugs," and found "bad company." However, all was not forever lost. Superintendent Davis assured the State that the girls' immoral and promiscuous status was not fixed, but rather could be remedied by marriage to a good man with sufficient money who also attended church regularly (Pasko, 2010, p. 1103).

While it may be tempting to dismiss these attitudes and sentencing patterns as Victorian hysteria, they persisted well into the 20th century, and influenced social/criminal justice policies still felt to this day. For example, in Los Angeles over the course of three decades (1920–1950), the majority of girls referred to the court system were there on status or immorality charges. Researchers noted that while truancy or incorrigibility might be the recorded charge, sexual promiscuity factored heavily into incarceration length and severity in a way that was not present for young men. Indeed, until the Juvenile Justice and Delinquency Act passed in 1974, the majorities of incarcerated or institutionalized young women (especially those of color or immigrants) were held for behavioral, rather than criminal offenses (Pasko, 2010).

Despite the changes in criminal law that prohibited the arrest of girls on charges of familial disobedience, promiscuity, or "waywardness," the incarceration of women continues to climb and some of the reasons are eerily similar to those of the past. Over the course of the last three decades, the rate of women being incarcerated has increased by over 800 percent (Ahmad & Iverson, 2013). Moreover, the majority (92%) of these women have suffered sexual abuse or assault, while many have also spent their adolescent years in and out of the juvenile justice system. Some researchers believe that, much like their predecessors, a large number of those early arrests stem from over-aggressive policing and charges of non-serious offences rooted in responses to earlier trauma (Saar, Epstein, Rosenthal, & Vafa, 2015). Indeed, in a direct throwback to the wayward, promiscuous girl of the early 19th Century, the leading cause of arrest for female adolescents are minor offenses such as misdemeanors, status offenses, outstanding warrants, and technical violations. The decision to arrest and detain girls in these cases is often based on the perceptions of how the girls are perceived as nonconforming to stereotypes of feminine behavior and societal norms.

Thus, current rates of incarceration still disproportionately target women and girls of color. African American women are three times as likely than their White peers to be incarcerated, and Latinx women are 69 percent more likely to be incarcerated in their lifetimes. The challenges facing incarcerated women, both during and after their sentences are myriad. A recent report from the Center for American Progress (2013) indicates that women have gender-specific needs that differ from incarcerated men, because they are "frequently the primary caregivers of their children before incarceration, and are disproportionately victimized by emotional, physical, and sexual abuse from their past" (p. 12).

Once they are released from prison, life circumstances can become even more difficult as they are denied access to governmental assistance programs such as housing, employment, education, and subsistence benefits. This can cause extraordinary hardship to recently-released women of color, especially those with young children. Statistics indicate that in state prisons alone, 62 percent of women have children under the age of 18, and 1 in 25 women were pregnant when they entered prison. Additionally, some convictions prevent future employment in care-giving fields where women of color are historically over-represented but underpaid.

While there are many individual, societal, and systemic reasons that young women may find themselves caught in the criminal justice system, one of the more recent and insightful perspectives is the adultification of Black children and adolescents. More importantly for this discussion is the highly sexualized characterization of young Black women. The twenty-first century finds that Black women in particular are regarded as aesthetic beings as they are so regularly disregarded for their intellect (Matthews, 2018), and the most drastic consequence of this belittling is the loss of a childhood for Black female children.

Childhood Erased – The Adultification of Black Girls

"I'm contemplatin' to myself asking God for some help—I got thoughts running through my head, because damn my brother's dead. Streets put his ass to sleep but he ain't even make his bed, so it's the same tear cycle over and over again…"

—Excerpt from "Over and Over Again"

In her song "Over and Over Again," Tia writes about the death of her brother, her time in the juvenile justice system, and the way she sees a cycle that perpetuates itself "over and over again." In many ways, she exemplifies the notion and theory of the erasure of Black childhood through adultification. Dating back to slavery, the idea that Black children were not entitled to typical childhood pursuits and harshly punished for them has remained brutal legacy still present in their treatment today.

In a 2014 study, Phillip Goff found that beginning at the age of 10, Black boys are misperceived by White adults, teachers, and police as being older, more prone to criminal activity, and more likely to be the target of police violence if suspected of a crime. Moreover, even experienced police officers tend to over-estimate the age of Black youth by as much as 4.5 years, while underestimating the age of White suspects by almost as wide a margin (Goff, 2014). Black girls are just as likely to be misperceived as far older chronologically and socially, while at the same time they are viewed as less capable academically (Morris, 2007). Black girls who assert themselves and their identities are frequently conflated with stereotypes of aggressive and dominating Black women (Morris, 2016).

To illustrate the pervasiveness of theories of adultification, Rebecca Epstein, Jamila Blake, and Thalia Gonzàlez (2017) surveyed 325 adults from various racial backgrounds (although 74% of respondents were White). The majority of respondents perceived Black girls (ages 5–14) as being less in need of nurturing, protection, comforting, and support. The same respondents also reported that Black girls were more independent, knew more about adult matters, and knew more about sex than their White counterparts. Although causal relationships between the adultification of Black girls and their treatment in schools and the juvenile justice system require more research, data demonstrate that although Black girls make up eight percent of the K–12 school population, they represent 13 percent of suspensions, and 37.9 percent of all arrests.

In addition to the criminalization of the Black girl, recent scholarship has illustrated the ways in which the overt sexualization of the Black female body, the subject of historical cultural fantasy, is also assigned to Black girls in a manner that negates their innocence (Dagbovie-Mullins, 2013). These paradigms of Black femininity are rooted in stereotypes dating to the Civil War, yet their legacy is felt today: "Sapphire," the loud, angry, brash, and emasculating woman; "Jezebel," the promiscuous seductress who victimizes men; and lastly, "Mammy," the self-sacrificing, doting, and asexual caregiver (Blake, Butler, & Smith, 2015). While the terminology may have changed in the twenty first century, Black women still carry the discriminatory labels of "angry Black woman" (Sapphire), or "fast-and-loose" (Jezebel), and finally "Black momma," such as Tyler Perry's popular character Madea (Mammy). These stereotypes, so permeated into the cloth of our collective consciousness, have far-reaching and potentially devastating effects. What is needed then, is a way to decenter and resist these images and assigned identities. What is needed is a counter-narrative. What is offered in this chapter and from this research is the opportunity for the reader to meet and learn from one young woman who disrupts all three paradigms of Black young womanhood and challenges us to question our own misperceptions of what it means to be a young Black woman in the juvenile justice system.

Tia

Image 1. Tia Self-Portrait: Good Girl Wasted

　Judith Dunkerly-Bean, Julia Morris, and Tom Bean

Over the course of the time the research team has been at Shoreline Youth Center, a residential co-ed facility, Tia was a resident, and thus part of this project, during two separate stays. Although it is not possible to ask any of the teens held there questions about their past, the researchers were permitted to listen to them talk about their alleged charges and backgrounds should they initiate the discussion or have it as a foci of their writings, drawings, etc. It was in this way that the research team learned some of Tia's story. Although Tia shared that her family was "from the hood," she said people "believed the stereotypes" but "didn't see the lives."

While she had hinted that she lost a brother when the research team first met her, it was not until she was sure that neither she, nor her brother, nor the circumstances would be judged that she finally shared what happened. Essentially, he was shot in the chest by a rival gang member but survived after weeks in the hospital. However, once he was released, he was set up by an ex-girlfriend and ambushed by another rival gang member, who shot him in the head. Tia was at the scene when he died. Understandably, she began to "act out" (in her words) and started doing drugs, engaging in self-injurious behavior (cutting), breaking into cars, and committing petty theft. During her stays in more restrictive detention centers, she would observe and interview other girls, and then turn their stories into songs or poems. Over the time the researcher team worked together with Tia, she added to her portfolio with a varied range of poetry and songs, and later recorded several using the app Garage Band. Tia dreamed of being a cardiologist but was not sure how she would go to college. More than anything else, though, she wants her life to mean something for her brother who had been murdered.

In the final song she wrote during our time together, she wrote about "not letting her thoughts cage her." During one of our last sessions together, Tia wrote that she "won't let thoughts cage her." Through her observations, poems, and songs she offers a counter-narrative to the stereotypical paradigms of Black femininity. Paradoxically, while creating beautiful, defiant, and heart-rending work that belies her age, she also holds up a mirror to a system that erased the innocence of her childhood. In the next sections, to the extent possible in this context, Tia's voice is put forth so it might be more readily heard. By presenting her works in their entirety, it is the hope of this chapter to engage in a resistance to the single story so often ascribed to Tia and her peers.

No Love Lost, No Wars Won: Tia's Work as Resistance

No matter the topic, Tia almost always tagged her writing with the line of "no love lost, no war won," which was sometimes accompanied by a sketch of a heart dripping blood. When asked about this, she said that it symbolized a perfect world—love is never lost, and if that is true, no wars are won, because none need to be fought. The bleeding heart represented her love for her brother and stories she held in her heart for and about him. Through her writing, Tia enacts an activism and resistance to what she sees as injustice in the world. In her research into the narratives of Black women in prison, Breea Willingham (2011) writes, narratives represent a unique form of activism and a continued struggle for freedom. Their stories fracture the stereotypical image of all women behind bars and reveal the mothers, sisters, wives, daughters and friends who are often forgotten once the iron bars close. (p. 57)

In positioning herself as a "researcher into other kids' lives," Tia engages in this type of activism and provides a voice for both herself and others like her. As Willingham continues, "While writing in prison may not be behavior that is always seen as explicitly political, it can become important to the resistance to structures of privilege, exploitation, and power" (p. 57). Thus, in resisting the three caricature paradigms of Black womanhood, even without that being her stated intent, Tia's writing becomes a powerful act of activism in a society and prison system rife with racism and sexism, where Black voices are intentionally silenced rather than encouraged to be heard.

The first of Tia's work shared here is a rap she created based on the experiences of another inmate in a more restrictive juvenile detention setting. This piece exemplifies Tia's self-positioning as a "researcher in other kid's lives." In "Runaway Love Remix," she tells the story of "Kay" who, as the 12 year-old daughter of a sex worker, runs away and tries to find love on her own by becoming pregnant. However, life on the street is brutal, so she turns to taking and selling drugs, but ultimately loses her baby. In presenting her work here, there is no attempt to alter her syntax in order to preserve her writing and voice. It is vital to provide some space where Tia is seen as a writer, an artist, and an activist in her authentic voice.

Runaway Love Remix

Her name is Lil' Kay and she was 12 years old

and steady tryna figure out exactly what she owed.

Her dad was never there and her momma was just a hoe

sleeping with whoever so Kay was all alone.

She gave up her virginity for a piece of love.

But really in the end, she was just a dub.

He ain't really love her, but his lies already sold.

Lil' did he know he took a toll on her soul.

Mom in and out, and Dad's never there,

First love lied so the world was never fair.

She's locked in her room all on her own,

Praying to her god that this is not her home.

Couple years later, she doesn't want love—

She just wants attention, she wanna feel above.

Above all the shit she's been through,

forgetting about the guys as she do what she do.

She never felt at home and she never felt love,

So there's no way she will stop doing drugs.

They make her feel safe and put her way above

Apples never fall far from the tree.

Momma sold her body and passed it down to Kay.

Give up green bands and you can have what's in mind

Depending on the money, determines your time.

It was never really for fun, she was doing it for her unborn.

She was going to name him Nas, but she didn't do it right

And he beat her real bad and now the baby's gone,

And she's gotta tell the dad.

Now she's locked up in her room, on her own,

Praying to her god not to take her baby home.

In the first verse of "Runaway Love," Tia sets up the story of "Kay" as a forgotten and perhaps unwanted child, who "trades her virginity for a piece of love." Yet in doing so, much like the "wayward girl" of the early 20th Century, she is trapped figuratively and literally as punishment, while the male in question disappears. In the next verse, Tia documents how drugs change Kay's life—she has become a different person from the girl wanting to be loved in the first verse. Drug use is portrayed as an escape, but also, ironically, as a way for Kay to have some control in her life. Tia explained that Kay did this as a means to mentally and emotionally escape from the literal confines of incarceration.

In her final verse, Kay's story comes full circle. She herself is now pregnant, but unlike her mother, she wants this baby. However, in the end she loses the baby and the love she so desperately wanted. Tia keeps the ending ambiguous, and never revealed whether the baby was lost to violence or to the State.

When asked what actually happened to the baby, she sighed and said she wrote it that way because "so many kids—either they die or get killed or they never get a second chance, so it doesn't really matter with this one, does it?" It is also evident that Tia changes the end of the verses from "praying to her god that this isn't her home" or hoping for a different outcome for herself in a literal and figurative sense, to "praying to god not to take her baby home." In other words, to spare the baby from both repeating her history or losing its life completely. Tia augmented this handwritten rap with a drawing of a sleeping, swaddled infant in a peace symbol in the middle of the words "Life Sucks." While Tia wrote this story partly as a cautionary tale, she also writes it as a complex counter-narrative to the single stories often ascribed to girls in the juvenile justice system. Additionally, she troubles the notion of the "Jezebel" paradigm by giving insight into the systemic injustices that keep young women like Kay trapped in a cycle of abuse and silencing.

Another prevalent theme in Tia's writing was the notion of a woman's body being her own. While Kay in "Runaway Love Remix" traded sex for an attempt at love, in writing about herself, Tia portrays physical love as the culmination of romantic love and commitment. She sees the act of sex as a gift to be given, not something to be taken, as was the case with Kay. In "Song of the Blue Bird," Tia asserts that her pride and her body are her own. Decentering the narrative of the stereotypically brash "Sapphire" who emasculates and is aggressive, or the brazen "Jezebel" who uses sex to gain power, Tia celebrates an assertive and joyful identity that she chooses to share with the man she marries—one who is worthy of her blue bird's song:

Song of the Blue Bird

The girl had a heart as good as a blue bird.

She'd never let you down and always stood by her word.

Her pride was something she could always obtain,

All her dreams awaited for no hurt must fade.

She'd never hurt a fly and wouldn't dare take God's name in vain.

She stayed away from trouble and out of harm's way,

And let God tell it, she'd pray everyday.

She'll never tell a lie and her body is her own,

for no one is worthy of her BLUE BIRD'S SONG!

She'll hold it 'til she's married, cherish it for life,

But whatever happens, she'll save it for that night.

The night of her wedding won't be gloom,

because she will know in her heart, she has that gift for her groom.

That special night all worthiness is brung,

when the love of her life hears her Blue Bird's Song!

By resisting the script written by an oppressive system, Tia literally writes her body as resistance. It is hers and hers alone. It has worth that cannot be degraded or taken without permission. She is "doing dangerous things with words" (Stanford, 2011) simply by not conforming to how society would like to frame her. This sense of her own worth and that of all women is exemplified in the final piece of her writing shared here. "A Woman's Worth" challenges all assumptions about women in the prison system, as well as the roles projected onto them. It is interesting to note that Tia wrote this last piece in one draft, as it is shown here. She penned it in the last few minutes of a session and handed it to the research team during egress from the Center. The nonchalant nature of that action belies the complexity of this piece. In it she provides a counter-narrative to any preconceived notion or misperceived identity. This piece is presented it here as it was given to the research team, so that the reader may experience firsthand the power of Tia's writing and the precision with which she is able to convey her beliefs.

Figure 2. A Woman's Worth

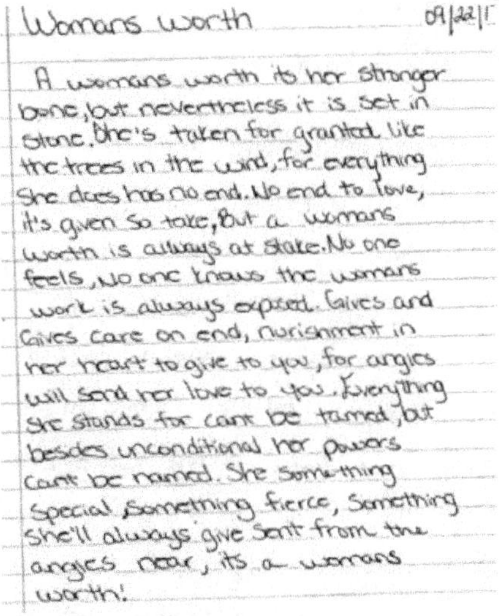

Womans worth   09/22/1

A womans worth is her stronger
bone, but nevertheless it is set in
stone. She's taken for granted. Like
the trees in the wind, for everything
She does has no end. We end to love,
it's given so take, but a womans
worth is always at stake. No one
feels, No one knows the womans
work is always expect. Gives and
Gives care on end, nurishment in
her heart to give to you, for angles
will send her love to you. Everything
She stands for cant be tamed. but
besides unconditional her powers
cant be named. She something
special. something fierce, something
she'll always give. Sent from the
angles near, its a womans
worth!

In this piece, Tia portrays herself, and indeed all women, as innately powerful. They love and are loved, they nurture but are fierce, and their power is unconditional. These are indeed "dangerous words" in a system designed to render girls as nameless and silently obedient or face the consequences. In her book *A Culture of Refusal*, Brett Elizabeth Blake (2004) speaks of a double jeopardy encountered by adolescent girls in the justice system: "Female adolescents in jail are doubly silenced, and thereby doubly punished, as they are not only held captive behind bars, but are also mentally held captive because of their gender. Their voices simply don't exist" (p. 109).

This erasure of voice, of childhood, through the adultification of Black children, and the ever-present school-to-prison pipeline that creates statistics rather than opportunities should be of concern to all. Yet, too often girls like Tia are seen as damaged, as not worthy of our consideration. Yet, as Willingham (2011) writes, the poems, stories, and narratives of Black women and, in this case, adolescents like Tia, are "deserving of more attention because these texts add a significant voice to this voiceless…they address broader social problems with race, gender, and sexual oppressions" (p. 64).

Tia herself echoes this plea in her song "Over and Over Again," where she admits her own culpability, but also addresses the broader social issues that contributed to her brother's death, as well as her own battle to escape a juvenile justice system that views her as a statistic. While the researchers do not currently know where Tia is or what her ultimate outcome will be (in this state, there is no follow-up once time and any probation are served), the hope is that she continues to advocate and resist the stereotypes and cycles that hold so many of her peers so tightly in its grasp. As educators and as activists there is a responsibility to engage with children like Tia, to resist the urge to misperceive them, and to create a space for voices unlike our own. So, to end this chapter, as took place in so many sessions, it seems most appropriate to give Tia the last word. The researchers echo her hope for a new tomorrow for all.

The Girl with the Curly Black Hair

Eyes go around when she's there—

the girl with the curly black hair

makes it hard not to stare.

Her body is like unburied treasure

with a questionable amount of pleasure.

It's hard to conquer yet easy to love,

she makes you wonder if she was sent from above.

Her presence gives you chills all right, as she slips off her red bottom heels.

She lays in her bed and from the look given, she's dead.

Not dead in her soul but dead to the world.

All the pain fades away for when sun rises she's a new girl.

All problems are gone with sorrow

because with every yesterday there's a new tomorrow.

REFERENCES

Ahmad, F. & Iverson, S. (2013). The state of women of color in the United States. Washington, DC: Center for American Progress.

Annamma, S. A. (2018). *The pedagogy of pathologization: Dis/abled girls of color in the school-prison nexus.* Routledge.

Blake, B. E. (2004). *A culture of refusal.* Peter Lang.

Blake, J. J., Butler, B. R., & Smith, D. (2015). Challenging middle-class notions of femininity: The cause of black females' disproportionate suspension rates. In D. J. Losen (Ed.), *Closing the school discipline gap: Equitable remedies for excessive exclusion.* Teachers College Press.

Cho, S., Crenshaw, K., & McCall, L. (2013). Toward a field of intersectionality studies: Theory, applications, and praxis. *Signs, 38*(4), 785–810. doi:10.1086/669608.

Dagbovie-Mullins, S. A. (2013). Pigtails, ponytails, and getting tail: The infantilization and hypersexualization of African-American females in popular culture. *Journal of Pop Culture. 46,* 745–771. doi:10.1111/jpcu.12047

Epstein, R., Blake, J. J., & Gonzalez, T. (2017). Girlhood interrupted: The erasure of Black girls' childhood. Washington, DC: Georgetown Law, Center on Poverty and Inequality.

Goff, P. A. (2014). The essence of innocence: Consequences of dehumanizing black children. *Journal of Personality & Social Psychology, 106*(4), 526–545.

Knupfer, A.M. (2001). *Reform and resistance: Gender, delinquency and America's first juvenile court.* Routledge.

Kincheloe, J., & Berry, K. (2004). *Rigour and complexity in educational research: Conceptualizing the bricolage.* Open University Press.

Matthews, A. D. (2018). Hyper-sexualization of Black women in the media. *Gender & Sexuality Studies Student Work Collection, 22.*

Morris, E. W. (2007). "Ladies" or "loudies"? Perceptions & experiences of black girls in classrooms. *Youth & Society, 38*(4), 490–515.

Morris, M. (2016). *Pushout: The criminalization of Black girls in schools.* The New Press.

Pasko, L. (2010). Damaged daughters: the history of girls' sexuality and the juvenile justice system. *Journal of Criminal Law & Criminology,100*(3),1099–1130.

Saar, M. K., Epstein, R., Rosenthal, L., & Vafa, Y. (2015). The sexual abuse to prison pipeline: The girls' story. Washington DC: Georgetown Law, Center on Poverty and Inequality.

Steinberg, S. (2018). Personal correspondence. April 2018. Norfolk, VA.

Steinberg, S. (2012). Critical pedagogy and cultural studies research: Bricolage in action. *Counterpoints, 422,* 230–254. Retrieved from http://www.jstor.org/stable/42981761

Thomas, W. I. (1923). *The unadjusted girl: With cases and standpoints for behavior analysis.* Little, Brown and Company. Retrieved from: https://archive.org/details/unadjustedgirlwi00thom/page/n13

Willingham, B. (2011). Black women's prison narratives and the intersection of race, gender and sexuality in US prisons. *Critical Survey, 23*(3), 55–66

Winn, M. (2011). *Girl time: Literacy, justice and the school-to-prison pipeline.* Teachers College Press.

Judith Dunkerly-Bean
Old Dominion University

Julia Morris
Old Dominion University

Tom Bean
Old Dominion University

Chapter Ten

Black Girls Have Their Say: Centering School-Based Sexual Violence as a Social Justice Issue in High School

Serena M. Wilcox

Schools that are in or near poor, chaotic communities experience more violence and disruption than schools in rural, suburban, or more affluent and organized communities (Jones, 2010; Leadbeater, 2008). The link between poverty, neighborhood duress, and sexual violence informs how harmful school climates are conceptualized and often overlooks gender challenges (Miller, 2008). Nan Stein (2005) suggests that school safety policies and reform interventions tend to focus on issues like fighting, weapons in schools, drug use and possession, and zero tolerance disciplinary actions. Meanwhile, gender violence is omitted from the discourse on school safety. Some scholars have noted how the organizational and ideological contexts of schools shape the way sexual violence is treated and reveal the harmful effects it has on the academic performance of students who survive school-based sexual violence (Miller, 2008; Stein, 2005). The reality that sexual violence exists in K-12 schools in the United States has been documented by federal court cases and research studies, as well as testimonials from students who are survivors of or witnesses to sexual violence. Research findings from the U.S. Department of Education's Office for Civil Rights (2020) reveal that sexual violence in K-12 school districts during the 2015-2016 and 2017-2018 academic years increased by 55%. The report also found that both boys and girls experience school-based sexual violence (SBSV), making it a policy issue that should encourage school officials and education policy analysts to consider how patriarchy, power, and control is operationalized in policy studies (Pillow, 2003).

This chapter will discuss the activism of a collective of Black girls known as Rise Up at a small urban high school and how their social justice class project raised awareness around sexual violence in their school district. Rise Up provides stories from themselves and other students at their high school who are victims of sexual violence. They seek to use their research to illustrate problems of sexual

E. Mikulec, D. Beichner (eds.), Distraction: Girls, School, and Sexuality, 149-163.
© *2021 DIO Press, Inc. All rights reserved.*

violence in their high school to educational leaders and recommend that classes on consent are added to the curriculum.

BLACK GIRLHOOD AND SCHOOL-BASED SEXUAL VIOLENCE IN URBAN SEETINGS

Nunn (2018) states that it is important to center the experiences of Black girls in schooling because they are rarely considered or discussed in the broader context of educational research. Although Black girlhood is not monolithic, scholars of Black girlhood studies have highlighted some common experiences and perceptions of Black girls in urban schools. The ways in which race and gender interact is important to explore within the SBSV context because studies show that Black girls are more prone to experiences SBSV than white girls and school personnel are less likely to respond to their complaints (Espelage et al., 2016; Harris & Kruger, 2020; Parks et al., 2016). Morris (2016) provides a collage of adolescent Black girls who are entangled in the criminal justice system and failing to achieve in school. Black girls are depicted as being loud and tough in order to gain recognition in the classroom (Evans-Winters & Esposito, 2010). Other scholars explore the ways girls of color assert agency and disrupt negative rhetoric and stereotypes in school through the performing arts (Brown, 2013; Endsley, 2018; Ladner, 1995). Black girls who live in urban communities are more vulnerable to the formal and informal consequences that are associated with gender violence (Cole & Guy-Sheftall, 2003; Collins, 2004; Jones, 2010; Richie, 1996). These studies reveal that Black girls are encountering harm and marginalization in their schools. However, it is also important to talk about the prevalence of sexual violence in school climate and education policy studies and how Black girls are impacted. More critical analyses are needed that situate gender-based violence as a system of oppression.

Sexualization is embedded in the cultural fabric of girls' lives and subjects all children to impoverished modes of thinking about gender and human relationships (Egan, 2013; Olfman, 2009). One example of this occurs through school dress codes that problematize female bodies, specifically female bodies of color that sends a message that their bodies are mainly sexual (Pavlakis & Roegman, 2018). Black bodies are bound to histories that influence the way public forms of Black femininity are objectified (Hill, 2018; McKittrick, 2006). Recently, a group of students in New Jersey started a hashtag #Iamnotadistraction to protest their school dress code that required female students to cover themselves by implying that their bodies were distracting male students from learning (Krischer, 2018). In the era of #MeToo, schools must find a more nuanced way to talk about issues of gender and sexuality that helps to create safe spaces for everyone. Black feminist theory, like intersectionality, points to systems of domination that produce and maintain other systems of oppression for Black girls. This work reveals the complexities and contradictions of different kinds of feminism and feminists messaging in public educational spaces. What is the utility of Black feminist theories and methods for disrupting and eventually abolishing SBSV in public schooling? What does it do as Black feminist scholars to write about Black girls' bodies as hypersexualized distractions embedded within structures of oppression? Black girls' complaints become a distraction because they refuse to accept the normalization of sexual violence in their school settings.

Schools are complicit in maintaining harmful school climates for SBSV survivors by consistently overlooking their needs and taking their complaints seriously (Harris & Kruger, 2020). Legal scholar Jody Miller (2008) asserts that public school officials are legally obligated to address sexual violence that take place on school grounds. The primary function of criminal law is to give guidance and to teach first, not punish (Dauda, 2010). The pedagogical role of the law in education systems is not to condemn the sexuality of students but provide procedures for making it clear and easy for them to report coercion or other forms of assault and harassment while protecting their choices, desires, and safety (Fischel, 2016). In 1992, the Supreme Court ruled in *Franklin v. Gwinnett County (Georgia) Public Schools* that schools could be financially liable for sexual harassment. In the case of *Davis v. Monroe County (Georgia) Board of Education* the Supreme Court in May 1999 decided that schools are liable for student-to-student sexual harassment when complaints are made, and when they fail to stop it. The law does not mean justice, nor does it mean justice will be served when it is broken. Former US Secretary of Education Betsy DeVos attempted to make changes to Title IX that would place barriers before students who have experienced SBSV and limit their ability to receive justice (Yoffe, 2018). However, during the last few months of DeVos' time as Education Secretary, a new Title IX rule was implemented that seeks to specifically combat sexual violence occurring in K-12 public schools (U.S. Department of Education & Office for Civil Rights, 2020). The Office for Civil Rights (OCR) will increase their efforts to ensure that schools districts under Title IX understand how to effectively respond to sexual violence. Sonja Tonnesen (2013) explains that under federal Civil Rights Law Title IX of Education Amendments of 1972, sexual harassment in schools is a form of illegal sex discrimination and school districts can be held liable for these incidents. Title IX law should guide the design and implementation of sexual harassment policies at the local school district level. However, local school districts construct and enact education policies based on their own social values and norms within their school culture.

Theoretical Framework

This study employs structural intersectionality from Black feminist thought as a theoretical framework for examining the experiences of sexual violence in urban schooling of Black girls. Structural intersectionality provides a theoretical and an analytical lens through which to interrogate the social context of sexual violence against Black girls and other girls of color and a means for gaining redress. Public protests reveal the limits of equality. It shows the nexus between intersectional forms of resistance in practice and its relationship with the law. Black women scholars often draw on Black feminist thought to provide nuance into educational challenges of race, class, and gender issues (Evans-Winters, 2015). The #MeToo movement seeks to offer a safe space and language for talking about sexual violence. It confronts the inherent ethos of sexual violence in the culture in the United States (Douglas, 2018). However, in many ways #MeToo has been co-opted as a movement that is about reporting sexual violence while leaving out one of the main aims of the movement: to create safe spaces for survivors to tell their stories and heal. Tarana Burke founded the #MeToo movement in 2006 and says that one of the underlying questions she wanted to answer was, "what does "survival" actually mean?" (Burke interview with Adetiba, *Nation*, 2017). Although Burke says the movement is inclusive of all women who have been sexually harassed or assaulted, she says the reason she centers Black women and girls in her work is because they have been socialized to view sexual violence as normal. She goes on to say that we need to think more critically about what justice should look like for survivors and perpetrators. She believes that communities will not be able to heal without taking a restorative justice approach to end the cycle of sexual violence.

Affirmative consent policies tend to focus on queer, Black and other people of color whose sexuality is deemed as deviant (Collins, 2004; Gilbert, 2018; Lamb et al., 2016). As Kimberlé Crenshaw (1991) explains, we cannot use feminist theories to describe the experiences of women and girls simply by analyzing patriarchy, sexism, or spheres of ideology. We must name and talk about race and racism in ways that can be applied to abolishing oppression. Oppression marks survivors in different ways based on their gender, race, and class status (Fay, 1987). Sexual violence is about gaining and maintaining power over subordinates by those in positions of authority. However, the sexual predator may not be in a position of authority over the survivor, but because of how structural mechanisms are arranged in schools, the predator may be allowed to get away with the harassment. Sexual harassment is not just about the perpetrator's erotic or perverse desire for the survivor, but in public institutions like schools, the actions of the perpetrator are designed to insult and degrade survivors (Fitzgerald & Shullman, 1993; Kohlman, 2004). When sexual harassment is normalized in public, girls learn that they cannot trust the adults around them to believe or protect them (Stein, 2005). Perpetrators are empowered to continue their behavior without fear of punishment.

METHODOLOGY

This study is a part of a larger critical ethnography conducted over a two-year period. Critical ethnography requires relationships with participants in the fieldwork. It is a cross sectional method that investigates human actions and experiences with social worlds and how those social worlds influence social behaviors. Critical ethnographers disrupt neutrality and assumptions projected onto groups of people by revealing obscure operations of power and domination (Madison, 2019). Thomas (1993) asserts that critical ethnography is ethnography with a political purpose. The aim of Madison's version of critical ethnography is to contribute to knowledge and discourses of restorative justice.

Participants and procedures

There were two participants in this participatory action research: the Rise Up researchers and the author researcher.

Rise Up

A high school social justice-oriented student group of Black girls called Rise Up decided to use their class project to raise awareness of school-based sexual violence in their high school. Their "portraits of marginality" (Simien, 2007) demonstrate how systemic patterns of discrimination are constructed and maintained and how girls in the school group/class project (Rise Up) disrupt policy scripts and practices around sexual violence in a small urban high school. What do their stories tell us about the need to improve school climates to become safe spaces? What do their narratives reveal about structural ways sexual violence is maintained by educational leaders against vulnerable students?

The Rise Up Project

The Black girls in Rise Up conducted a mixed methods participatory action research project over the course of the Fall school term during the 2017-2018 academic year. The goal of the research project was to capture data regarding SBSV at the high level in their school district. The small urban school district has (N=10,000) students with only two high schools. The girls used convenience sampling to select students for interviews who they knew had were survivors of SBSV. Boys and girls were participants for the survey, but only girls who were known to be survivors of SBSV between the two high schools were interviewed. Quantitative survey data were collected from boys and girls across the two high schools to examine their knowledge of consent procedures, school-based sexual violence in the two high schools, and the source of the information. Quantitative survey data were collected and analyzed using Survey Monkey. The sample sizes for the survey data vary due to the fluctuation in responses from participants. Data cited in this chapter labeled "Rise Up data" comes from their written presentations and reports from their research project.

Author Researcher Procedures

Data were collected by the author researcher, referred to hereafter as the author, during a series of meetings and presentations with district educational leaders where Rise Up presented their findings during the months of February 2018 and May 2018. All other data such as interviews, fieldnotes, and observations were taken by the author from 2016-2018. The meeting minutes were written by the district secretary and provided to the author to use in this research as well as published on the school district's website. The purpose of the meetings and presentations were to petition for changes to the sexual harassment and abuse policy and procedures in the school district. The meetings were open to the public. The author attended the meetings as a participant observer taking field notes and asking questions of the Black girls in Rise Up and school leaders regarding the policy changes. Narrative excerpts used in this chapter will not be edited in order to allow the voices of the participants to be represented authentically. This study is under an IRB protocol that requires that all participant names and locations be pseudonyms. The author does not use pseudonym names when citing participants from Rise Up's interview data. Citations used in this chapter from Rise Up's data are noted as such to give them credit for their work.

Language Policy

I do not capitalize the term "white" when using it to describe a racial category unless it is the first word in a sentence. Here, I follow the Du Boisian (2007; 1930) tradition of capitalizing the word Black to acknowledge and render respect on the page for African Americans. The narratives presented in this research from participants in this study are presented as they said them or wrote them without alteration.

FINDINGS AND DISCUSSION

Black girl activism and the logics of SBSV as a social justice issue

Black youth activism programs are sites where critical consciousness can be developed and where transformative work occur (Carey et al., 2020). The work of Rise Up centers school-based sexual violence (SBSV) as a social justice issue that demands attention. Their study found that the school district did not have a form or even a clear procedure for students to submit complaints of sexual violence. There were several key issues that the girls raised, and one of them was for training on consent to be added to sex education classes. The girls presented their work to district-level school administrators asking for policy changes to their sexual harassment policies and procedures manual. Survey data results conducted by Rise Up asked respondents if they or anyone they knew had experienced sexual harassment while at high school? Sixty two percent of respondents answered yes to the question. Respondents were asked if they or anyone they know experienced sexual assault while in high school? Forty two percent of respondents answered yes to that question.

What follows are excerpts from interviews conducted by Rise Up with Black schoolgirls about their experiences in high school with school-based sexual violence.

> I have been sexually harassed in this school, at other schools, and outside of schools in stores. I'm in 9th grade and my whole school career I have had experiences with witnessing sexual assault or being assaulted.

> When I walk through the halls, I feel like I have to constantly pull my shirt down to cover my butt. Bending down to use the water fountain as a group of people walk by is the most stressful thing because I never know what they might say to/about me.

> While walking down the hallways I hear inappropriate comments being yelled at to anybody and everybody. After having been yelled inappropriate comments at, I feel the need to keep my head down, earbuds in and try to ignore what is going on around me.

As shown through the excerpts above, sexual harassment happens in public and is a form of sexual discrimination that is illegal as defined by Title IX. Sexual harassment is a violation of students' rights to receive an educational opportunity without fear of sexual harassment or discrimination. Sexual violence contaminates the entire school climate that reach far beyond intended targets (Stein, 2005). The primary site for SBSV primarily occurs in hallways, followed by classrooms, gym locker rooms and classes, lunchrooms, and outside of the school (Espelage et al., 2016). SBSV encompasses unwanted verbal, nonverbal, and physical sexual violence. Consent is the ability to reject or accept proposals for sexual behaviors whether physical or verbal. Research on Black schoolgirls in the United States are entangled within socio-historical processes that render them invisible, exploited, hypersexualized, and blamed for their own subjugation (Crenshaw et al., 2015; Harris & Kruger, 2016; Morris, 2016; Nyachae & Ohito, 2020; Wilcox, 2021). The ways that traditional sex education courses in school address the idea of affirmative consent is entrenched in gendered notions of fear whereby boys ask girls for consent to engage in sexual activity, thus rendering all sexuality for girls as a danger or moment of degradation for girls (Gilbert, 2018; Halley, 2016; Hess, 2010; Irvine, 2004; Kipnis, 2017; Luker, 2007). Why is it important to teach consent in high school sex education?

The Black girls in Rise Up believe "failing to educate young students on what consent means leads to higher instances of sexual violence." (Interview data, 2018). Scholarship on sexual consent among high school adolescents reveal that cultivating an understanding of sexual consent is important due to their findings showing most adolescent girls often lack the skills to resist peer pressure (Righi et al., 2019; Salvy et al., 2014;), sexual assertiveness (Rickert et al., 2002), and sexual agency (Mann, 2016) is often lacking in the sexual experiences of girls. Title IX guidance recommends education on consent become a major part of sexual assault prevention programs (U.S. Department of Education, Office for Civil Rights, 2014). A clear understanding regarding sexual consent among high school adolescents is vital to interventions of sexual violence in high schools (Righi et al., 2019). The Rise Up survey data revealed that out of (N=113) respondents, (68%) of them said they had received some education on consent. However, when asked where they had received the training regarding consent respondents identified either home (39%) or social media (26%) their top two sources of information. Only (8%) of respondents said that they had learned or received any education about consent in school. A black schoolgirl participant told Rise Up that:

> A close friend of mine has experienced sexual assault, and it was difficult to see how little the school did for her. Rather than punishing the perpetrator, the victim had to work around her attacker['s] schedule instead of him working around hers. The treatment is unfair and biased, and more needs to be done for victims, (Rise Up interview data, 2018).

Black girls are less likely to report sexual violence because of the racial beliefs of some teachers and fear of retaliation from the perpetrator (LeMoncheck, 1997). Black schoolgirls' perpetrators are more likely older and romantic partners while white schoolgirls' perpetrators tend to be same-age peers and friends (Espelage et al., 2016). The testimonies from the survivors of SBSV in this study complicate traditional ideas of the role of sex education in school climate studies.

Black Girl Activism as Transformative Policy Action for Survivors of SBSV

Black feminist activism offers a social justice critique of that acknowledges the intersections of gender-based violence and other interpersonal forms of violence and its connections with institutional violence (Kim, 2020). The school culture determines what goals and problems will be addressed and which will not (Sarason, 1982). School officials will not challenge existing values and practices that are meaningful to them (Villenas & Angeles, 2013). Juanita Epp (1996) asserts that structural violence is not intended to cause harm but, an unintentional consequence of policies and procedures invoked by well-meaning leaders. Discourse between Rise Up and school officials at Blakesdale School District reveal that structural violence can be intentional. Pillow (2008) notes that [Black] feminist poststructuralist analyses of schooling and education policy demonstrate that policies are all about controlling and dominating bodies. The students' examination of the policy problems in their school district is a discursive construction of the problems and the lived effects of the policies on their lives.

At the committee meeting with district education leaders, Rise Up presented their research on SBSV cases in their high schools. The Black schoolgirls requested that some of the language in the Student Code of Conduct manual change or be deleted to support clearer procedures for sexual harassment complaints. For instance, one sentence in the manual states,

> 'students who feel they or other students have been subjected to sexual harassment are encouraged to advise the student to stop his/her offensive behavior'. Rise Up asked that this be changed because a "survivor' shouldn't have to confront a 'perpetrator" (Fieldnotes, 2018).

Some committee members disagreed with the use of the term perpetrator because "the 'perpetrator' may not realize the behavior is unwanted and without the 'survivor' informing him/her, would not necessarily know to change his/her behavior in the future" (School district meeting minutes, 2018). The school officials' narrative in this situation places the responsibility on the survivors to confront the perpetrator for the sexual harassment to end. However, gendered harassment often targets girls at school by policing physical, verbal, and psychological behaviors of heterosexual gender norms (Meyer, 2008). School leaders do not take into consideration that the girls may fear further abuse and consequences by confronting the perpetrator (Liston & Rahimi-Moore, 2005). What is concealed in this policy narrative is the lack of attention school officials give to investigating claims of sexual harassment by Black schoolgirls and protecting all students from it in their school district.

Rise Up asked if students would be allowed "to/elect to drop a class because of sexual misconduct from a teacher" (School district meeting minutes, 2018). One school official said that the topic would need to be discussed with high school administrators because it would impact high school curriculum procedures and the awarding of credit. School officials did not inquire about the possible sexual misconduct of their staff, or the students who may be experiencing sexual violence. They chose to focus on how the change would impact achievement data procedures instead. It was noted at the meeting that the school district did not have a form that victims could use to report sexual violence to administrators. One of the school board members said,

> she talked to some of the girls in her daughter's peer group about sexual harassment/abuse at the high school and their experiences do not seem to mirror those of the girls in [Rise Up]. It was noted that girls of color and girls with disabilities may encounter more harassment/abuse than girls from the majority race who are from upper-middle class backgrounds (School district meeting minutes, 2018).

Why are Black girls' and other marginalized girls' bodies more of a distraction than girls from affluent backgrounds? Sexual harassment is often perceived and acknowledged based on class and racial stereotypes (Harris & Kruger, 2020; Rahimi & Liston, 2011). The fact that the socioeconomic positions of school officials often do not match those of the students they work with can conceal forms of harassment taking place at school (Rahimi & Liston, 2011). The racialized socioeconomic rhetoric during this meeting reveals how intersectional fatalities continue to occur for the same group of disadvantaged students. The girls in Rise Up confronted school administrators and asked them why they allow sexual violence to persist in their high schools. Rise Up's petition to their educational leadership to address SBSV in their high school and implement a sex education curriculum that teaches students about consent was met with disregard. The Black schoolgirls assert that "[they] want to change the idea that bodies are "distracting" and to be "controlled," (Rise Up interview, 2018).

Resistance strategies are conceptualized as a refusal to believe certain information about oneself (Pitt, 1997) or the development of a critical consciousness of myths and stereotypes about marginalized groups (Ward, 2007). Black feminist scholar bell hooks (1992) call this an oppositional gaze, which empowers marginalized people with the ability to organize and act in ways that reform, undermine, and overthrow systems of oppression (Mansbridge & Morris, 2001). Collective prevention and resistance strategies against structural SBSV represent the action arm of intersectional transformative work for survivors (Crenshaw, 2000; Wilcox, 2021). The policy narrative in this conversation provides an example of how race, class, and gender intersect in ways that prohibit school officials from thinking about developing a safe school climate for all students. It suggests that school officials may not have a clear understanding of consent or the desire to protect the kind of girls in Rise Up from harassment or abuse because the girls "from the majority race who are from upper-middle class backgrounds" (School district meeting minutes, 2018) are not affected. The collective activism of Rise Up demonstrates how race, class, and gender-based violence intersects structurally to create and maintain harmful educational environments.

Sexual comments and gestures towards young women are viewed as attention from males as praise (Weitz, 1998). This position is problematic for young girls who find themselves confronted within dominant heterosexual patriarchal frameworks that define masculinity by sexual experiences with reverberation, while girls' sexual activities brand them with negative sexual labels such being a ho, slut, or bitch (Rahimi & Liston, 2011; Tolman et al., 2003). There are intersectional implications to centering a gendered, classed, and racialized analysis on SBSV (Purkayastha & Ratcliff, 2014). It suggests and exposes a level of structural violence that asks, who is safe in high school from sexual assault and why? Whose bodies are a distraction and why? Irene MacDonald (1996) asserts that in many schools, young people accept psychological and physical abuse as a normal part of their adolescent experience because they feel powerless to change things.

The only change the school district made to their policies and procedures manual regarding sexual violence was to update the date on the manual. However, four implications from Rise Up's work occurred. Rise Up's work provided another example of the importance of including social justice education within the curriculum in urban schooling. The Black schoolgirl activism provided a space where survivors' stories could be told and where a record of the events would be documented and archived for other to know that SBSV happens within their school district. The design and carried out evidence-based research on the problem of SBSV in their district. Their presentations at school district leadership meetings allowed the voices of the survivors to be amplified beyond the district and illuminated ways in which SBSV is maintained discursively and put SBSV at the center of social justice issues occurring in their high schools.

CONCLUSION

The discourse in this study demonstrates the need for training on consent in sex education in high school and raises broader questions about sex education curriculum and policies. The interview excerpts from victims of sexual violence in a small urban high school reveal policy gaps institutionally that prohibit their high school from being a safe space for all students. However, their stories illuminate how adolescent gender and sexuality issues are framed within a heterosexual patriarchal framework. Class and racial biases of school administrators make it difficult to develop sex education curriculum that is inclusive of non-heterosexual relations structures. School administrators have a difficult task of navigating decision and policymaking around sex curriculum and the law.

What can we learn from the resistance strategies used by Black girls in Rise Up that illuminate the problem of sexual violence in urban schooling? How are pedagogical and legal procedures around sex education, particularly consent limited by refusing to speak honestly and responsibly about childhood sexuality in schooling? The narratives of survivors of SBSV are the centerpiece of the social justice work of Rise Up and is a powerful form of agency that reveal prevention and resistance strategies that show that Black girls are not only political but intellectual. The research context of the stories from Black girls in this study illuminate their experiences with SBSV is rooted in feminist trauma studies or endarkened feminism (Dillard, 2006; Gardner, 2015) that require one to listen to the stories of survivors and see sexual violence as a social justice issue. Rise Up's research is a powerful tool for studying the intersections of race, class, gender, and sexuality issues in education. The Black girls in this work want to become more than a distraction at their high school. The Black schoolgirls in this group suggest that sexual education curricula reform can be both a prevention and resistance strategy to remedy school-based sexual violence. They seek to challenge school officials to be accountable for antiquated sex education curriculum and passive attention given to survivors of sexual violence in their high school. They want to be heard.

REFERENCES

Adetiba, E., & Burke, T. (2017). Q&A Tarana Burke. *Nation, 305*(15), 5.

Brown, R.N. (2013). *Hear our Truths: The Creative Potential of Black Girlhood*. Urbana: University of Illinois Press.

Carey, R.L., Akiva, T., Abdellatif, H., & Daughtry, K.A. (2020). 'And school won't teach me that!' Urban youth activism programs as transformative sites for critical adolescent learning. *Journal of Youth Studies*. DOI: 10.1080/13676261.2020.1784400.

Crenshaw, K., & Ocen, P., & Nanda, J. (2015). *Black girls matter: Pushed out, overpoliced, and underprotected*. Center for Intersectionality and Social Policy Studies. Columbia University.

Crenshaw, K. (2000). *Background paper for the expert meeting on the gender-related aspects of race discrimination*. New York: United Nations.

Crenshaw, K. (1991). Mapping the margins: Intersectionality, identity, and violence against women of color. *Stanford Law Review, 43*(6), 1241–1300.

Cole, J.B., & Guy-Sheftall, B. (2003). *Gender Talk: The Struggle for Women's Equality in African American Communities*. New York: One World/Ballatine Books.

Collins, P.H. (2004). *Black sexual politics*. New York Routledge.

Dauda, C. (2010). Childhood, age of consent and moral regulation in Canada and the UK. *Contemporary Politics, 16*(3), 227-247.

Davis v. Monroe County (Georgia) Board of Education, 526 U.S. 629 (1999).

Dillard, C.B. (2006). *On Spiritual Strivings Transforming an African American Woman's Academic Life*. Albany State University of New York Press.

Douglas, D. (2018). Black women say #MeToo. Retrieved from www.thecrisismagazine.com.

Du Bois, W.E.B. (2007). *The Philadelphia Negro*. (The Oxford W.E.B. Du Bois). New York: Oxford University Press.

Endsley, C.L. (2018). "Something good distracts us from the bad" Girls cultivating disruption. *Girlhood Studies, 11*(2), 63-78.

Egan, R. D. (2013). Becoming Sexual: *A Critical Appraisal of the Sexualization of Girls*. Cambridge, Polity Press.

Epp, J.R. (1996). Schools, complicity, and sources of violence. In Epp, J.R., & Watkinson, A. (Eds.), *Systemic Violence: How Schools Hurt Children* (pp. 1-23). Washington, DC: The Falmer Press.

Espelage, D.L., Hong, J.S., Rinehart, S., & Doshi, N. (2016). Understanding types, locations, & perpetrators of peer-to-peer sexual harassment in US middle schools: A focus on sex, racial and grade difference. *Children and Youth Services Review, 71*, 174-183. Doi: 10.1016/j.childrenyouth.2016.11.010.

Evans-Winters, V.E. (2015). Black feminism in qualitative education research. In In Evans-Winters, V.E., & Love, B.L. (Eds.), *Black Feminism in Education: Black Women Speak Back, Up, and Out* (pp.129-142). New York Peter Lang.

Evans-Winters, V.E., & Esposito, J. (2010). Other people's daughters: Critical race feminism and Black girls' education. *Educational Foundations, 24*(1), 11-24.

Fay, B. (1987). *Critical Social Science*. Ithaca Cornell University Press.

Fischel, J. (2016). *Sex and Harm in the Age of Consent*. Minneapolis: University of Minnesota Press.

Fitzgerald, L. F., & Shullman, S. L. (1993). Sexual harassment: A research analysis and agenda for the 1990's. *Journal of Vocational Behavior, 42*, 5-27.

Franklin v. Gwinnett County (Georgia) Public Schools, 112 S. Ct. 1028 (1992).

Gardner, R.P. (2015). If you listen, you will hear: Race, place, gender, and the trauma of witnessing through listening in research contexts. In Evans-Winters, V.E., & Love, B.L. (Eds.), *Black Feminism in Education: Black Women Speak Back, Up, and Out* (pp. 121-128). New York Peter Lang.

Gilbert, J. (2018). Contesting consent in sex education. *Sex Education, 18*(3), 268-279.

Halley, J. (2016). The move to affirmative consent. *Signs: Journal of Women in Culture and Society, 42*(1), 257-279.

Harris, J., & Kruger, A.C. (2020). "We always tell them, but they don't do anything about it!" Middle school Black girls experiences with sexual harassment at an urban middle school. *Urban Education*, 1-27. DOI: 10.1177/0042085920959131.

Hess, A. (2010). Hold the sex please: The discursive politics between national and local abstinence education providers. *Sex Education, 10*(3), 251-266.

Hill, D.C. (2018). Black girl pedagogies: Layered lessons on reliability. *Curriculum Inquiry, 48*(3), 383-405.

hooks, b. (1992). *Black Looks: Race and Representation*. Boston: South End Press.

Irvine, J.M. (2004). *Talk about Sex: The Battles over Sex Education in the United States*. Berkeley: University of California Press.

Jones, N. (2010). *Between Good and Ghetto: African American Girls and Inner-City Violence*. New Brunswick Rutgers University Press.

Kim, M.E. (2020). Transformative justice and restorative justice: Gender-based violence and alternative visions of justice in the United States. *International Review of Victimology*, 1-11. Doi:10.1177/0269758020970414.

Kipnis, L. (2017). *Unwanted Advances: Sexual Paranoia Comes to Campus*. New York: Harper.

Kohlman, M.H. (2004). Person or position: The demographics of sexual harassment in the workplace. *Equal Opportunities International, 23*, 143-161.

Krischer, H. (2018, April 17). Is your body appropriate to wear to school? *New York Times*.

Ladner, J.A. (1995). *Tomorrow's Tomorrow: The Black Woman*. Lincoln University of Nebraska Press.

Lamb, S., Roberts, T., & Plocha, A. (2016). *Girls of Color, Sexuality, and Sex Education*. New York, Springer.

Leadbeater, B.J. (2008). Urban girls: Building strengths, creating momentum. In Leadbeater, B.J., & Way, N. (Eds.). *Urban Girls Revisited: Building Strengths* (pp. 1-15). New York: University Press.

LeMoncheck, L. (1997). *Loose Women, Lecherous Men: A Feminist Philosophy of Sex*. Oxford: Oxford University Press.

Liston, D., & Rahimi-Moore, R. (2005). A disputation of a bad reputation. The impact of adverse sexual labels on the lives of five southern women. In Bettis, P., & Adams, N. (Eds.), *Geographies of Girlhood: Identities in-between* (pp. 211-230). Mahwah Lawrence Erlbaum Associates.

Luker, K. (2007). When Sex Goes to School: *Warring Views on Sex-and Sex Education-Since the Sixties*. New York: W.W. Norton.

Lyons, N., & LaBoskey, V.K. (2002). Why narrative inquiry or exemplars for a scholarship of teaching? In Lyons, N., & LaBoskey, V.K. (Eds.), *Narrative inquiry in practice: Advancing the knowledge of teaching* (pp. 11-27). New York Teachers College Press.

MacDonald, I.M. (1996). Expanding the lens: Student perceptions of school violence. In Epp, J.R., & Watkinson, A.M. (Eds.), *Systemic violence: How schools hurt children* (pp. 84-93). London Falmer Press.

Madison, D. S. (2019). *Critical ethnography: Method, ethics, and performance* (3rd ed.). Thousand Oaks SAGE.

Mann, E.S. (2016). Latina girls, sexual agency, and the contradictions of neoliberalism. *Sexuality Research and Social Policy*, 13, 330-340.

Mansbridge, J., & Morris, A. (Eds.). (2001). *Oppositional Consciousness: The Subjective Roots of Social Protest*. Chicago: University of Chicago Press.

McKittrick, K. (2006). *Demonic grounds: Black women and the cartographies of struggle*. Minneapolis: University of Minnesota Press.

Miller, J. (2008). *Getting Played: African American Girls, Urban Inequality, and Gendered Violence*. New York: New York University Press.

Morris, M.W. (2016). Pushout: *The Criminalization of Black Girls in Schools*. New York The New Press.

Meyer, E.J. (2008). Gendered harassment in secondary schools: Understanding teachers' (non) interventions. *Gender and Education*, *20*, 555-570.

"NEGRO" WITH A CAPITAL "N.". (1930, Mar 07). New York Times (1923-Current File) Retrieved from https://search-proquest-com.proxy2.library.illinois.edu/docview/98721509?accountid=14553.

Nunn, N.M. (2018). Super-girl: Strength and sadness in Black girlhood. *Gender and Education*, *30*(2), 239-258.

Nyachae, T.M., & Ohito, E.O. (2020). No disrespect: A womanist critique of respectability discourses in extracurricular programming for Black girls. *Urban Education*. DOI: 10.1177/00420859198937.

Olfman, S. (2009). The sexualization of childhood: Growing older younger/Growing younger older. In Olfman, S. (Ed.), *The Sexualization of Childhood* (pp. 1-6). Westport Praeger.

Parks, C., Wallace, B.C., Emdin, C., & Levy, I.P. (2016). An examination of gendered violence and school push-out directed against urban Black girls/adolescents: Illustrative data, cases and a call to action. *Journal of Infant, Child, and Adolescent Psychotherapy*, *15*(3), 210-219. DOI: 10.1080/15289168.2016.1214451.

Pavlakis, A., & Roegman, R. (2018). How dress codes criminalize males and sexualize females of color. *Phi Delta Kappan*, *100*(2), 54–58.

Pillow, W.S. (2008). Exposed methodology: The body as deconstructive practice. In St. Pierre, E.A., & Pillow, W.S. (Eds.). *Working the ruins: Feminist poststructural theory and methods in education* (pp. 199-219). New York: Routledge.

Pillow, W. (2003). 'Bodies are dangerous': Using feminist genealogy as policy studies methodology. *Journal of Education Policy*, *18*(2), 145-159.

Pitt, A. (1997). Reading resistance analytically: On making the self in women's studies. In Roman, L., & Eyre, L. (Eds.), *Dangerous Territories: Struggles for Difference and Equality in Education* (pp. 127-142). New York: Routledge.

Purkayastha, B., & Ratcliff, K.S. (2014). Routine violence: Intersectionality at the interstices. In Segal, M.T., & Demos, V. (Eds.), *Gendered perspectives on conflict and violence part B* (pp.19-43). United Kingdom: Emerald Group Publishing Limited.

Rahimi, R., & Liston, D. (2011). Race, class, and emerging sexuality: teacher perceptions and sexual harassment in schools. *Gender & Education, 23*(7), 799–810.

Richie, B. (1996). *Compelled to Crime: The Gender Entrapment of Battered Black Women.* New York: Routledge.

Rickert, V., Sanghvi, R., & Wiemann, C. (2002). Is the lack of sexual assertiveness among adolescent and young adult women a cause for concern? *Perspectives on Sexual and Reproductive Health, 34,* 178-183.

Righi, M.K., Bogen, K.W., Kuo, C., & Orchowski, L.M. (2019). A qualitative analysis of beliefs about sexual consent among high school students. *Journal of Interpersonal Violence.* DOI: 10.1177/0886260519842855.

Salvy, S.J., Pedersen, E.R., Miles, J.N., Tucker, J.S., & D'Amico, E.J. (2014). Proximal and distal social influence on alcohol consumption and marijuana use among middle school adolescents. *Drug and Alcohol Dependence, 144,* 93-101.

Sarason, S. (1996). *Revisiting the Culture of the School and the Problem of Change.* New York: Teachers College Press.

Simien, E.M. (2007). Doing intersectionality research: From conceptual issuesto practical examples. *Politics & Gender, 3*(2), 264-271.

Stein, N. (2005). Still no laughing matter: Sexual harassment in K-12 schools. In Buchwald, E., Fletcher, P.R., & Roth, M. (Eds.). *Transforming a Rape Culture: A Revised Edition* (pp. 59-74). Minneapolis Milkweed Editions.

Tolman, D.L., Spencer, R., Reynoso-Rosen, M., & Porche, M. (2003). Sowing the seeds of violence in heterosexual relationships: Early adolescents narrate compulsory heterosexuality. *Journal of Social Issues, 59*(1), 159-178.

Thomas, J. (1993). *Doing critical ethnography.* Thousand Oaks SAGE Publications.

Tonnesen, S. C. (2013). "Hit It and Quit It": Responses to Black girls' victimization in school. *Berkeley Journal of Gender, Law & Justice, 28*(1), 1-29.

U.S. Department of Education, Office for Civil Rights. (2020). 2017-2018 Civil rights data collection: Sexual Violence in K-12 Schools. Retrieved from https://www2.ed.gov/about/offices/list/ocr/docs/sexual-violence.pdf

U.S. Department of Education, Office for Civil Rights. (2014, April 29). Questions and answers on Title IX and sexual violence. Retrieved from https://www2.ed.gov/about/offices/list/ocr/docs/qa-201404-title-ix.pdf.

Villenas, S.A., & Angeles, S.L. (2013). Race talk and school equity in local print media: The discursive flexibility of whiteness and the promise of race-conscious talk. *Discourse: Studies in the Cultural Politics of Education, 34*(4), 510-530.

Ward, J.V. (2007). Uncovering truths, recovering lives: Lessons of resistance in the socialization of Black girls. In Leadbeater, B.J., & Way, N. (Eds.). *Urban Girls Revisited: Building Strengths* (pp. 243-259). New York: New York University Press.

Weitz, R. (1998). *The politics of women's bodies: Sexuality, appearance and behavior*. Oxford: Oxford University Press.

Wilcox, S.M. (2021). Political intersectionality and Black girls' #MeToo movement in public K-12 schools. *Journal of Black Sexuality and Relationships, 7*(1), 21-34. DOI: 10.1353/bsr.2020.0009.

Yoffe, E. (2018). Reining In the Excesses of Title IX. *The Atlantic*. Accessed at https://www.theatlantic.com/ideas/archive/2018/09/title-ix-reforms-are-overdue/569215/

Serena M. Wilcox
University of Kentucky

Chapter Eleven

Campus Sexual Assault in the USA: A Call for a Restorative, Survivor-Centered, Intersectional Approach

Dawn Beichner

> Too often in this country, victims of rape are humiliated and harassed when they report and prosecute the rape. Bullied and cross-examined about their prior sexual experiences, many find the trial almost as degrading as the rape itself. Since rape trials become inquisitions into the victim's morality, not trials of the defendant's innocence or guilt, it is not surprising that it is the least reported crime. It is estimated that as few as one in ten rapes is ever reported.

These are the words of then Representative Elizabeth Holtzman in 1978, addressing Congress more than four decades ago, as an advocate in support of the Privacy Protection for Rape Victims Act (124 Cong. Rec. 34,913 1978, cited in Galvin, 1986, p. 764). Holtzman's comments came in a time of vociferous lobbying efforts by feminist and political associations across the United States, including the National Organization for Women, the League of Women Voters, and the American Civil Liberties Union to affect change on the handling of rape cases. These efforts propelled nationwide attention and legislative reform of rape statutes across the nation. Victim advocates sought and demanded change of a system that suffered from case attrition, produced under-reporting, favored the accused, and traumatized and re-victimized victims through the justice process (See Beichner, 2015 for a complete review). As a result of these efforts, the United States underwent sweeping reform of rape statutes: rape was redefined as sexual assault or similar terminology and expanded to include an array of graduated offenses, such as attempted, first, and second degree. Importantly, corroboration requirements were removed or significantly altered, and the methods used to determine consent were redefined. Additionally, rape shield laws emerged, limiting the use of the victim's past sexual history in court proceedings.

E. Mikulec, D. Beichner (eds.), Distraction: Girls, School, and Sexuality, 165-189.

These reforms notwithstanding, serious issues remain with sexual assault in the Unites States—particularly those involving students on university and college campuses. If Representative Elizabeth Holtzman's comments were amended so that the term "sexual assault" was used in place of "rape," there would be no way of distinguishing her concerns in 1978 from those of present times. This chapter provides an overview of campus sexual assault in the United States, including problems with current approaches. The review includes an overview of Title IX and how it and sexual assault policies have changed over time. The chapter concludes with a call for an approach to sexual assault that is restorative, centered on the survivor-victims,[12] and intersectional.

THE PREVALENCE OF CAMPUS SEXUAL ASSAULT

Empirical research on campus sexual assault in the United States overwhelmingly indicates that it is among the most prevalent forms of gender-based violence in the country. Studies also reveal that—consistent with wider patterns of sexual assault in the general population—campus sexual assault is highly underreported. A significant number of the incidents of campus sexual assault involve drugs and alcohol. In one of the most comprehensive studies completed to date, slightly less than half of the student respondents indicated that they witnessed a drunk person heading for a sexual encounter; however, most did not try to intervene (Cantor et al., 2019).

In their study of 33 universities, the Association of American Universities (AAU) Climate Survey on Sexual Assault and Sexual Misconduct reported that whereas 13% of students reported sexual assault, the prevalence of sexual assault among undergraduate women was 25.9% (Cantor et al., 2019). Other research on campus sexual assault shows consistent patterns; current predictions are that over 16% of college women will be assaulted at some point during their time on campus (Washington Post, Kaiser Family Foundation, 2015; Corey, Durney, Shepardson, & Curey, 2015; England, 2015; University of Oregon Sexual Violence and Institutional Betrayal Survey, 2014; George Washington University Unwanted Sexual Behavior Survey, 2014).

Consistent with previous research on sexual assault reporting in the criminal justice system, underreporting of campus sexual assault is quite common. The AAU report found that only eleven percent or less of the assaults—including the most serious incidents—were reported to campus police (11.2%) or local law enforcement (9.4%) (Cantor et al., 2019). The Bureau of Justice Statistics (2014) estimates that 80% of people sexually assaulted on college campuses do not report the incident to law enforcement. Although there was variation in the reasons for not reporting, respondents of all types of incidents indicated that they did not perceive their sexual victimization to be serious enough to mandate reporting or they were ashamed and embarrassed by the incident and did not believe that anything would be done about it (Bureau of Justice Statistics, 2014; RAINN, 2019).

THE HIDDEN FIGURE OF CAMPUS SEXUAL ASSAULT AMONG LGBTQ STUDENTS

Sexual assault figures in the United States indicate that transgender people and bisexual women are sexually victimized at high rates, with many offenses dating back to childhood (Human Rights Campaign, 2019). In fact, the 2015 Transgender Survey revealed that almost half of all transgender people (47%) will be sexually assaulted in their lifetimes (National Center for Transgender Equality, 2019). The Association of American Universities (AAU) Climate Survey on Sexual Assault and Misconduct indicated that the rate of sexual assault among all students was 13%, but for Transgender men, Transgender women, Nonbinary or genderqueer, the rate was 22.8% for undergraduates and 14.5% for graduate and professional students (Cantor et al., 2019). The overall marginalization of LGBTQ people undoubtedly makes survivor-victims much less trusting of law enforcement, medical personnel, and other victim advocates (HRC, 2019). Research from the National Coalition of Anti-Violence Projects (NCAVP) revealed that 85% of victim advocates indicated that they had worked with LGBTQ survivors who were denied services because of their gender identity or sexual orientation (HRC, 2019).

Considered in this context, underreporting of campus sexual assault is even more severe among LGBTQ students. Current research suggests that LGBTQ students' rates of campus sexual assault is even higher than those of other students (EROC, 2019). Moreover, in terms of students' confidence in university response and prevention, LGBTQ students have lower confidence than others. These trends are consistent with the larger research examining sexual victimization among LGBTQ survivor-victims.

Wooten (2016) purports that the heteronormative framing that characterizes most campus sexual assault policies is a byproduct of the feminist influence on such policies. Though there is a clear gendered pattern with university women being the most often sexually assaulted, campus sexual assault policies must be inclusive of all survivor victims. The current heteronormative approach to campus sexual assault largely ignores sexual violence among the LGBTQ community.

RAPE CULTURE AND VICTIM BLAMING ON COLLEGE CAMPUSES

One of the most influential catalysts for contemporary activism on campus sexual assault in the United States was the documentary film *The Hunting Ground* (Dick et al., 2015). The film's title likens campuses in the United States to hunting grounds for rapists. The filmmakers described how predatory men—often in fraternities or university athletics—would seek out and sexually assault intoxicated women. The documentary, and the many showings that took place around the nation, demanded attention to the problem of campus sexual assault and the treatment of survivor-victims. It was also instrumental in showcasing the volumes of campus sexual assaults that were reported by students and the failure to respond by university administrators. One of the startling statistics from the film indicated that in 2012, 45% of universities and colleges reported 0 sexual assaults, a figure that is impossible, given the prevalence of the crime. The film also illustrated the ways in which Title IX could be successfully used to hold universities accountable for failing to respond to reported campus sexual assaults, through the documentation of an actual class action lawsuit.

Victim Blaming

One of the survivor-victims in the documentary *The Hunting Ground* described her experience telling a university administrator about her rape. She said that the administrator used the metaphor of a football game, saying "rape is like a football game. Looking back, what would you have done differently, if you could replay the situation again?" (Dick et al., 2015). Another common theme among survivor-victim narratives in the film was that they were repeatedly asked how much they had to drink, implying that their alcohol consumption contributed to their sexual assault. Many survivor-victims said that they felt like they were being lectured by university officials, who were asking questions like "Did you say no? How did you say it?" (Dick et al., 2015). The film also includes reflections from a survivor-victim from Harvard University. After the student described that she and her friend were sexually assaulted while they were passed out, the Dean of Students told the survivor-victim not to talk to anyone about what happened. The administrator went on to ask, "Did you give [the perpetrator] the wrong message with your friendship? Why didn't you fight him?"

Patterns of victim blaming such as these have existed for decades and are not unique to campus sexual assault. Studies on the effects of victim characteristics have examined what researchers consider "blame and believability" of the victim—factors that might lead criminal justice decisionmakers to blame her/him for being victimized or question her credibility as a complainant (see Beichner & Spohn, 2012 for a complete review). These factors—using of alcohol or illicit drugs at the time of the incident, willingly accompanying the suspect to his residence, and inviting the suspect to her residence—are especially influential in simple sexual assault cases, such as those that occur on college campuses which involve students who are acquaintances and center on consent.

Rape Culture on College and University Campuses

There are a number of characteristics unique to college campuses that make them conducive to sexual violence, such as the cultures fostered by student athletics and fraternities (Crosset, 2016; Martin, 2016). Lasky and her colleagues outline the ways in which the university culture is conducive to binge drinking, both in terms of the emphasis on campus party culture, as well as participation in Greek life membership and events (Lasky, Fisher, Henriksen, & Swan, 2017). The atmosphere of heavy drinking at bars or house parties, otherwise known as pregaming (drinking at home before going out), both increases the risk of sexual assault, and the overall risk of drugging victimizations or administering alcohol or drugs to someone without their consent or knowledge (Lasky, Fisher, Henriksen, & Swan, 2017). Contemporary research reports that an estimated 1 in 13 university students report experiencing drugging (Coker, Follingstad, Bush, & Fisher, 2016; Swan et al., 2016). These risks are reportedly higher among first year undergraduate students, those who binge drink, and those who are members of a Greek sorority (Lasky et al., 2017).

Fraternities. Many campus sexual assault reformers point to the problems that are posed by Greek fraternities. Universities often allow for special consideration of Greek organizations that is not afforded to other students (Jozlowski & Wiersma-Mosley, 2017). Fraternities dominate the social scene on campus; not only are their houses lining the campus, they have the ability to host mixed-gender parties with alcohol,[13] something that is prohibited among sororities (Jozlowski & Wiersma-Mosley, 2017). Accordingly, universities are contributors to this system of male dominance and control.

In their exploration of axes of power on college campuses, Jozlowski and Wiersma-Mosley (2017) identify White men as having the most power on college campuses. More specifically, the predominantly White male-dominated party culture of the Greek system has been identified as a campus subculture that is conducive to sexual assault (Jozkowski & Wiersma-Mosley, 2017). Fraternity-sponsored events provide spaces of high risk for sexual assault (Boyle & Walker, 2016; Minow & Einolf, 2009) and the culture within has been criticized as being disrespectful of women and encouraging sexual competition (Boyle, 2015; Boyle & Walker, 2016; Jozlowski & Wiersma-Mosley, 2017), as well as having a higher propensity to subscribe to rape myths (Bannon, Brosi, & Foubert, 2013; Canan et al., 2016). Moreover, the heterosexist culture perpetuated by fraternities also underscores gender expectations (Tolman, 2006). Often, students and parents arriving to campus on drop-off day are greeted by fraternities' signage like "Freshmen Daughter Drop Off" (Jozkowski & Wiersma-Mosley, 2017; Rotuno-Johnson, 2016) and "Drop Your Mothers Off Too" (New, 2015; Saucier, 2017). Not only are the signs misogynistic, they send a clear message that women are sexual objects. Moreover, with few exceptions, this kind of behavior has gone unchallenged.

One of the reasons that such behaviors are tolerated and that universities do not disassociate with fraternities is because of the money they receive. In 2013, nearly 60% of all donations of more than 100 million dollars made to universities came from fraternity alumni (The Chronicle of Philanthropy, 2014). Many of the wealthiest alumni, including politicians, were involved in fraternities; most U.S. Senators and Congressmen, Supreme Court Justices, Fortune 500 executives, and U.S. Presidents have been fraternity members (Chang, 2014). One such politician, Representative Matt Salmon of Arizona, authored legislation designed to protect students accused of sexual assault, whose victims do not report the incident to police (Kingkade, 2015). In his proposed "Safe Campus Act," colleges and universities would only be able to investigate sexual misconduct if the survivor-victim reported the incident to law enforcement officials. In sexual assaults where the survivor-victim did not report the incident to law enforcement, campus administrators would not be permitted to investigate or punish sexual misconduct.

The rape culture perpetuated in male-dominated spaces is reinforced by the all-male support peer model (Schwartz & DeKeseredy, 1998). The male peer support group, which is characterized by groupthink, can contribute to fraternity members contributing to rape culture by endorsing rape-supportive attitudes and behaviors (e.g., covering up sexual assault, fostering loyalty, encouraging secrecy), all of which perpetuate sexual assault and contribute to victim blaming (Jozkowski & Wiersma-Mosley, 2017, p. 96). This can also be problematic in campus athletics; both exude aggression and masculinity.

Campus Athletics. Both fraternities and athletics exude aggression and masculinity, which can set the stage for campus sexual assault. In the documentary film *The Hunting Ground*, the filmmakers provided an in-depth examination of the many ways in which universities protect athletes who are accused of sexual assault (Dick et al., 2015). The exposé revealed that campus athletes were treated with a privilege not offered to other students. For example, one of the interviewees in the film, a Notre Dame Campus Police Officer, said that officers were not permitted to contact athletes at any athletic facility (Dick et al., 2015). One of the survivor-victims of a sexual assault was told by a university administrator, "This is a really big football town, you really should think long and hard before you decide to press charges."

In 2015, Brock Turner, a student athlete was found guilty of sexually assaulting an unconscious woman behind a dumpster (Kebodeaux, 2017). One of the key pieces of evidence in the case was the testimony of two students who saw Brock Turner raping the victim. Although Turner was eventually convicted of three counts of sexual assault, he was only sentenced to six months in county jail and was released after only three months (Kebodeaux, 2017). The case sparked a public outcry that resulted in California passing a bill to impose a mandatory minimum sentence for individuals who sexually assault someone who is unconscious. Brock Turner's lenient sentence is consistent with what happens to most student athlete rapists. *The Hunting Ground* also discussed the problems with punishments. Some perpetrators were assigned community service hours, suspended for one semester, suspended for summer break, given small fines ($25 or $75), given warnings, or required to write a paper about why their behavior was wrong—all of which are no comparison to the trauma and harm to the survivor-victim.

CAMPUS STRATEGIES TO PREVENT AND PUNISH SEXUAL ASSAULT

When confronted with concerns of unsafe campuses, many colleges and universities focused efforts on improvements of increased lighting around the campus and walkways, as well as the installation of emergency blue light phones, which are located around campus and offer passers-by a direct line to the campus police department. What is problematic about these approaches is that increased lighting and blue light phones do nothing to solve the issue of campus sexual assault. Research examining campus sexual assault consistently reveals that sexual violence is not a problem along campus walkways—it happens in student housing on and off-campus—places not illuminated by pathway lights or accessible to blue light phones.

Another common campus strategy to confront sexual assault is the promotion of self-defense classes, which implicitly builds on the victim-blaming model that if a student is well-trained, s/he will be able to fend off a potential attacker. Self-defense classes have been part of the campus arsenal against sexual assault for decades, and yet, like the efforts to shine lights or provide phone access, they are mere distractions. Rather than focusing on the behavior or abilities of students to ward off attackers, campus sexual assault strategies should focus on the behaviors of those committing acts of sexual violence.

Efforts such as these are not only misguided, they also perpetuate the myth that sexual assaults—including those on college and university campuses—are carried out by strangers lurking in the bushes. If campuses are motivated to eliminate sexual assault, much more must be done. Acknowledging the true nature of campus sexual assaults, the perpetration by acquaintances, and the role that campuses play in perpetuating rape culture are critical, as are the strategies to punish perpetrators.

Although the current guidelines by the Association of Title IX Administrators (2018) recommends either suspension or expulsion for nonconsensual sexual intercourse (ATIXA, 2018), this is not the typical punishment in many universities. Whereas suspension allows for a perpetrator to eventually re-enroll at the college or university, expulsion does not. Recent coverage of campus-based sexual assault reveals that expulsion is not always a common punishment and, instead, that a rapist may be permitted to re-enroll after only two or three semesters of suspension (Stannard, 2018). It can be very stressful to survivor-victims, when they learn that the perpetrator is returning to campus to resume classes.

Moreover, given that universities have discretion to set standards for punishment, there is wide variation in the punishments used across schools—including those within the same geographic region. Whereas one campus may have a very punitive approach to sexual assault, another may dole out lenient punishments. For example, at Yale, the University of New Haven, and Quinnipiac University, suspension is given as a punishment in some of the most severe sexual assaults, whereas at Southern Connecticut State University and the University of Connecticut, punishment for the same kinds of sexual assault is likely to be expulsion (Stannard, 2018). Although states cannot be held liable for failure to act, colleges and universities that fail to prevent gender-based wrongdoing can be held accountable via Title IX and Campus Sexual Violence Act (Novkov, 2016).

CAMPUS SEXUAL ASSAULT POLICIES AND TITLE IX AMENDMENTS

Title IX was signed into law in 1972 by then President Nixon (Novkov, 2016). The amendment, which is part of the Educational Amendments of 1972, stated: "No person in the United States shall, on the basis of sex, be excluded from participation in, be denied the benefits of, or be subjected to discrimination under any education program or activity receiving Federal financial assistance" (20 USC §§ 1681-1688, 2012). Initially, the law was used narrowly as a mandate for gender parity in athletics and university admissions system; however, the scope grew considerably through Supreme Court decisions and Department of Education guidance (Cyphert, 2018).

The act required that universities take action to prevent and process allegations of sexual harassment, assault, and abuse (Brodsky, 2018). The primary purpose of the act was to encourage educational institutions to stop sex discrimination by denying federal funding to those institutions that supported it (Novkov, 2016). Title IX requires that institutions of higher education provide safe and equitable learning environments for all students (Wood, Sulley, Kammer-Kerwick, Follingstad, & Busch-Armendariz, 2017). This emphasis on safe campuses requires a different approach to sexual assault than that taken in the larger community, which relies on the use of civil and criminal justice systems (Brubaker, 2018).

The Clery Act

As a supplement to Title IX, Congress passed and amended the Crime Awareness and Campus Security Act, commonly known as the Clery Act, in 1990 and 1992 (Novkov, 2016). The act required that campuses receiving federal financial aid address sexual violence, by making individuals reporting victimizations aware of their options to report the incident to law enforcement (Novkov, 2016). The Clery Act also required that campus staff disclose information on disciplinary processes and victims' rights to all students. Students reporting sexual assault must be made aware of available counseling services and have an option to change classes or living arrangements, to avoid the accused (Novkov, 2016). Campuses must maintain and publish annually records of all crimes reported to security and police, including acts of sexual violence. Similar to Title IX, the implementation of the Clery Act lies in the Department of Education. Accordingly, students bringing allegations of violations, must do so directly to the Department of Education.

Although Title IX and the Clery Act provide methods for addressing campus sexual assault and providing access to services for survivors, some advocates and scholars view the reforms as being insufficient (Novkov, 2016; Fisher, Hartman, Cullen, & Turner, 2003). Whereas the acts collectively provide significant monetary penalties for non-compliant universities, they did nothing to address the pressures that colleges and universities have in maintaining their public images (see Novkov, 2016 for a review). Response to concerns about institutional reputation emerged in two forms: the 2011 Dear Colleague Letter from the Department of Education and 2013 statutory reform.

The "Dear Colleague Letter"

Although Title IX is an educational policy, there are distinct criminal justice connections when we consider the impact it has had on the handling of sexual offenses on college campuses (Brubaker, 2018; Koss, Wilgus, & Williamson, 2014). The Department of Education's policy memorandum in 2011, commonly referred to as the "Dear Colleague Letter" (DCL), was sent out to the nation's approximately 4,600 institutions of higher education. The DCL clarified the Office of Civil Rights' intent in increasing enforcement efforts to address sexual violence and how failure to do so is a form of sex discrimination under Title IX (Novkov, 2016). The letter, which was intended as a guidance document for the Office for Civil Rights' enforcement directives under Title IX, defined sexual assault and included recognition that impairment of the victim renders her/him incapable of giving consent, and demanded that schools take immediate steps to end sexual violence (Koss et al., 2014; Novkov, 2016).

The stipulations in the letter also made clear that campuses could not simply rely on existing policies or shift responsibility for handling sexual assault cases to local law enforcement (Novkov, 2016). It also made explicit that mediation, even if done voluntarily, could not be used as a resolution in sexual assault cases (Cyphert, 2018). This restriction, some believe, is why many schools steered clear of instituting and developing restorative justice practices—though they are distinct from mediation (See Coker, 2016 for an overview). Lastly, the letter suggested that campuses and local law enforcement agencies take a coordinated effort to address sexual victimization, including efforts to enhance reporting, and improve the treatment of complainants (Koss et al., 2014).

The Department of Education guidelines and regulations required the services and accommodation that survivor-victims of sexual harassment and assault need to continue their education—including mental health services, academic support, housing changes, flexibility in scheduling courses, and keeping accused students and survivors apart (Brodsky, 2018, p. 135). These campus-specific approaches are seen as being distinct from the standard criminal justice approach of seeking evidence, determining criminal culpability, and prosecuting suspects (Brubaker, Keegan, Guadalupe-Diaz, & Beasley, 2017).

In comparing the Title IX approach to sexual assault with the traditional criminal justice response, Brubaker (2019) contends that there are many differences that exist across the two approaches. Rather than requiring proof beyond a reasonable doubt, Title IX requires only a preponderance of evidence (Harper et al., 2017; Konradi, 2017; Loschiavo & Waller, n.d.; Triplett, 2012). The investigation and adjudication of sexual assault incidents on campus is much shorter than that in the criminal justice system (Brubaker, 2018; Kaminer, 2014). Although there is an investigation and sometimes an adjudication hearing, there is no trial (Bennett, Gregory, Loschiavo, & Waller, 2014). Also, the most serious punishment that can be imposed via Title IX is expulsion, compared to potential jail or prison time in the criminal justice system (Bennett et al., 2014; Brubaker, 2018).

If survivor-victims or accused perpetrators believe that they were treated unfairly in the Title IX process, they may file civil complaints (Anderson, 2019). Students may file lawsuits in the federal courts or lodge complaints through the Department of Education's Office for Civil Rights. According to a recent exposé in *Inside Higher Ed*, some claims are for perceived unfair disciplinary sanctions, whereas others are related to perceived procedural failings at universities (Anderson, 2019). At public universities, where accused perpetrators have due process rights in Title IX proceedings, students can sue the universities for violations. Other accused perpetrators have made claims that the university's process is biased against them as men, thereby creating reverse gender discrimination claims.

Safe Campus Act

In 2013, two years after the "Dear Colleague Letter," Congress enacted the Campus Sexual Violence Act (CSVA) (Brodsky, 2018; Novkov, 2016). This legislative act, which updated the crime reporting requirements of the Clery Act, requires federally funded higher educational institutions to include information about the prevalence of sexual violence on their campuses and the policies that have been developed to address such victimizations. Schools must provide an overview of their efforts to promote awareness about sexual assault and outline the policies and procedures that will be followed in reported cases of sexual violence. The CSVA also requires schools to advise victims how to file a claim on campus, as well as how to decide whether or not to file a report through the criminal justice system. The act mandates that institutions advise survivor-victims that they will provide assistance, if s/he chooses to make an official report of the incident.

Universities that fail to comply with Title IX and the CVSA's standards can be held accountable. In 2014, The Office of Civil Rights published a list of higher education institutions with open Title IX investigations (Novkov, 2016; U.S. Department of Education, 2014). The initial report, which included all public and private colleges and universities under investigation for the handling of sexual assault cases, included 55 schools in total, ranging in size and geographic location. This public acknowledgment of problems in Title IX compliance represents an advance over the previous system of ignoring the problem; however, many institutions have expressed concern about the impact the listing may have on public relations and student recruitment.

Under the Title IX parameters, faculty and staff must report knowledge/disclosures of sexual assault to the school. Only confidential counselors do not have to report it. This has caused some feminists and legal scholars to question whether or not Title IX proceedings provide adequate victim protection (Brubaker, 2018). There has been a long-standing dialogue in the scholarly literature regarding Title IX and victim-survivor empowerment. Although it may seem like a solution to the historical neglect of campus sexual assault, mandatory referral laws may discourage survivors from reporting to schools, to avoid triggering a criminal investigation of the case. In Brodsky's terms (2018, p. 133), such policies "threaten rather than serve" sexual assault survivor-victims. Students might have a real interest in reporting to the university, so that they can attain counseling and/or housing changes, but avoid doing so, knowing the long-standing problems with survivor-victim treatment in the criminal justice system. This skepticism is also observed among some campus-based advocates. In her study of campus-based victim advocates, Brubaker (2019) found that whereas some advocates viewed Title IX negatively, in terms of issues with victim assistance and the harmful effects on marginalized communities, others believed the Title IX approach provided more options and supports for survivors than the traditional criminal justice approach.

Betsy DeVos's Withdrawal of the DCL and Proposed Changes to Title IX

On September 7, 2017, the Secretary of Education, Betsy DeVos, delivered comments that called into question the application of Title IX. In her description of campus sexual assault handlings since the 2011 Dear Colleague Letter (DCL), she used the terms "failed system" 13 times (Schneider, 2017). Many critics have emerged and refuted claims that DeVos made in her speech and have indicated that some of the sexual assault cases she referenced in her speech were not accurately portrayed. It is not within the purview of this chapter to provide an overview here, but interested readers can see an overview in Schneider (2017).

Dawn Beichner

Approximately two weeks following DeVos's speech, on September 22, 2017, the Department of Education withdrew the guiding DCL and the 2014 Q&A, which was created to help explain the DCL (Cyphert, 2018). At that same time, the Department of Education issued the 2017 Q&A, which was intended as an interim directive on the new approach for Title IX. Given the focus of this book, it is important to note that, in her term as Secretary of Education, Betsy DeVos revoked more than 20 sets of guidelines on anti-discrimination, including those that protected transgender students (Gersen, 2019). Moreover, in 2018, the Violence Against Women Act was not renewed. Many feminists, including the editors of this volume, view these gendered strikes as purposeful—and, in the case of Title IX, directed at giving more power to the accused than the accuser.

The newly-implemented 2017 Q&A document outlines 12 questions and answers related to Title IX coverage and complaints of sexual misconduct (Department of Education, 2017). It was introduced as a "new interim Q&A" to guide schools on the procedures for investigation and adjudication of campus sexual misconduct (US Department of Education News, 2017). Table 1 provides an overview of the questions. On November 29, 2018, DeVos unveiled her proposal to amend the regulation requirements of Title IX (Department of Education, 2018; Gersen, 2019). Opponents of DeVos's proposal point out that the proposal is a marked shift from the DCL in favor of the accused (Adams, 2018). It is important to acknowledge that restructuring to protect those accused of sexual assault perpetuates the myth that false allegations are common; empirical research on false allegations shows that only 2–10% of reported sexual assaults are false (EROC, 2019). There are fears that the changes will make schools unsafe (Gersen, 2019; North, 2018) and ignore claims from survivor-victims who are from historically and currently disenfranchised and minoritized groups (EROC, 2019). There are also concerns about what the changes mean for survivor-victims, given the decades of research that show how certain justice system practices traumatize and revictimize complainants.

Table 1. Questions from the September 2017 Department of Education "Q&A on Campus Sexual Misconduct"

What is the nature of a school's responsibility to address sexual misconduct?	After a Title IX complaint has been opened for investigation, may a school facilitate an informal resolution of the complaint?
What is the Clery Act and how does it relate to a school's obligations under Title IX?	What procedures should a school follow to adjudicate a finding of responsibility for sexual misconduct?
What are the interim measures and is a school required to provide such measures?	What procedures should a school follow to impose a disciplinary sanction against a student found responsible for a sexual misconduct violation?
What are the school's obligations with regard to complaints of sexual misconduct?	What information should be provided to the parties to notify them of the outcome?
What time frame constitutes a "prompt" investigation?	How may a school offer the right to appeal the decision on responsibility and/or any disciplinary decision?
What constitutes an "equitable" investigation?	In light of the rescission of the Office of Civil Rights' (OCR) 2011 Dear Colleague Letter and 2014 Questions and Answers guidance, are existing resolution agreements between OCR and schools still binding?

Definitionally, the changes redefine the definition of hostile environment. Rather than using the standard language of "conduct of a sexual nature...sufficiently severe or pervasive to alter the conditions" of the environment, the new definition replaced "severe or pervasive" with "severe, pervasive, and objectively offensive" (Gersen, 2019, p. 6). As opponents readily point out, this exclusionary definition is unacceptable and restricts the behaviors intended in the original definition, which included all unwelcome conduct of a sexual nature (Adams, 2018). The amended definition fails to ensure that campuses are free from sexual violence of all types and makes campuses less safe (North, 2018).

Among concerns generated about the guidelines is a change in the standard for establishing misconduct (Mangan, 2017). Under the 2011 DCL, colleges and universities were required to adopt a "preponderance of the evidence" standard, which meant that it was more likely that the misconduct occurred than not. With the 2017 guidelines, schools get to choose the standard that they use (Adams, 2018). They have the discretion to apply either the "preponderance" standard or the "clear and convincing evidence" standard, which is higher. Many opponents to the change believe that the more rigorous standard of proof is unwarranted and will dissuade survivor-victims from coming forward with claims.

Another significant departure between the 2011 DCL and the 2017 Q&A relates to the use of mediation (Cyphert, 2018; Mangan, 2017). Whereas the 2011 guidelines explicitly stated that mediation of sexual assault was not appropriate, even on a voluntary basis, the 2017 stipulations permit informal resolution processes, such as mediation, as long as all parties are informed of all other options for a formal resolution. The application of mediation or other informal resolutions are to be determined on a case-by-case basis. Critics of mediation believe that the practice produces a power imbalance, does not hold the perpetrator accountable, and makes the survivor-victim vulnerable to re-traumatization through the process. It also sets the stage for campus sexual assault to be swept under the rug (Saul & Taylor, 2017).

The timeframe for investigations is also different under the guidelines (Mangan, 2017). Instead of the 60-day limit imposed through the DCL in 2011, the 2017 guidelines provide no such limits for the investigation. Schools are bound to conduct a good-faith effort to complete the Title IX investigation in a timely manner. Opponents warn that delayed investigations may jeopardize the complainant's safety and well-being. Moreover, if the delays are consistent with those in criminal investigations, university proceedings may last more than a year.

The live-hearing requirement is different than the former system in which a hearing is not required. One of the most controversial aspects of the hearing is the provision for cross-examination (Gersen, 2019; Sarappo, 2018). This is controversial because of how traumatizing it can be for the survivor-victim to be questioned and challenged. Many opponents point to how this change of mimicking an adversarial trial may preclude survivor-victims from coming forward, so that they can avoid this experience. Victim advocates, among others, see the potential trauma and intimidation inherent in such a practice (Adams, 2018; Sarappo, 2018).

A final problem with the is that colleges and universities are only responsible for responding to sexual violence that occurs within their educational programs and activities (Gersen, 2019). Given the aforementioned prevalence of sexual assaults that occur off campus—in apartment buildings and fraternity houses—limiting the realm of coverage to ignore "off campus" sexual assault is highly problematic. There is also the possibility that religiously affiliated schools may invoke religious exemption, thereby putting lesbian, gay, bisexual, transgender, queer, intersex, and asexual students at risk (EROC, 2019). This, like many of the other with "so-called "reforms seem to be taking a step back in time in terms of progress. The previous guidelines made clear that schools were responsible for investigating all sexual assaults involving students (Adams, 2018; North, 2018). Moreover, because the DeVos-era reforms say that schools are legally responsible for investigating formal complaints only, meaning those that are made to an official who has the authority to institute corrective measures, many of the sexual assaults that are reported to someone other than staff in the Title IX office will be outside of the purview of responsibility (Adams, 2018).

A CALL FOR A RESTORATIVE, SURVIVOR-CENTERED, INTERSECTIONAL APPROACH

For many years, proponents of restorative justice have advocated for its use in sexual assault case processing and, more recently, in campus sexual assault. Novkov (2016), among others, advocates for restorative justice approaches to campus sexual assault, which shifts the focus from the individual to the structural factors that contribute to sexual assault. In its simplest form, restorative justice brings together all stakeholders in an event to collectively identify the harm that has been done and seek solutions for healing (Zehr, 2015). Implicit within restorative justice is the acknowledgement that the harm or wrongdoing extends beyond the survivor-victim and the perpetrator, to have ripple effects on both parties' loved ones and the community (Koss et al., 2014). Considered another way, although the damage caused by sexual assault is direct to the survivor-victim, the circle of damage includes friends and acquaintances of both parties (Kebodeaux, 2017; Novkov, 2016). As Novkov (2016) indicates, some sexual assault cases may make the university community "feel threatened, unwelcome, disrespected, or distrusted" (p. 615). Restorative justice practices work to address all the aforementioned harms.

Importantly, proponents of restorative justice practices make clear that the model does not preclude a survivor-victim from seeking a remedy in the criminal justice system. Ideally, restorative justice practices would be one of many remedies from which survivor-victims of campus sexual assault could choose (Cyphert, 2018; Novkov, 2016). The survivor-victim would be counseled on all the options available for the case: the on-campus restorative justice practice and the formal processing through the criminal justice system. If, after learning the details and processes available, a survivor-victim believes that the standard disciplinary proceedings—including the newly-proposed requisite hearing and cross-examination—would be re-traumatizing, then the survivor-victim could choose the restorative resolution.

Restorative Justice (RJ) as a reintegration process for campus sexual misconduct would take place after the responsible person completes his/her period of separation or suspension from the institution (Koss et al., 2014, p. 253). After the perpetrator fulfills the conditions of his/her sanction and takes all requisite actions to rejoin the campus community, he/she will be permitted to re-enroll in courses. At this stage, campus officials can facilitate a reintegration process that is consistent with the previously discussed circles of support, whereby the responsible party is assisted in seeking access to services and other items necessary for reintegration to the campus.

Restorative Justice Approaches for Sexual Assault

Koss and her colleagues (2014, pp. 247–248) provide an overview of four different restorative practices which have potential applications in campus sexual assault cases: Victim-offender dialogue, sentencing circles, circles of support and accountability, and conferencing. In victim-offender dialogue, which involves a face-to-face meeting between the survivor-victim and perpetrator, the survivor-victim sets the agenda for the meeting. S/he may seek acknowledgement for the crime, ask questions, and provide a statement of how the crime has impacted her/his life (Koss et al., 2014, p. 247).

Sentencing circles bring together the survivor-victim, the responsible person, friends, family members, community members, social service providers, and criminal justice officials (law enforcement officers, attorneys, and judges) to develop a plan of response for the wrongdoing (Koss et al., 2014, p. 247). Circles of support and accountability, which operate as auxiliary practices to the criminal justice process, may occur in many contexts, including when a responsible person has already completed her/his sentence and are returning to the community. These circles bring together key stakeholders in the responsible person's life, so that a formal support network can be formed to help the person acquire necessary resources. The approach also includes involvement of individuals who will provide bystander observation in situations in which the person faces high risks. Although acknowledgment of the survivor-victim and her/his need for healing is at the center of the practice, s/he does not have to be directly involved in the circle.

Conferencing, which incorporates elements of the other practices, involves consensual agreement of all impacted parties (i.e., the survivor-victim, responsible person, family, and friends) to convene for a meeting together, which is guided by a trained facilitator (Koss et al., 2014, p. 248). The agenda in the meeting includes the responsible person explaining the incident and taking responsibility for her/his actions, the survivor-victim detailing the harm that she/he suffered by the incident, followed by statements by the friends and family members in the conference. At the conclusion of the meeting, there is a written redress plan outlining how the responsible person will be held accountable for her/his actions, including remedies to the survivor-victim and the community. The plan is monitored to ensure that the responsible person fulfills the obligations outlined in the agreement.

As a resolution process, RJ requires that both the survivor-victim and the perpetrator enter into the resolution voluntarily. If the survivor-victim does not wish to attend a face-to-face meeting with the responsible party, s/he may identify a surrogate to attend on her/his behalf. Similar to the conferencing model explained previously, the RJ resolution would include an opportunity for the survivor/victim or surrogate to explain the impact of the incident on her/his life and a written redress model will be established and monitored through completion. In the campus model of RJ resolution, the student conduct professional—either the Title IX officer or the student misconduct officer—would serve as the facilitator and ensure compliance with the redress plan, which may include campus community service, reparations to the survivor-victim, counseling, and avoidance of classes or social events in which the survivor-victim will participate (Koss et al., 2014).

The RJ approach espoused by Koss and her colleagues (2014) requires that universities develop memorandums of understanding with local criminal justice personnel to articulate arrangements in how incidents will be handled. Special consideration must be given to keep the survivor-victims' interests at the center and share responsibility in eliminating sexual misconduct, preventing its recurrence, and addressing the harm that it produces in the campus and larger community. Although some campus administrators may be remiss in using RJ practices in criminal matters, it is important to recognize the potential benefits to students, including enhancing accountability. Cyphert (2018) believes that restorative practices must also incorporate exclusionary protections to alleged perpetrators, protecting their admissions of guilt from being used against them in later civil or criminal suits. The evidentiary exclusionary rule proposed by Cyphert (2018) is similar to those used in medical apologies and truth and reconciliation commissions.

Potential Benefits to Survivor-Victims

Although restorative practices have not yet been applied specifically to campus sexual assault, there have been applications to incidents of sexual assault among adults (Daly & Curtis-Fawley, 2005; Koss & Achilles, 2008; Madsen, 2004; Skelton & Batley, 2006). The limited research that has been conducted examining restorative justice approaches shows that there are many potential benefits to survivor-victims. For example, in a small study by Stubbs (2009, cited in Koss et al., 2014, p. 247), when given the choice, survivor-victims chose restorative justice practices over traditional responses. Another study, examining victims' participation in sentencing hearings, revealed that through participation in the sentencing hearing, survivor-victims felt that "they had moved beyond the rape in some emotional way" (Konradi, 2010, p. 52). Positive effects also emerged in findings from a post-conference survey of participants, including survivor-victims; the survey revealed that over 90% of participants felt supported, treated with respect, and believed the conference was a success (Koss, 2014). RJ approaches may be used as an alternative to the criminal justice approach or in addition to it (McGlynn et al., 2012). Because the focus is victim-survivor centered, RJ provides an advance over the current approach, which centers on the perpetrator and his/her conviction, punishment, and imprisonment (Kebodeaux, 2017). The power in the situation is redistributed so that the survivor-victim has a say in what happens and can ask the offender specific questions about the impact his/her actions have had.

The Need for an Intersectional Approach: Recognizing All Survivor-Victims and Affording Due Process to All Accused Perpetrators

Strategies to address campus sexual assault must move away from enhanced lighting on walkways, blue-light emergency phones, and self-defense classes. Instead, consistent with the proposal of the United Nations Women (2019), campuses must adopt strategies to educate members of the campus and larger community about harmful masculinity and gender stereotypes. Intervention strategies to end campus sexual assault must promote respectful, healthy relationships among students and recognize violent behavior (UN Women, 2019).

The individuals who are entrusted to be first-responders to survivor-victims of campus sexual assault must be trained in methods that do not produce further harm. For example, Illinois passed the Preventing Sexual Violence in Higher Education Act in 2015, which requires that campus personnel are trained on the neurobiological effects of trauma (Yoffe, 2017). Other states have considered or are considering similar legislation. There is a National Center for Campus Public Safety that was established in 2013, funded by a grant from the US Department of

Justice and the Bureau of Justice Assistance, which provides educational resources for campus administrators that espouses a trauma-informed approach (NCCPS, 2019).

The United Nations Women (2019) report on addressing campus violence calls for a human rights-based approach, which considers the needs of all victim-survivors, including individuals who are facing multiple forms of bias and discrimination. Many individuals on college campuses face multiple forms of discrimination and bias related to their physical disabilities, race, ethnicity, sexual orientation, and gender identity. Campus programming and services must be designed to be inclusive of all victim-survivors.

It is also essential that we have support staff available with whom students can identify. The campus staff serving survivor-victims must be diverse, look like, and be relatable to the students whom they serve (Jozkowski & Wiersma-Mosley, 2017). Without these purposeful measures in place, campus staff will not be poised to see privilege-based biases in the ways that they make decisions. Without purposeful intersectional[14] methods, some survivor-victims may be recognized, but not others. Moreover, some alleged perpetrators may be singled out or treated more harshly than alleged perpetrators from other privileged groups.

It is critical that the strategies to end campus sexual assault operate from a position of recognizing implicit and institutionalized bias and discrimination. Privileging and biasing systems have been in existence for so long, that many architects of change do not see them or acknowledge them. For example, in the documentary *The Hunting Ground*, which has been instrumental in affecting change and bringing national attention to the problems inherent in campus sexual assault, the only accused rapist who is featured in the film is an African American man—Jameis Wilson of Florida State University—who allegedly assaulted a White woman. Inter-racial sexual assault is not common. The United States' focus on it and the inherent racism that underlies it, however, has been a historical constant. Efforts to address sexual victimization on campus—including those that are centered on educating the masses—should not contribute to existing marginalization or criminalization of some groups of students.

CONCLUSION: CONSIDERING THE FUTURE OF CAMPUS SEXUAL ASSAULT

This chapter has provided a comprehensive overview of the problems associated with campus sexual assault, including the problematic "reforms" made by Department of Education Secretary, Betsy DeVos, that changed the way Title IX functions on college and university campuses. The level of attention being paid right now to sexual assault and specifically campus sexual assault hearkens back to the 1970s, when activists like Representative Holtzman, among others, were demanding what became the most vast and sweeping change to rape laws this country had ever witnessed. For all of the reasons presented here, there is no doubt that this era will be remembered as essential to campus sexual assault reform—it is not yet known whether the record will reflect a time of instrumental, lasting change or one in which "reform" efforts set the country back a half of a century by reinstituting a system that protects the accused—read privileged White male—and makes no attempt at trauma-informed strategies. At present, there are a number of large universities, including Ohio State, the University of California, and Michigan State, that are accused of failing to protect students from sexual misconduct and covering up the behaviors of the accused (Adams, 2018). Without purposeful action, there will be additional collateral damages to sexual assault survivor-victims from the changes made to Title IX during the Trump administration.

To this end, it appears that restorative justice (RJ), whether used alone or in conjunction with traditional criminal justice methods, provides a potential advance to current campus sexual assault responses. Although restorative justice practices are not without criticism (see for example McGlynn, Westmarland, & Godden, 2012; Daly & Nancarrow, 2010), RJ presents a number of advantages over current practices. As this chapter makes clear, the present approach to campus sexual assault is rife with problems. There is case attrition, due in part to underreporting by victims, but also by founding decisions by law enforcement officers and charging decisions by prosecutors (for an overview see Beichner & Spohn, 2012; see also Holleran, Beichner, & Spohn, 2010). Survivor-victims' interactions with criminal justice officials often involve victim blaming, and few cases result in guilty pleas. Also, in cases like that involving Brock Turner, light sentences send the message that rapists can get away with only a slap on the wrist (Kebodeaux, 2017). RJ proponents believe that instituting RJ approaches to sexual assault may reduce victim-blaming, offer more validation and empowerment to victims, and present an additional opportunity for justice in the incident (Kebodeaux, 2017; McGlynn et al., 2012). When done correctly, restorative justice teaches offenders that what they did was wrong and has impacts on the victim-survivor and others. The RJ approach also redirects the focus from the state as the harmed entity to the survivor-victim, thereby giving voice back to her/him (Kebodeaux, 2017). Research suggests that strategies that use such a centered-approach encourage individuals to report their victimizations (Brubaker, 2009; Richards, Branch, Fleury-Steiner, & Kafonek, 2017; Walsh, Banyard, Moynihan, Ward, & Cohn, 2010).

Research indicates that survivor-victims' wishes are often in opposition to the requirements in formal legal proceedings (Herman, 2005). Other findings indicate that survivor-victims' lack of confidence in the justice process is related to their perceptions of being denied a voice in the proceedings and not having an active role in the proceedings (Jülich, 2006). Through restorative justice approaches to sexual assault, survivor-victims are empowered. Those who select RJ are given an opportunity to tell their stories how they choose to do so and in a safe space, both of which leads to empowerment (Herman, 2005; Hudson, 2002; Jülich, 2006). This can be critical to survivor-victims, who have been victimized and disempowered by their perpetrators.

Another potential benefit of the restorative justice approach to sexual assault is that the offender is required to acknowledge his/her actions, which is not part of most criminal justice or quasi-criminal justice proceedings. Research indicates that the offender's acknowledgement of guilt may be more significant to survivor-victims than the actual punishment itself (Konradi, 2010). As Hopkins and

Koss (2005) point out, restorative justice practices that initiate some consequence on offenders may also help to increase community understanding of sexual assault and encourage more survivor-victims to report their victimizations. Not only does RJ provide some therapeutic benefit to survivor-victims who recount and work through their victimizations, it also contributes to an overall sense of justice in the incident (McGlynn, 2011). Considered together, restorative justice could carry out the traditional elements of the justice process—retribution, reintegration, individual protection, and societal protection—in a more effective way than the existing system (Hudson, 2002).

The use of restorative justice also offsets the influence of economic resources of wealthy male students hiring attorneys to help them circumvent justice (Konradi, 2017; Jozkowski & Wiersma-Mosley, 2017). Because this remedy can exist without adjudication in the criminal justice system, it is available to all people, irrespective of their individual financial circumstances. Also, of critical importance to campus sexual assault, RJ takes into account what other elements in the environment played a role. For example, this expansive view of campus sexual assault would examine the role of fraternities and university athletics, which are often in the backdrop of these victimizations. Accordingly, RJ-based remedies in this community- and campus-based approach would examine fraternity culture and athlete culture to target sexual assault prevention efforts toward these groups. For fraternities, it would also require that campus administrators explore how to hold national fraternity offices accountable and how to stop fraternities from manipulating charter arrangements or taking other actions to evade legal liability (Novkov, 2016, p. 618). For athletics, special attention would be made to prevent the intimidation tactics that are often used against complainants who bring accusations against athletes. Considered together, these efforts represent an attempt to build a campus environment and community that facilitate healthy and egalitarian sexual relationships (Novkov, 2016). Because universities have a duty to their communities to prevent a culture of sexual violence and to ensure that student groups and athletic teams reject sexual assault, restorative justice can be quite effective.

REFERENCES

Anderson, G. (2019, October 3). More Title IX lawsuits by accusers and accused. *Inside Higher Ed*. Retrieved from https://www.insidehighered.com/news/2019/10/03/students-look-federal-courts-challenge-title-ix-proceedings

Bannon, R. S., Brosi, M. W., & Foubert, J. D. (2013). Sorority women's and fraternity men's rape myth acceptance and bystander intervention attitudes. *Journal of Student Affairs Research and Practice, 50*, 72–87.

Beichner, D. (2015). Rape/sexual assault as crime. In G. Ritzer (Ed.), *The encyclopedia of sociology* (2nd Ed.). Wiley-Blackwell.

Beichner, D. & Spohn, C. (2012). Modeling the effects of victim behavior and moral character on prosecutors' charging decisions in sexual assault cases. *Violence and Victims, 27*(1), 3–24.

Bennett, L., Gregory, D. M., Loschiavo, C., & Waller, J. (2014). Student conduct administration & Title IX: Gold standard practices for resolution of allegations of sexual misconduct on college campuses. College Station, TX: Association of Student Conduct Administrators.

Boyle, K. M. (2015). Social psychological processes that facilitate sexual assault within the fraternity party subculture. *Sociological Compass, 9*, 386–399.

Boyle, K. M., & Walker, L. S. (2016). The neutralization and denial of sexual violence in college party subcultures. *Deviant Behavior, 37*(12), 1392–1410. https://doi.org/10.1080/01639625.2016.1185862

Brubaker, S. J. (2009). Sexual assault prevalence, reporting, and policies: Comparing college and university campuses and military service academies. *The Security Journal, 22*, 56–72.

Brubaker, S. J. (2018). Campus-based sexual assault victim advocacy and Title IX: Revisiting tensions between grassroots activism and the criminal justice system. *Feminist Criminology, 14*(3), 307–329.

Brubaker, S. J., Keegan, B., Guadalupe-Diaz, X. L., & Beasley, B. A. (2017). Measuring and reporting campus sexual assault: Privilege and exclusion in what we know and what we do. *Sociology Compass, 11*(12), e12543.

Bureau of Justice Statistics (2014). Rape and sexual assault higher among college-age nonstudent females than female college students in 1995. Retrieved from https://www.bjs.gov/content/pub/press/rsavcaf9513pr.cfm

Canan, S. N., Jozkowski, K. N., & Crawford, B. L. (2016). Sexual assault supportive attitudes: An analysis of rape myth acceptance and token resistance in Greek and non-Greek college students from two university samples. *Journal of Interpersonal Violence, 33*, 1–29.

Cantor, D., Fisher, B., Chilbnall, S., Harps, S., Townsend, R., Thomas, G., Lee, H., Kranz, V., Herbison, R., & Madden, K. (2019). Report on the AAU climate survey on sexual assault and sexual misconduct. Retrieved from https://www.aau.edu/key-issues/campus-climate-and-safety/aau-campus-climate-survey-2019

Chang, C. (2014). Separate but unequal in college Greek life. Century Foundation. Retrieved from http://www.tcf.org/work/education/detail/separate-but-unequal-in-college-greek-life

Cleary, T. (2016, June 6). Judge Aaron Persky: 5 fast facts you need to know. Heavy News. Retrieved from http://heavy.com/news/2016/06/aaron-persky-brock-turner-judge-standford-recall-petition-election-photos-sentence

Coker, D. K. (2016). Crime logic, campus sexual assault, and restorative justice. *Texas Tech Law Review, 49*, 147.

Coker, A. L., Follingstad, D. R., Bush, H. M., & Fisher, B. S. (2016). Are interpersonal violence rates higher among young women in college compared with those never attending college? *Journal of Interpersonal Violence, 31*(8), 1413–1429. doi:10.1177/0886260514567958

Collins, P. H. (2000). Gender, black feminism, and black political economy. *Annals of the American Academy, 568*, 41–53.

Crenshaw, K. (1989). Demarginalizing the intersection of race and sex: A black feminist critique of antidiscrimination doctrine, feminist theory and antiracist politics. *The University of Chicago Legal Forum*, 139–167.

Crenshaw, K. (1991). Mapping the margins: Intersectionality, identity politics, and violence against women of color. *Stanford Law Review, 43*(6), 1241–1299.

Crosset, T. W. (2016). Athletes, sexual assault, and universities' failure to address rape-prone subcultures on campus. In S. C. Wooten & R. W. Mitchell (Eds.), *The crisis of campus sexual violence: Critical perspectives on prevention and response* (pp. 74–92). Routledge.

Cyphert, A. B. (2018). The devil is in the details: Exploring restorative justice as an option for campus sexual assault responses under Title IX. *Denver Law Review, 96*(1), 51–85.

Daly, M. (2014, October 3). The math that keeps helping college rapists. Daily Beast. Retrieved from http://www.thedailybeast.com/articles/2014/10/03/the-math-that-keeps-helping-college-rapists.html

Daly, K. & Curtis-Fawley, S. (2005). Restorative justice for victim-survivors of sexual assault. In K. Heimer & C. Kruttschnitt (Eds.), *Gender and crime: Patterns of victimization and offending* (pp. 230–260). New York University Press.

Daly, K., & Nancarrow, H. (2010). Restorative justice and youth violence toward parents. In J. Ptacek. (Ed.), *Restorative justice and violence against women* (pp. 150–174). Oxford University Press.

DeKeseredy, W. S. & Schwartz, M. D. (1998). *Woman abuse on campus: Results from the Canadian national survey.* Sage.

DeMatteo, D., Galloway, M., Arnold, S., & Patel, U. (2015). Sexual assault on college campuses: A 50-state survey of criminal sexual assault statuses and their relevance to campus sexual assault. *Psychology, Public Policy & Law, 21*, 227–238.

Department of Education. (2017). Q&A on campus sexual misconduct. Retrieved from https://www2.ed.gov/about/offices/list/ocr/docs/qa-title-ix-201709.pdf

Department of Education. (2018). Nondiscrimination on the basis of sex in education programming or activities receiving federal financial assistance: A proposed rule by the education department. Retrieved from https://www.federalregister.govdocuments/2018/11/29/2018-25314/nondiscrimination-on-the-basis-of-sex-in-education-programs-or-activities-receiving-federal

Dick, K., Ziering, A., Herdy, A., Scully, R. K., Blavin, P., Wadleigh, T., Kopp, A., (2015). *The hunting ground.* United States: Minerva Productions.

End Rape on Campus. (2019). End rape on campus comment on Devos' Title IX rule. Retrieved from https://endrapeoncampus.org/new-blog/2019/1/30/end-rape-on-campus-comment-on-devos-title-ix-rule

End Rape on Campus. (2019). LGBTQ pride. Retrieved from ttps://endrapeoncampus.org/lgbtq-pride-blog

Fisher, B. S., Hartman, J. L., Cullen, F. T., & Turner, M.G. (2003). Making campuses safer for students: The Clery Act as a symbolic legal reform. *Stetson Law Review, 32*(1), 61–90.

Galvin, H. (1986). Shielding rape victims in the state and federal courts: A proposal for the second decade. *Minnesota Law Review, 70*, 763–916.

Harper, S., Maskaly J., Kirkner A., & Lorenz K. (2017). Enhancing Title IX due process standards in campus sexual assault adjudication: Considering the roles of distributive, procedural, and restorative justice. *Journal of School Violence, 16*, 302–316.

Herman, J. L. (2005). Justice from the victim's perspective. *Violence Against Women, 11*(5), 571–602.

Holleran, D., Beichner, D., & Spohn, C. (2010). Modeling the charging decision between police and prosecutors in rape cases. *Crime & Delinquency, 56* (3), 365–413.

Hopkins, C. Q. & Koss, M. K. (2005). Incorporating feminist theory and insights into a restorative justice response to sex offenses. *Violence Against Women, 11*(5), 693–723.

Hudson, B. (2002). Restorative justice and gendered violence—diversion or effective justice? *British Journal of Criminology, 42*(3), 616–634.

Human Rights Campaign. (2019). Sexual assault and the LGBT community. Retrieved from https://www.hrc.org/resources/sexual-assault-and-the-lgbt-community

Jozkowski, K. N. & Wiersma-Mosley, J. D. (2017). The Greek system: How gender inequality and class privilege perpetuate rape culture. *Family Relations, 66*(1), 89–103.

Jülich, S. (2006). Views of justice among survivors of historical child sexual abuse – implications for restorative justice in New Zealand. *Theoretical Criminology, 10*(1), 125–138.

Kaminer, A. (2014, November 19). New factor in campus sexual assault cases: Counsel for the accused. *New York Times*. Retrieved from https://www.nytimes.com/2014/11/20/nyregion/new-factor-in-campus-sexual-assault-cases-counsel-for-the-accused.html?_r+0

Karp, D. R., Shackford-Bradley, J., Wilson, R. J., Williamsen, K. M., Llewellyn, J. J., Kallem, H., & Koss, M. P. (2016). Campus PRISM: A report on promoting restorative justice initiatives for sexual misconduct on college campuses. Saratoga Springs, NY: Skidmore College Project on Restorative Justice.

Kebodeaux, C. (2017). Rape sentencing: We're all mad about Brock Turner, but now what? *Kansas Journal of Law & Public Policy, 27*(1), 30–47.

Kingkade, T. (2015, August 4). Fraternity groups push bills to limit college rape investigations. *Huffington Post*. Retrieved from http://www.huffingtonpost.com/entry/fraternity-groups-college-rape_us_55c10396e4b0e716be074a7f

Konradi, A. (2010). Creating victim-centered criminal justice practices for rape prosecution. In S.L. Burns & M. Peyrot (Eds.), *New approaches to social problems treatment* (pp. 43–76). Emerald Group.

Konradi, A. (2017). Can justice be served on campus? An examination of due process and victim protection policies in the campus adjudication of sexual assault in Maryland. *Humanity & Society, 41*(3), 373–404.

Koss, M. P. (2014). The RESTORE program of restorative justice for sex crimes: Vision, process, and outcomes. *Journal of Interpersonal Violence, 24*, 1623–1660.

Koss, M. P. & Achilles, M. (2008). Restorative justice responses to sexual assault. Retrieved from www.vawanet.org/Assoc_Files_VAWnet/AR_RestorativeJustice.pdf

Koss, M. P., Wilgus, J. K., & Williamsen, K. M. (2014). Campus sexual misconduct: Restorative justice approaches to enhance compliance with Title IX guidance. *Trauma, Violence, & Abuse, 15*, 242–257.

Lasky, N. V., Fisher, B. S., Henriksen, C. B., & Swan, S.C. (2017). Binge drinking, Greek life membership, and first-year undergraduates: The "perfect storm" for drugging victimization. *Journal of School Violence, 16*(2), 173–188.

Loschiavo, C. & Waller, J. (n.d.). The preponderance of evidence standard: Use in higher education campus conduct processes. Association for Student Conduct Administration. Retrieved from http://www.theasca.org/files/The%20Preponderance%20of%20Evidence%20Standard.pdf

Madsen, K. S. (2004). Mediation as a way of empowering women exposed to sexual coercion. *NORA-Nordic Journal of Women's Studies, 12*(1), 58–61.

Mangan, K. (2017, September 22). What you need to know about the new guidance on Title IX. *The Chronicle of Higher Education*. Retrieved from https://www.chronicle.com/article/What-You-Need-to-Know-About/241277

Martin, P. Y. (2016). The rape prone culture of academic contexts of fraternities and athletics. *Gender & Society, 30*, 30–43.

McGlynn, C. (2011). Feminism, rape and the search for justice. *Oxford Journal of Legal Studies, 31*, 825–842.

McGlynn, C., Westmarland, N., & Godden, N. (2012). "I just wanted him to hear me": Sexual violence and the possibilities of restorative justice. *Journal of Law and Society, 39*, 213–240.

Minow, J. C., & Einolf, C. J. (2009). Sorority participation and sexual assault risk. *Violence Against Women, 15*, 835–851.

National Center for Campus Public Safety. (2019). Retrieved from https://www.nccpsafety.org/

National Center for Transgender Equality. (2019). 2015 U.S. Transgender Survey. Retrieved from: http://www.ustranssurvey.org/

New, J. (2015). A common sign. *Inside Higher Ed.* Retrieved from: https://www.insidehighered.com/news/2015/08/28/sexist-banners-old-dominion-point-practice-many-campuses

North, A. (2018, November 16). 'This will make schools less safe': Why Betsy DeVos's sexual assault rules have advocates worried. Vox. Retrieved from https://www.vox.com/policy-and-politics/2018/11/16/18096736/betsy-devos-sexual-assault-harassment-title-ix

North American Interfraternity Council (2018). NIC fraternities ban hard alcohol in decisive action. Retrieved from https://nicfraternity.org/nic-fraternities-vote-to-ban-hard-alcohol/

Novkov, J. (2016). Equality, process, and campus sexual assault. *Maryland Law Review, 75*, 590–619.

RAINN. (2019). Campus sexual violence: Statistics. Retrieved from https://www.rainn.org/statistics/campus-sexual-violence

Rotuno-Johnson, M. (2016). Sexually-explicit banner at off-campus house prompts Ohio state university response. NBC. Retrieved from: https://www.nbc4i.com/news/sexually-explicit-banner-at-off-campus-house-prompts-ohio-state-university-response/

Sarappo, E. (2018, November 16). Betsy Devos wants to overhaul Title IX procedures. What will that mean for campus assault survivors? Pacific Standard. Retrieved from https://psmag.com/education/betsy-devos-wants-to-overhaul-title-ix-procedures-what-will-that-mean-for-campus-assault-survivors

Saucier, S. (2017). Misogynist banners at UMaine underscore a lack of support for women on campus. Beacon. Retrieved from https://mainebeacon.com/misogynist-banners-at-umaine-underscore-a-lack-of-support-for-women-on-campus/

Saul, S. & Taylor, K. (2017, September 22). Betsy Devos reverses Obama-era policy on campus sexual assault investigations. *New York Times.* Retrieved from https://www.nytimes.com/2017/09/22/us/devos-colleges-sex-assault.html

Schneider, S. (2017, September 11). What DeVos got wrong in her speech on the 'dear colleague' letter. *Chronicle of Higher Education.* Retrieved from https://www.chronicle.com/article/What-DeVos-Got-Wrong-in-Her/241145

Students Ending Rape Culture. (2018). 2018 proposed changes to Title IX: A guide to understanding from students ending rape culture (SERC). Retrieved from https://endrapeoncampus.org/new-blog/2019/1/30/end-rape-on-campus-comment-on-devos-title-ix-rule

Skelton, A. and Batley, M. (2006). Charting progress, mapping the future: Restorative justice in South Africa. Pretoria, South Africa: Institute for Security Studies.

Swan, S. C., Lasky, N. V., Fisher, B. S., Woodbrown, V. D., Bonsu, J. E., Schramm, A. T. (2016). Just a dare or unaware? Outcomes and motives of drugging ("drink spiking") among students at three college campuses. *Psychology of Violence, 7*(2), 253.

Stannard, E. (January 19, 2018). Expulsion not always the punishment for campus sexual assault. *New Haven Register*. Retrieved from https://www.nhregister.com/news/article/Expulsion-not-al-ways-the-punishment-for-campus-12531199.php

Stubbs, J. (2009). Meanings of justice: Sexual assault and the appeal to restorative justice. Australian & New Zealand Society of Criminology Conference, University of Western Australia, Perth, Australia.

Title IX 20 U.S.C. §§ 1681-1688 (2012).

Tolman, D. L. (2006). In a different position: Conceptualizing female adolescent sexuality development within compulsory heterosexuality. *New Directions for Child and Adolescent Development, 112*, 71–89.

Triplett, M. R. (2012). Sexual assault on college campuses: Seeking the appropriate balance between due process and victim protection. *Duke Law Journal, 62*, 487–527.

United Nations Women (2019). Guidance note on campus violence prevention and response. New York City, NY: UN Women. Retrieved from http://www.unwomen.org/-/media/headquarters/attachments/sections/library/publications/2019/campus-violece%note_guiding_principles.pdf?la=en&vs=3710

U.S. Department of Education (2014). Press Release. U.S. department of education releases list of higher education institutions with open Title IX sexual violence investigations. Retrieved from http://www.ed.gov/news/press-releases/us-department-education-releases-list-higher-education-institutions-open-title-ix-sexual-violence-investigations.

U.S. Department of Education (2017). Press Release. Department of education issues new interim guidance on campus sexual misconduct. Retrieved from https://www.ed.gov/news/press-releases/department-education-issues-new-interim-guidance-campus-sexual-misconduct

Walsh, W. A., Banyard, V. L., Moynihan, M. M., Ward, S., & Cohn, E. S. (2010). Disclosure and service use on a college campus after an unwanted sexual experience. *Journal of Trauma & Dissociation, 11*, 134–151.

Women's Law Project. (2018, December 17). WLP analysis of the proposed Title IX regulations & invitation for you to submit comment. Retrieved from https://www.womenslawproject.org/2018/12/17/wlp-analysis-of-the-proposed-title-ix-regulations-invitation-for-you-to-submit comment/?fbclid=IwAR1QCaDkHFnHEXFUYEI rekAx8-mcGOzOAzIaXUFNbxBUyh7fktpf-wRLLXdU

Wood, L., Sulley, C., Kammer-Kerwick, M., Follingstad, D., & Busch-Armendariz, N. (2017). Climate surveys: An inventory of understanding sexual assault and other crimes of interpersonal violence at institutions of higher education. *Violence Against Women, 23*, 1249–1267.

Wooten, S. C. (2016). Heterosexist discourses: How feminist theory shaped campus sexual violence policy. In S. C. Wooten & R. W. Mitchell (Eds.), *The crisis of campus sexual violence: Critical perspectives on prevention and response* (pp. 33–51). Routledge.

Yoffe, E. (2017). The bad science behind campus response to sexual assault. *The Atlantic*. Retrieved from https://www.theatlantic.com/education/archive/2017/09/the-bad-science-behind-campus-response-to-sexual-assault/539211/

Zehr, H. (2015). *The little book of restorative justice*. Revised and updated. Simon and Schuster.

Dawn Beichner
Illinois State University

FOOTNOTES

12. The author uses the term "survivor-victim" to offset the potentially derogatory connotations of the term victim. In her experiences working with women who have experienced trauma and abuse, several identify more with the term "survivor" than the term "victim."

13. Due to a number of hazing-related and binge-drinking deaths, the North-American Interfraternity Conference enacted a hard alcohol ban prohibiting the use of alcohol products about 15% by volume, which began implementation on September 1, 2019 (North-American Interfraternity Conference, 2018). Fraternities were tasked with adopting, implementing, and enforcing policies that limit alcohol not served by an outside licensed vendor to beer, malt liquor, wine and other products that meet the proscribed limit.

14. Intersectionality refers to the intersectionality theoretical perspectives developed by Crenshaw (1989, 1991) and later expanded by Collins (2000). The theory explains how social identities, at both the micro-level (race, ethnicity, gender identity, sexual orientation) and the macro-level (socio-economic status, poverty) overlap and create unique experiences for women.

About the Authors

Emily Bailin Wells holds an Ed.D. in Communication & Education from Teachers College at Columbia University. Her interests lie at the intersections of gender, race, and class; youth multimodal literacies practices and media literacy education; and storytelling as a means of socially just pedagogies. Emily's research is situated at the intersection of gender and communication studies. More specifically, she examines how notions of "girls" and "girlhood" are constructed through the images and messages of an institution and, in turn, how students take up, question, reject, and/or redefine these representations as a form of agency and action. Emily is an adjunct assistant professor at Teachers College, Columbia University and New York University.

Thomas W. Bean, Ph.D., is the Roseanne Keely Norris Professor of Literacy and Graduate Program Director in the Department of Teaching and Learning, Darden College of Education and Professional Studies, Old Dominion University. Tom's research is centered on content area literacy, critical literacy, and global young adult literature in the classroom. Dr. Bean is considered a leading scholar in content area literacy. He is the co-author of 15 books, 23 book chapters, and over 100 journal articles. He may be contacted at tbean@odu.edu.

Dawn Beichner, Ph.D., is a professor in the Criminal Justice Sciences Department and Women's and Gender Studies Program at Illinois State University. Her research interests include victimology, women offenders in the criminal justice system, and prisoner re-entry. Her current research centers on incarcerated mothers and the role of family reunification in women's successful re-entry into society. She is a member of the executive committee of the World Society of Victimology, an international nongovernmental organization with Special Category consultative status with the Economic and Social Council of the United Nations and the Council of Europe.

E. Mikulec, D. Beichner (eds.), Distraction: Girls, School, and Sexuality, 191-195.
© *2021 DIO Press, Inc. All rights reserved.*

Brianna Boehlke is an undergraduate student at the University of Mount Union, where she is majoring in history with minors in Adolescent to Young Adult Education and Gender Studies. She is the former research assistant of Dr. Jennifer Martin. She is the Vice President of Philanthropy for Delta Sigma Tau, the saxophone section leader in the marching band, a member of the music honorary Kappa Kappa Psi, and a member of the education honorary Kappa Delta Pi. She was honored with the Alliance YMCA's Volunteer of the Year award for 2017–2018, and she was the recipient of the Martin Luther King Jr. Award for her work in social justice at the University of Mount Union in 2018. She has presented at various international conferences, such as the International Association of Research on Service Learning and Community Engagement and the Race and Pedagogy Institute. Ms. Boehlke may be reached at boehlkebri@gmail.com.

Courtney Cepec is an undergraduate student at the University of Mount Union majoring in English and minoring in Writing and Adolescent Young Adult Education, and a former research assistant of Dr. Jennifer Martin. She is president of her Kappa Delta Pi chapter, Omega Iota, which is a national education honorary on her campus. She has presented nationally three times at Kappa Delta Pi convocation in Indianapolis, Indiana in November of 2018, and has presented internationally at the Race & Pedagogy Institute in Tacoma, Washington in September of 2018. Courtney plans to pursue a career in the field of education with hopes of working in an urban environment. Ms. Cepec can be reached at ctcepec@gmail.com.

Cara Crandall, currently a middle school English teacher in Longmeadow, Massachusetts, has taught in a variety of school settings and grade levels. Cara taught at the collegiate level for seven years and served for two years as Emerson College's Director of First-Year Writing. She has continued to teach at the university-level as an adjunct at Westfield State University and Springfield College, where she continued works that she had begun in Boston preparing new teachers for the professional work of the classroom. Cara's research interests center on gender; power relations; and analyzing the personal, societal, and ideological functions of narrative. Cara has a chapter forthcoming in This Ground Covered: Opportunities and Challenges in Holocaust and Social Justice Education Lessons from Teachers in the Memorial Library Summer Seminars as well as articles and chapters in *Teaching/Writing: The Journal of Writing Teacher Education* and *Teaching Towards Democracy with Postmodern and Popular Culture Texts*.

Judith Dunkerly-Bean, Ph.D., is an Associate Professor of Literacy, Language and Culture and Co-Director of the Literacy Research and Development Center in the Department of Teaching and Learning, Darden College of Education and Professional Studies at Old Dominion University. Judith's research utilizes transnational feminist and cosmopolitan theory to explore the intersection of critical literacy, social justice and human rights. Her work has been published in the *Journal of Literacy Research*, the *Journal of Adolescent and Adult Literacy*, *Comparative Issues in Education* and *Language and Literacy*, as well as in several edited volumes and handbooks. She is the co-author of *Teaching Young Adult Literature: Developing Students as World Citizens*. She may be contacted at jdunkerl@odu.edu.

Abiola Farinde-Wu is an Assistant Professor of urban education in the Department of Leadership in Education at the University of Massachusetts Boston. Her research examines the educational experiences and outcomes of Black women and girls. Highlighting how racial, social, and cultural issues impact the educational opportunities and treatment of Black women and girls, she investigates policies, structures, and practices that influence the recruitment, matriculation, and retention of this particular group. Complementing her research, her teaching and service focus on preparing pre-service and in-service teachers for diverse student populations. Farinde-Wu has authored and co-authored numerous studies published in journals, including *Urban Education, Urban Review*, and *Teaching and Teacher Education*. She is also a co-editor of *Black Female Teachers: Diversifying the United States' Teacher Workforce* (Emerald, 2017). She can be reached at abiola. farinde@umb.edu.

DaVonna L. Graham is a third-year doctoral student in the Department of Instruction and Learning at the University of Pittsburgh and serves as a graduate research and teaching associate in the Center for Urban Education. Her research interests include learning Black teachers' perspectives on race talk with students and positive racial identity development. She can be reached at DLG76@pitt.edu.

Heidi L. Hallman is a Professor in the department of Curriculum and Teaching at the University of Kansas. Her research interests include studying "at risk" students' literacy learning as well as how prospective English teachers are prepared to teach in diverse school contexts. Dr. Hallman is co-author of *Secondary English Teacher Education in the United States* (Bloomsbury, 2018) and *Reconceptualizing Curriculum, Literacy and Learning for School-age Mothers* (Routledge, 2019), as well as author of several journal articles and book chapters. At the University of Kansas Dr. Hallman teaches undergraduate and graduate courses in teacher education.

Stephanie Jones-Fosu is a second-year doctoral student in Curriculum and Instruction for Urban Education at the University of North Carolina at Charlotte. She attended Morgan State University where she received a B.A. in Political Science. She then earned her M.A. in Education and Human Development at George Washington University. Stephanie has taught middle and high school social students for nine years. She has also coached over 100 first- and second-year teachers through a non-traditional teaching organization. She is currently a research assistant and Holmes Scholar, writing and presenting nationally and internationally on her research. She has several publications under review with *Journal of Equity and Excellence in Education, Journal of African American Males in Education*, and *Multicultural Education Journal*. Her research interests include preservice, teacher preparation, and evaluation with an emphasis on culturally sustainable pedagogy. She can be reached at sjonesfo@uncc.edu.

Tülay Kaya, Ph.D., is an Assistant Professor of the Department of Sociology, Istanbul University. She received her Master's and Ph.D. degrees in the field of sociology from Istanbul University in 2005 and 2011, respectively. After receiving her Ph.D., she expanded her research interests to the sociology of education and visited Pennsylvania State University, Department of Education Policy Studies, for postdoctoral studies to conduct research on homeschooling for one year. She has published academic papers and book chapters on vocational education and alternative education as well as history of sociology. Currently, she is engaged in a European Union research project on upskilling immigrant adults. Dr. Kaya can be reached at tulay.kaya@istanbul.edu.tr or tulaykayatr@gmail.com.

Abigail Kindelsperger is a lecturer and Associate Director of English Education at University of Illinois at Chicago. Her research interests include the literacy practices of urban adolescents, as well as the preparation of socially engaged teachers. Dr. Kindelsperger is co-author of *Reconceptualizing Curriculum, Literacy and Learning for School-age Mothers* (Routledge, 2019), as well as a contributing author to *Rethinking Sexism, Gender, and Sexuality* (Rethinking Schools, 2016). At the University of Illinois at Chicago, Dr. Kindelsperger teaches undergraduate English Education methods courses and first-year writing.

Jennifer L. Martin, Ph.D., is an Assistant Professor in the Department of Teacher Education at the University of Illinois at Springfield. Prior to working in higher education, Dr. Martin worked in public education for 17 years, 15 of those as the department chair of English at an urban alternative high school for students labeled at-risk for school failure in metropolitan Detroit. She is the editor of *Racial Battle Fatigue: Insights from the Front Lines of Social Justice Advocacy* (Recipient of the 2016 AERA Division B's Outstanding Book Recognition Award), and co-author of *Teaching for Educational Equity: Case Studies for Professional Development and Principal Preparation, Volumes 1 and 2* (Rowman & Littlefield). Her most recent edited volume is *Feminist Pedagogy, Practice, and Activism: Improving Lives for Girls and Women* (Routledge, 2017). Dr. Martin may be reached at jmart315@uis.edu.

Erin Mikulec, Ph.D., is a Professor in the School of Teaching and Learning at Illinois State University. Dr. Mikulec received her Ph.D. in Curriculum and Instruction with an emphasis in foreign language education from Purdue University. Her research interests include pre-service teacher education, developing diverse clinical field experiences, working with LGBTQ youth, and teaching for global engagement. In 2014, Dr. Mikulec was a Fulbright Scholar at the University of Helsinki, where she studied Finnish education and taught English in area schools. Dr. Mikulec is President Elect for the International Society for Language Studies, where she also serves as conference co-chair and co-editor for the Readings in Language Studies book series. Dr. Mikulec teaches classes in secondary teacher education, student diversity and educational practices, ESL methods and materials, and English as a Foreign Language for visiting groups on campus and abroad.

Julia D. Morris, MS.Ed. (ABD), is an award-winning educator and the Roseanne Keely Norris Doctoral Scholar in the Department of Teaching and Learning, Darden College of Education and Professional Studies at Old Dominion University. Her research utilizes critical theories to explore the literacies and education available or denied to collegiate student Athletes of Color. She is the co-author of several articles and book chapters. She may be reached at jmorr005@odu.edu.

Irda Nalls, Ph.D., is lecturing at Nanyang Technological University (NTU), Singapore. She received a B.A. in Education with specialization in English and Literature from NTU, and an M.A. in Applied Linguistics from the University of Colorado (CU) in Colorado, America. She also has a Ph.D. in Education and Human Development from CU. She is passionate about bilingualism and multilingualism and is interested in educational studies, identity, and critical theories. She speaks five languages and reads and writes in three of the five languages. Currently, she is learning Hieroglyph with the goal of visiting Egypt to study writings on the tombs. In addition, she believes in empowering the marginalized communities through education. Dr. Nalls may be contacted at cookies264@yahoo.com.

Gwendolyn Nuding is a middle-level English Language Arts educator in Illinois. She holds a Bachelor's degree in Elementary Education and a Master's in Teaching and Learning both from Illinois State University. She serves as the sponsor of two club divisions of Girls Who Code. Winnie advocates for gender equity in computer science and partners with community organizations to increase opportunities for young women to engage in coding and mentoring.

Serena M. Wilcox earned her Ph.D. from the University of Illinois at Urbana-Champaign in Social Science and Education Policy Studies with a graduate minor in Gender and Women's Studies. She is currently a Postdoctoral Scholar in Sociology of Education at the University of Kentucky. Her research interests examine the influence of racial thought on public education policy, particularly in small rural and urban schools globally.

CPSIA information can be obtained
at www.ICGtesting.com
Printed in the USA
LVHW041246051221
705332LV00004B/170